The Handbook of French Fantastic Cinema

OTHER RELEVANT TITLES FROM BLACK COAT PRESS

by Jean-Marc & Randy Lofficier
The French Fantasy Treasury 1: The World's Edge (ISBN 978-1-61227-544-4)
The French Fantasy Treasury 2: Myths & Legends (ISBN 978-1-61227-545-1)
The French Fantasy Treasury 3: Far Realms (ISBN 978-1-61227-546-8)
Shadowmen: Heroes and Villains of French Pulp Fiction (ISBN 978-0-9740711-3-8)
Shadowmen 2: Heroes and Villains of French Comics (ISBN 978-0-9740711-8-3)
The Handbook of French Science Fiction (ISBN 978-1-64932-161-9)
The Handbook of French Fantasy & Supernatural Literature (ISBN 978-1-64932-165-7)
The Handbook of French Fantastic Radio & Television (ISBN 978-1-64932-196-1)

by Brian Stableford
The Plurality of Imaginary Worlds: The Evolution of French Roman Scientifique (ISBN 978-1-61227-503-1)
Tales of Enchantment and Disenchantment: A History of Faerie, with an Exemplary Anthology of Tales (ISBN 978-1-61227-838-4)

The Handbook of French Fantastic Cinema

by

Jean-Marc & Randy Lofficier

A Black Coat Press Book

Acknowledgements: Portions of this book have appeared in *French Science Fiction, Fantasy, Horror & Pulp Fiction* published in 2000 by McFarland.

Copyright © 2023 by Jean-Marc & Randy Lofficier.
Cover illustration Jane Fonda & John Philip Law in *Barbarella* photograph Copyright © 2023 Colette Forest.

Visit our website at www.blackcoatpress.com

ISBN 978-1-64932-166-4. First Printing: April 2023. Published by Black Coat Press, an imprint of Hollywood Comics.com, LLC, 18321 Ventura Blvd., Suite 915, Tarzana, CA 91356. All rights reserved. Except for review purposes, no part of this book may be reproduced or transmitted in any form or by any means, electronic or mechanical, including photocopying, recording, or by any information storage and retrieval system, without permission in writing from the publisher. The stories and characters depicted in this novel are entirely fictional. Printed in the United States of America.

TABLE OF CONTENTS

Foreword 7
Overview 11
The Pioneers 19
Feature Films 31
List of Films 237
Index 251

EDDIE CONSTANTINE
ALPHAVILLE
UNE ÉTRANGE AVENTURE DE LEMMY CAUTION
JEAN-LUC GODARD
ANNA KARINA
AKIM TAMIROFF

Foreword

When embarking on any study about science fiction or fantasy, it is often customary to start with an attempt to define these genres.

In French, the word "*fantastique*" carries with it a much larger definition, or "semantic field", than its approximate English equivalent—fantasy. Because it is easy to lose oneself in complex arguments about definitions, about what belongs to the genre and what does not, we subscribe to Pierre Gripari's simple definition: "The *fantastique* is everything that is not rational".

Within this definition, science fiction can be viewed, as Belgian writer Jacques Sternberg once did, as nothing more than a *succursale* [a branch] of the *fantastique*.

For the purpose of these handbooks, science fiction is defined as works appealing to the head, the intellect and the mind, and not the heart. Its true roots lie with humanism, the Renaissance, and the 18th century *Esprit des Lumières*, or Age of Enlightenment. It is, ultimately, based on logic, on science and on testing hypotheses. Science fiction, even when used as a social allegory, which it often is, always relies on a shared pretense of verisimilitude between the writer and his reader.

Fantastique, on the other hand, encompasses all of that which appeals to the heart, to the emotions, to the soul. It relies on irrational beliefs, a sense of the *merveilleux*. It stems from faith; faith in established religions as well as in folkloric legends; faith in ancient or modern myths, such as what is commonly known as the occult or, more accurately, what the French dub *ésotérisme* [*esoterica*], meaning that which is hidden, occult, obscure or secret. Faith traditionally opposes science and material progress, which science fiction, naturally, embraces and advocates.

These, then, are our terms of reference, the canvas against which we propose to paint the history of French fantastic cinema and television.

It will not escape the knowledgeable reader's attention that large sections of this book (and its two companion volumes, *The Handbook of French Fantasy & Supernatural Fiction* and *The Handbook of French Science Fiction*) first appeared in our 800-page bibliographical work, *French Science Fiction, Fantasy, Horror and Pulp Fiction: A Guide to Cinema, Television, Radio, Animation, Comic Books and Literature from the Middle Ages to the Present*, published 2000 by McFarland. According to *The Encyclopedia of Science Fiction*, "the Lofficier text covers the French fantastic with a comprehensiveness and intensity equaled only by the central texts of English-language bibliography and reference".

It should also be understood that, throughout this book, we have used the word "French" in the sense of French-language, that is to say, including Belgian, Swiss and French-Canadian works whenever appropriate. We have, however, strived to identify such non-French-national works and/or authors. Also, animated theatrical features and television programs will be the subject of a fourth book in this series; only live action films and television are included in this volume.

Finally, no project of this type is ever perfect, or complete. We have tried to be as comprehensive as possible and correct all mistakes that appeared in the McFarland tome. Nevertheless, in a book of this scope, no matter how careful one is, omissions are still bound to creep in, as well as the occasional mistake. We will be grateful to anyone pointing out such errors or omissions to us, for future reference and inclusion in subsequent reprints.

While we have listed new films and television up to 2022, we have wisely left the analysis of French Fantastic cinema in this new century to future genre historians.

Jean-Marc & Randy Lofficier

Overview

Arguably, France is, with the United States, the country that has contributed the most to the artistic development of the cinema.

If the credit for the invention of cinema itself can be fairly divided between Thomas Edison's *Kinescope* (1891) and Auguste & Louis Lumière's *Cinématographe* (1895), there can be no doubt that fantasy and science fiction cinema was born in France. Its pioneer was Georges Méliès, who virtually created the genre with *Le Voyage dans la Lune* [A Trip to the Moon] (1902), a loose adaptation of Jules Verne's classic novel, but also based on a popular fairground attraction of the times.

Méliès' success helped launch the careers of several "rivals" who exploited the same vein. Among these were Gaston Velle, Ferdinand Zecca and Spanish director Segundo de Chomon, who produced his own *Voyage à la Lune* [Journey to the Moon] (1909), followed by another Verne adaptation, *Voyage au Centre de la Terre* [Journey to the Center of the Earth] (1909).

Pioneers of French fantasy and science fiction cinema also included Jean Durand, the creator of the comic character of *Onésime*, Alice Guy-Blaché, the first woman director, and Victorin Jasset, the "father" of serials and author of an adaptation of a genre story about a "missing link" creature accused of murder, Gaston Leroux' *Balaoo* (1913).

In the 1920s, various artistic influences, such as Dadaism and Surrealism, as exemplified by writers André Breton and Antonin Artaud, and painters such as Fernand Léger and Marcel Duchamp, helped foster a Surrealist cinema which became known as the *avant-garde*. Among its most representative authors were Marcel L'Herbier, with *L'Inhumaine* [The Inhuman] (1923), Henri Chomette with *Reflets de Lumière et de Vitesse* [Reflections of Light and Speed] (1925), Jean Epstein with *La Chute de la Maison Usher* [The Fall of the House of Usher] (1928), based on the classic Edgar Allan Poe story, Germaine Dulac, another pioneering woman, with *La Coquille et le Clergyman* [The Seashell and the Clergyman] (1928), written by Artaud himself.

Other French filmmakers who experimented with the *avant-garde* included Abel Gance with *La Folie du Dr. Tube* [The Madness of Dr. Tube] (1915), René Clair with *Entr'acte* [Intermission] (1924) and *Le Voyage Imaginaire* [*The Imaginary Journey*] (1926), and Jean Renoir with *La Petite Marchande d'Allumettes* [The Little Match Girl] (1928).

Finally, French cinema also welcomed expatriate *avant-garde* artists such as Russian Dimitri Kirsanov, whose *Ménilmontant* (1924) featured the most visual murder scene ever prior to Alfred Hitchcock's *Psycho*, American artist Man Ray, who made a series of surreal shorts such as *Le Retour à la Raison* [The Return to Reason] (1925), *Emak Bakia* (1926), *L'Étoile de Mer* [The Starfish] (1928) and *Les Mystères du Château de Dé* [The Mysteries of the Castle of Dice] (1929), and Spanish director Luis Buñuel, who had apprenticed with Epstein on *La Chute de la Maison Usher* and made both *Un Chien Andalou* (1928) in collaboration with fellow Spanish Surrealist Salvador Dali, and *L'Age d'Or* [The Golden Age] (1930) in Paris.

Buñuel's *L'Age d'Or* and Jean Cocteau's *Le Sang d'un Poète* [The Blood of a Poet] marked both the culmination and the end of the *avant-garde*. Political reasons, such as the rise of fascism, as well as economic ones, such as the closure of many French movie studios, caused the movement to fragment and, ultimately, vanish. But it had forced a re-evaluation of the medium of film and freed it from the artistic shackles of conventional stage melodrama.

Unfortunately, after this auspicious beginning, fantasy and science fiction became marginalized in French cinema until the late 1970s, when the imports of big budget American productions such as *Star Wars* and *Close Encounters of the Third Kind* made them respectable again in the eyes of both producers and critics. Also, the dominance of realism in French cinema, as in French literature, if not totally excluding the *fantastique*, as long as it remained within tasteful boundaries or juvenile forms, practically ruled out any serious science fiction films.

In this review of French genre cinema, we will, therefore, find no series of films comparable to the Universal monster movies of the 1930s, the giant monster movies of the 1950s, or the Hammer films of the 1960s. No commercial recipes, no classic monsters, no school of B movies. It is worth noting that a large number of these types of foreign-made films were either not distributed in France, or distributed in cheap, exploitation houses, and could not, therefore, pull the genre out of its commercial ghetto.

French filmmakers who did make incursions, no matter how timid, into the *fantastique*, were consequently motivated more by literary pretensions than by the mere desire of thrilling their audiences. Overwhelmingly, the themes of early French genre films revolved around the three "Ds": Death, Dream and the Devil (Religion), or traditional folk legends. Abel Gance's *J'accuse* [I Accuse, translated as They May Live] (1918, rem. 1937), Julien Duvivier's *La Charrette Fantôme* [The Ghost Cart] (1939), Maurice Tourneur's *La Main du Diable* [The Devil's Hand, translated as Carnival of Sinners] (1942), René Clair's *La Beauté du Diable* [The Beauty and the Devil] (1949), or the films of Serge de Poligny, were good illustrations of this high-brow approach.

The continued influence of the surrealist movement was nevertheless still felt in genre films by Cocteau, such as the classic *La Belle et la Bête* [Beauty and the Beast] (1945) and *Orphée* [Orpheus] (1949), and, later, Claude Chabrol, Alain Robbe-Grillet and Juan Luis Buñuel, the son of the Spanish director.

Filmmakers who chose a more popular approach, starting with the great Louis Feuillade, who virtually pioneered the art of the serial, and others like him, relied on material drawn from pulp literature: Marcel Allain & Pierre Souvestre's master criminal, *Fantômas*, the novels of Gaston Leroux, Maurice Leblanc and Arthur Bernède, etc.

Georges Franju's horror masterpiece *Les Yeux Sans Visage* [Eyes Without a Face, translated as The Horror Chamber of Dr. Faustus] (1959) or, in a strikingly different vein, Roger Vadim's *...Et Mourir de Plaisir* [...And To Die From Pleasure, translated as Blood and Roses] (1960) and *Barbarella* (1967), (an adaptation of Jean-Claude Forest's popular graphic novel) were all representative of that approach.

In the 1960s, the great directors of the so-called French "New Wave" made sparse use of the genre, and always as a form of allegory to address social or philosophical concerns: Jean-Luc Godard's *Alphaville* (1965), François Truffaut's *Fahrenheit 451* (1966) (based on Ray Bradbury's novel) and Alain Resnais' *Je t'aime, Je t'aime* [I Love You, I Love You] (1968) were all serious films using the trappings of science fiction to make a point about life and society.

Virtually the only French filmmaker who could be said to have worked consistently in the genre was Jean Rollin who, starting in the late 1960s, began producing a series of mildly erotic vampire films. Rollin's love for the *fantastique* is not in question; however, his relatively undistinguished skills as a filmmaker and his subject matter relegated him and his films to the exploitation (not to say X-rated) distribution circuits, thus furthering the ghettoization problem.

In spite of Méliès' glorious beginnings, science fiction, in the more classic form of space travel and/or alien encounters, remained virtually absent from French movie screens. It is striking to note that, the year before the ground-breaking *2001: A Space Odyssey* impacted the fans' consciousness, French cinema was offering Henri Delanoe's trite comedy *Ne Jouez Pas Avec Les Martiens* [Don't Play with the Martians] (1967).

As always, there were a few exceptions. André Zwoboda's *Croisières Sidérales* [Star Cruises] (1941) was only remarkable because it dealt with space/time travel at all. More worthy of notice were Abel Gance's grandiose treatment of Camille Flammarion's *La Fin du Monde* [The End of the World] (1930) or documentarian Chris Marker's remarkable short feature about time travel, *La Jetée* [The Jetty] (1964), which inspired Terry Gilliam's *Twelve Monkeys* (1996).

In the 1980s, the genre received a boost from the commercial success of imported American films. Some French filmmakers made occasional tries to follow in the footsteps of their American colleagues, but such attempts remained sporadic at best, and were often hampered by the lack of budget and special effects know-how.

In that vein, one might mention Francis Leroi's *Le Démon Dans l'Île* [The Demon on the Island] (1982) and Jean-Louis Bertucelli's *Stress* (1984), two effective sci-fi/horror thrillers; Yves Boisset's *Le Prix Du Danger* [The Prize of Peril] (1982), based on a Robert Sheckley story similar to, but predating *The Running Man* (1987) and finally, Arnaud Sélignac's *Gawin* (1990), a feel-good movie making clever use of modern science fiction icons.

Despite their good intentions, most of these films often seemed to lack a certain conviction and the French public did not embrace them in the way their producers had hoped. The box office instead continued to support the "real thing", i.e.: American films.

Modern French filmmakers have produced far more interesting genre films when they have pursued their own path, with stories often strikingly different from Anglo-Saxon models. Over the years, sweveral French (or French-language) films have thus struck an original note, although, sad to say, commercial success has more often than not eluded them.

Among these, one would single out Pierre Kast's *Les Soleils de l'Île de Pâques* [The Suns of Easter Island] (1971), Belgian filmmaker Harry Kumel's *Malpertuis* (1972) (based on the novel by Jean Ray); Jean Pourtalé's *Demain les Mômes* [Tomorrow the Kids] (1975); Luc Besson's first film, *Le Dernier Combat* [The Last Combat] (1982); Alain Jessua's *Para-*

dis pour Tous [Paradise for All] (1982); Claude Lelouch's *Viva la Vie* [Hurray for Life] (1984); Luc Besson & Didier Grousset's *Kamikaze* (1986); Enki Bilal's *Bunker Palace Hotel* (1989), Jean-Pierre Jeunet & Marc Caro's *Delicatessen* (1992) and René Manzor's *Un Amour de Sorcière* [A Witch's Love] (1997).

French co-productions with other countries have also made it possible for French directors to profit from more lavish budgets and better production values. *Fahrenheit 451* (1966), *Barbarella* (1967), *Le Joueur de Flûte* [The Pied Piper of Hamelin] (1971) and Pierre-William Glenn's *Terminus* [End of the Line] (1986), were all co-productions. To these, one must add two remarkable films, Bertrand Tavernier's sole incursion into the genre, the uncompromising *La Mort en Direct* [*Death on Live TV*, translated as *Death Watch*] (1980) (based on a novel by D. G. Compton) and Jean-Jacques Annaud's recreation of J.-H. Rosny Aîné's prehistoric saga, *La Guerre du Feu* [*Quest for Fire*] (1981). Interestingly, Hollywood took notice. Luc Besson wrote and directed a major French-American science fiction co-production, *Le Cinquième Élément* [*The Fifth Element*] (1997), and Jean-Pierre Jeunet was hired by 20th Century Fox to direct *Alien Resurrection* (1997).

As the 20th century camer to a close, two authentic fantasy films broke French box office records: Jean-Marie Poiré's comedy *Les Visiteurs* [The Visitors] (1994) and Jeunet & Caro's *La Cité des Enfants Perdus* [The City of Lost Children] (1995), heralding at last a new and successful era for French genre cinema.

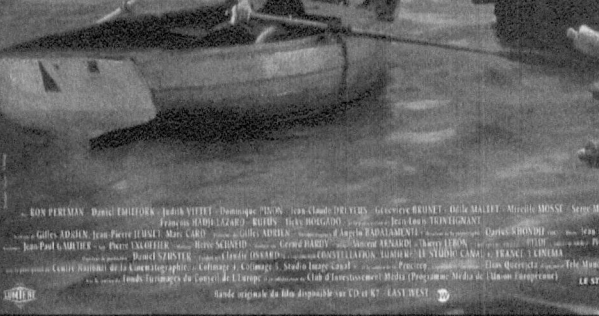

Georges Méliès

The Pioneers

Fantastic cinema was present at the very inception of cinema itself. In this chapter, we shall cover major filmmakers who contributed significantly the developmednt of genre cinema before World War I.

Georges Méliès (1861-1938), the son of a shoe manufacturer, became interested in art, sculpture and puppetry while in school. After completing his military service, and against his father's wishes, he attended the École des Beaux-Arts, one of France's most prestigious art schools. In 1884, he traveled to London, where he became acquainted with the tradecraft of stage magicians. In 1888, after receiving his father's inheritance, Méliès purchased Robert Houdin's theater and embarked on a full-time career as a stage magician, often incorporating "magic lanterns" as part of his elaborate illusions. In 1895, after witnessing the Lumière Brothers' first cinematographic exhibition,[1] he decided to become a filmmaker.

Méliès' first short films (about 20 meters in average length), which he began producing in 1896, were nothing more than recorded daily events, occasionally sprinkled with doses of stage magic for spice. But soon—allegedly following an accidental jamming of his camera—he discovered the potential of trick photography. He began experimenting with studio shooting and artificial lighting, and pioneered virtually all modern special effect techniques: multiple exposures, matte paintings, etc. From magic to fantasy and science fiction was but a small step, and it was therefore not surprising that

---

[1] Including *La Marmite Diabolique* [The Devil's Cooking-Pot] (1'30"), in which the Devil appears in cauldron, perhaps the first fantasy/horror film ever made.

Méliès quickly came to rely on fantasy and science fiction themes for his work. Most of the genre's classic themes were first featured in his films: ghosts and haunted castles, wizards and witches, space travel, airships and submarines, the conquest of the Pole and the tunnel under the British Channel, transcontinental car races, flying men and mermaids, giants and microscopic men, living dolls, men turning into monsters, and many, many more.

Méliès can also be credited for being the first filmmaker to adapt the works of H. Rider Haggard (*She*), Jonathan Swift (*Gulliver's Travels*), Jules Verne, Washington Irving (*Rip van Winkle*), Charles Perrault (*Cinderella*) Goethe (*Faust*), the *Adventures of Baron of Munchausen* and the *Thousand and One Nights*.

Eventually, Méliès' career waned. Financial difficulties forced him to sell his studio in 1923, and subsequently, he left the business entirely. However, he was rediscovered in the 1930s, and awarded the Legion of Honor medal. Most of his films contain elements of fantasy and science fiction. A partial list of titles follows:

L'Hallucination de l'Alchimiste (*The Alchemist's Hallucination*, 1897)
Le Château Hanté (*The Haunted Castle*, 1897)
Magie Diabolique (*Diabolical Magic*, 1898)
La Damnation de Faust (*The Damnation of Faust*, 1898)
Le Rêve d'un Astronaute ou La Lune à un Mètre (*An Astronaut's Dream or the Moon a Meter Away*, 1898) (the first space travel film ever.)
La Caverne Maudite (*The Haunted Cavern*, 1898)
Le Spectre (1899)
Le Diable au Couvent (*The Devil in the Convent*, 1899)
La Danse du Feu (*The Fire Dance*, 1899) (loosely based on *She*)
Le Miroir de Cagliostro (*The Mirror of Cagliostro*, 1899)
Évocation Spirite (*Summoning the Spirits*, 1899)
Cendrillon (*Cinderella*, 1899)

La Forêt Enchantée (*The Enchanted Forest*, 1900)
Le Livre Magique (*The Magic Book*, 1900)
Spiritisme Abracadabrant (*Amazing Spirits*, 1900)
Mésaventures d'un Aéronaute (Misadventures of an Aeronaut, 1900)
Chez la Sorcière (*The Witch's House*, 1901)
Le Temple de la Magie (*The Temple of Magic*, 1901)
Le Diable Géant (*The Giant Devil*, 1901)
L'Oeuf du Sorcier (*The Sorcerer's Egg*, 1901)
La Danseuse Microsocopique (*The Microscopic Dancer*, 1901)
L'Homme Mouche (*The Fly-Man*, 1902)
La Femme Volante (*The Flying Woman*, 1902)
Les Voyages de Gulliver (*Gulliver's Travels*, 1902)
Le Voyage dans la Lune (*A Trip to the Moon*, 1902) (loosely based on Jules Verne's novel.)
Les Filles du Diable (*The Devil's Daughters*, 1903)
La Statue Animée (*The Living Statue*, 1903)
La Flamme Merveilleuse (*The Wondrous Flame*, 1903)
Le Sorcier (*The Wizard*, 1903)
Le Monstre (*The Monster*, 1903)
Le Royaume des Fées (*The Faerie Kingdom*, 1903)
Le Revenant (*The Revenant*, 1903)
Faust aux Enfers (*Faust in Hell*, 1903) (a sequel to the 1898's *La Damnation de Faust*.)
Le Coffre Enchanté (*The Enchanted Chest*, 1904)
Le Voyage à travers l'Impossible (*The Impossible Journey*, 1904)
La Damnation du Dr. Faust (*Dr. Faust's Damnation*, 1904) (a remake of 1898's *La Damnation de Faust*)
La Sirène (*The Mermaid*, 1904)
La Dame Fantôme (*The Lady Ghost*, 1904)
Le Diable Noir (*The Dark Devil*, 1905)
Le Palais des Mille et Une Nuits (*The Palace of the Thousand and One Nights*, 1905)
La Légende de Rip van Winkle (*The Legend of Rip Van Winkle*, 1905) (based on Washington Irving's tale.)

Le Dirigeable Fantastique (*The Fantastic Airship*, 1906)
La Magie à travers les Âges (*Magic through the Ages*, 1906)
Le Fantôme d'Alger (*The Ghost of Algiers*, 1906)
Les 400 Farces du Diable (*Satan's Merry Frolics*, 1906)
L'Alchimiste Parafaragaramus (1906)
La Fée Carabosse (1906)
200,000 Lieues sous les Mers, ou le Cauchemar d'un Pêcheur (*200,000 Leagues under the Sea, or a Fisherman's Nightmare*, 1907) (loosely based on Verne's novel.)
Le Tunnel sous la Manche, ou le Cauchemar Franco-Anglais (*The Tunnel Under The Channel, or the Franco-British Nightmare*, 1907)
Satan en Prison (*Satan in Jail*, 1907)
Le Rêve d'un Fumeur d'Opium (*The Dream of an Opium Smoker*, 1908)
La Prophétesse de Thèbes (*The Seeress of Thebes*, 1908)
Le Raid Paris-New York (*The Paris-New York Race*, 1908)
Au Pays des Jouets (*Toyland*, 1908)
La Poupée Vivante (*The Living Doll*, 1908)
Le Fakir de Singapour (*The Singapore Fakir*, 1908)
Le Locataire Diabolique (*The Diabolical Tenant*, 1909)
Le Papillon Fantastique (*The Fantastic Butterfly*, 1910)
Les Hallucinations du Baron de Munchausen (*Baron Von Munchausen's Hallucinations*, 1911)
Cendrillon (*Cinderella*, 1912) (another remake.)
La Conquête du Pôle (*The Conquest of the Pole*, 1912).

Alice Guy-Blaché (1873-1968) was the first woman director in motion picture history. As Alice Guy (her maiden name), she made numerous one-reelers for Gaumont between 1896 and 1907, including numerous fantasy films such as:

La Fée aux Choux (*The Cabbage Fairy*, 1896)
Faust et Mephistopheles (1902)
La Fiancée Ensorcelée (*The Bewitched Fiancée*, 1903)
La Fève Enchantée (*The Magic Bean*, 1904) (an adaptation of *Jack and the Beanstalk*)

La Fée Printemps (*The Spring Fairy*, 1906)
The Pit and the Pendulum (1907)
And the full-length feature, *La Vie du Christ* (*The Life of Christ*, 1908), with over 300 actors.

After marrying American cameraman Herbert Blaché Bolton, Alice, now Alice Guy-Blaché, moved to the United States, where she formed her own production company. Most of her other genre output was produced in the United States:

In The Year 2000 (1912),
The Pit and the Pendulum (remake, 1913),
The Vampire (1915)

In 1922, she returned to France but was not able to continue her career in the film industry. However, she went on to write several children's books under the pseudonym of Guy Allix.

Georges Méliès' success helped launch the careers of a number of lesser-known filmmakers, who largely mined the same vein as he did. Among these was **Ferdinand Zecca** (1864-1947). Mostly an imitator of Méliès, Zecca strove not to innovate but to make more commercial films. He eventually became a director of the Pathé organization in 1910. Some of his most famous genre films included:

Un drame au fond de la mer (*A Drama at the Bottom of the Sea*, 1901)
La Soupière merveilleuse (*The Marvelous Pot*, 1901)
Les Sept Châteaux du diable (*The Devil's Seven Castles*, 1901)
Rêve et Réalité (*Dream and Reality*, 1901)
Plongeur fantastique (, 1901)
À La Conquête de l'Air (*The Conquest of the Air*, 1901),
Ce Que Je Vois dans mon Télescope (*What I See in my Telescope*, 1902)

La Fée des roches noires (*The Fairy of Black Rock*, 1902)
Ali-Baba et les Quarante Voleurs (*Ali-Baba and the Forty Thieves*, 1902),
La Belle au Bois Dormant (*Sleeping Beauty*, 1902)
Le Chat Botté (*Puss in Boots*, 1903),
Rêve à la Lune (*Moon Dream*, 1905)
Le Spectre Rouge (*The Red Spectre*, 1907)
L'Album Magique (*The Magic Album*, 1908)
Le Roi de l'Air (*The King of the Air*, 1913).

Gaston Velle (1868–1948) was another prominent director and pioneer of special effects. Like his father, the Hungarian entertainer Joseph "Professor" Velle, he began his career as a traveling magician, before putting his illusionist skills to work in cinema and ultimately creating more than fifty films between 1903 and 1911. He worked under Auguste and Louis Lumière, before serving as the head of production for the Italian film studio Cines. But he is best remembered for his work at Pathé, where he was hired to produce trick films that rival those of his contemporary. He also created some of the first *féerie* films, and collaborated with Segundo de Chomon and Ferdinand Zecca to create such silent film classics as *The Moon Lover* (1905), *The Raja's Casket* (1906), and *The Hen that Laid the Golden Egg* (1905), the latter of which was featured in the 1997 Martin Scorsese film, *Kundun*. Some of his genre contributions include:

Un drame dans les airs (*A drama in the air*, 1904)
Le Chapeau magique (*The Magic Hat*, 1904)
La Poule aux œufs d'or (*The Hen that Laid the Golden Egg*, 1905)
La Fée aux fleurs (*The Flower Fairy*, 1905)
Le Garde fantôme (*The Phantom Guard*, 1906)
Les Invisibles (*The Invisibles*, 1906) (first known invisible man film)
La Fée aux pigeons (*The Pigeon Fairy*, 1906)

Voyage autour d'une étoile (*Journey around a star*, 1906) (a scientist travels to Jupiter)
Le Secret de l'Horloger (*The Clockmaker's Secret*, 1907)
Au pays des songes (*In the Land of Dreams*, 1907)
Le Spectre (1908)
Cagliostro (1910)
L'Armure de feu (*The Armor of Fire*, 1911)
Le Cauchemar de Pierrot (*Pierrot's Nightmare*, 1911)
La Nuit rouge (*Red Night*, 1913)

Velle mysteriously retired from film production in 1913, and little is known about the last several decades of his life.

Another filmmaker who mined the same vein as Méliès was Spanish director **Segundo de Chomon** (1871-1929), who worked in France from 1906 to 1909, during which he produced several, semi-plagiarized Jules Verne adaptations. His genre films of the period include:

Voyage à la Planète Jupiter (*Travel to Jupiter*, 1907)
Le Chevalier Mystère (*The Mystery Knight*, 1907)
La Maison Hantée (*The Haunted House*, 1907)
Cauchemar et Doux Rêve (*Nightmare and Sweet Dream*, 1908)
Mars (1908),
Cuisine Magnétique (*Magnetic Kitchen*, 1908)
Voyage à la Lune (*Journey to the Moon*, 1909)
Voyage au Centre de la Terre (*Journey to the Center of the Earth*, 1909).

Victorin Jasset (1862-1913) was Alice Guy-Blaché's assistant before becoming himself a director, specializing in early serials, westerns, and adaptations of popular novels and Grand-Guignol plays (often by André de Lorde). His genre contributions include:

Nick Carter, le Roi des Détectives (*Nick Carter, King of the Detectives*) (6 épisodes, 1908)
Les Merveilleux Exploits de Nick Carter (*The Amazing Exploits of Nick Carter*) (3 épisodes, 1908)
Docteur Phantom (6 episodes, 1909)
Zigomar (1910) (based on Léon Sazie's novel, a predecessor of Fantômas)
Au Fond du Gouffre (*At the Bottom of the Pit*, 1910)
Un Cri dans la Nuit (*A Scream in the Night*, 1910)
Le Crime d'un Fils (*The Crime of a Son*, 1910)
Dans la Cave (*In the Cellar*, 1910)
Zigomar, Roi des voleurs (*Zigomar, King of Thieves*) (1911)
Dans la Fournaise (*In the Furnace*, 1911)
Destin Tragique (*Tragic Fate*, 1911)
Fatalité (*Fate*, 1911)
Le Système du Dr. Goudron et du Professeur Plume (*The System of Dr. Tarr and Professor Fether*) (not to be confused with Maurice Tourneur's 1912 version)
La Justice du Mort (*Dead Man's Justice*, 1912)
L'Invisible (1912)
Zigomar contre Nick Carter (1912)
La Justicière (*The Avenging Woman*, 1912)
Une Nuit d'Épouvante (*A Night of Terror*, 1912)
Le Mystère de Notre-Dame de Paris (*The Mystery of Notre-Dame*) (with Émile Chautard)
Le Semeur de Ruines (*The Sower of Ruins*, 1913)
Zigomar, Peau d'anguille (*Zigomar, The Eel*) (1913) (the film was removed after Sazie sued and won, having deemed the adaptation too unfaithful)
Balaoo (1913) (based on the novel by Gaston Leroux)
Protéa (1913)
Le Collier de Kali (*Kali's Necklace*, 1913)

Émile Chautard (1864-1934) was both a director and an actor, directing more than 100 films (many being adaptations of André de Lorde's Grand-Guignol plays) and appearing in more than 60. He started as an assistant to Victorin Jasset at the Éclair studio before emigrating to the United States in January 1915. From 1915 to about 1918, he worked for the World Film Company in New Jersey, alongside Maurice Tourneur, Léonce Perret, George Archainbaud, Albert Capellani, Lucien Andriot, and hired Josef Von Sternberg to be his assistant director on his adaptation of Gaston Leroux' *The Mystery of the Yellow Room*. His genre contributions include:

Fumeur d'Opium (*Opium Smoker*, 1911)
Une Nuit d'Épouvante (*A Night of Terror*, 1911)
Le Cercueil de Verre (*The Glass Coffin*, 1912)
Le Mystère de Notre-Dame de Paris (*The Mystery of Notre-Dame*) (with Victorin Jasset)
Le Sculpteur aveugle (*The Blind Sculptor*, 1913)
La Malédiction (*The Curse*, 1913)
Le Mystère de la chambre jaune (*The Mystery of the Yellow Room*, 1913)
La Fiancée Maudite (*The Accursed Fiancée*, 1913)
Bagnes d'enfants (*Children's Labor Camp*, 1914)
L'Homme qui a oublié (*The Man Who Forgot*, 1917)
La Sirène (*The Eternal Temptress*, 1917)
La Maison de verre (*The House of Glass*, 1918)
Les Marionnettes (*The Marionnettes*, 1918)
Le Mystère de la chambre jaune (*The Mystery of the Yellow Room*, 1919) (remake)

Jean Durand (1882-1946) was important in the development of the slapstick comedy. Between 1907 and 1929, he turned out scores of silent shorts, including the *Calino* (1907-11) and *Onésime* (1912-13) series. Several contained fantasy elements, such as *Onésime Horloger* (*Onesime Clock-Maker*, 1912), *Onésime aux Enfers* (*Onesime in Hell*, 1912) and *Onésime et la Maison Hantée* (*Onesime and the Haunted House*, 1913).

No one knows who made *La Police en l'An 2000* [*The Police in the Year 2000*], a 4'35" silent short film released iby

Gaumont in 1910. It is one of the very first science fiction/anticipation films produced at the time. In it, the police of the year 2000 use a dirigible balloon to travel across and above Paris and spot criminals. Officers use long claws to grab them and place them in a cage before dropping them off at the station.

Abel Gance (1889-1981) began his career as an actor, then a screenwriter, then he began directing short films such as *Le Masque d'Horreur* (*The Horror Mask*, 1912). A pioneer of film technique with his use of close-ups and tracking shots, Gance is better remembered today for his experimental shorts such as *La Folie du Dr. Tube* (*The Madness of Dr. Tube*, 1916), *Les Gaz Mortels* (*Deadly Gasses*, 1916), *La Zone de la Mort* (*The Zone of Death*, 1917) and *Au Secours!* (*Help!*, 1923). His more ambitious film projects include *J'accuse* (*I Accuse*, 1918, remade in 1937), *La Roue* (*The Wheel*, 1923), his unqualified masterpiece, *Napoléon* (1927), and the classic science fiction picture, *La Fin du Monde* (*The End of the World*, 1930), reviewed in our next chapter.

Finally, **Louis Feuillade** (1873-1925) began his film career as a screenwriter in 1906. The following year, he was appointed production chief at Gaumont, but continued to direct his own projects, including such genre shorts as:

L'Homme Aimanté (*The Magnetized Man*, 1907)
La Chatte Métamorphosée en Femme (*The Cat Transformed into a Woman*, 1909)
Le Mort Vivant (*The Living Dead*, 1912)
L'Anneau Fatal (*The Deadly Ring*, 1912)
Le Revenant (*The Revenant*, 1913)
La Gardienne du Feu (*Guardian of the Fire*, 1913)

Today, Feuillade is considered the father of the serials, a forerunner of German expressionism, and a master of suspense. His pulp fantasy serials featuring colorful master villains, masked avengers, secret societies, and the like, such as the classic *Fantômas* (5 eps., 1913-14), *Les Vampires* (10 eps., 1915-16) and *Judex* (12 eps., 1915-16) are all reviewed separately in our next chapter).

Feature Films

We have attempted to list virtually every French genre feature film. Our criteria for inclusion in this list have been as follows:

(1) *French*: in an age of international co-productions, it is sometimes hard to determine a film's nationality. In most cases, we have been guided by the director's nationality, which, but for a few exceptions, ruled out many French/Italian, French/Spanish and French/Eastern European co-productions, such as Mino Loy's *Flashman* (1967), Peter Fleischmann's *Un Dieu Rebelle* [Hard to be a God] (1990), Lars Von Trier's *Melancholia* (2011), but did allow us to include *Barbarella* (1967), *Fahrenheit 451* (1966), *Le Joueur de Flûte* [The Pied Piper of Hamelin] (1971) and *Lucy* (2014). We have also included French-language Belgian, Swiss, and the occasional French Canadian, films.

There are, however, two major exceptions to the above rule:

(a) Luis Buñuel was a Spanish filmmaker who was forced to make films in France, written by French author Jean-Claude Carrière, acted by a French cast and produced with French money. We have therefore included his French-produced genre films in this compilation. His son, Juan Luis Buñuel, is treated as a French filmmaker.

(b) Jesus (Jess) Franco is a prolific Spanish B-movie director. Like Buñuel (but for different reasons), he, too, has made several French-produced films, as well as French/Spanish co-productions, usually gore and/or X-rated pictures. We have listed his French productions, but not his foreign co-productions.[2]

(2) *Genre*: to be included in our list, a film generally had to contain a clear element of *fantastique*: supernatural, fantasy, horror or science fiction. We have not always deemed it necessary to include minor films with only a very tenuous genre connection, usually in the form of an allegory, e.g.: *Haine* [Hatred] (1980) or films dealing purely with religious matters and miracles, e.g.: *Bernadette* (1987), because most people do not consider them *fantastique*. However, we made an exception for Godard's *Je Vous Salue Marie* [*Hail Mary*] (1984).

On the other hand, we have included films about serial killers and gory murders, such as Bernard Blier's *Buffet Froid* [Cold Cuts] (1979), Claude Chabrol's *Le Boucher* [The Butcher] (1969), Henri-Georges Clouzot's *Les Diaboliques* [Diabolique] (1954), Rémy Belvaux, André Bonzel & Benoît Poelvoorde's *C'est Arrivé Près De Chez Vous* [It Happened Near Where You Live, translated as Man Bites Dog] (1992) and Paul Vecchiali's *L'Étrangleur* [The Strangler] (1970), because they have a good claim to be at least marginally part of the *fantastique*.

We have also included films based on well-known, popular "pulp" / superheroes, such as *Fantômas*, *Arsène Lupin*, *Rouletabille*, and superspies *Coplan FX-18* and *OSS 117*, for the same reasons as *Sherlock Holmes, The Shadow* and *James Bond* are often listed in similar works in the English language.

Running times vary slightly according to the sources. When in doubt, we have relied on Jean Tulard's authoritative *Guide des Films*. The year given here is that of the first French release.

---

[2] Readers interested in a more detailed study of Franco's idiosyncratic career are invited to check the following books: *Immoral Tales* by Cathal Tohill & Pete Tombs (St. Martin's, 1995) and the remarkable *Obsession: The Films of Jess Franco* by Lucas Balbo & Peter Blumenstock (in English, Hauffen & Trebbin, Munich, Germany, 1993).

(3) To list each and every French genre short feature—even limiting ourselves to those actually screened or broadcast—would have been literally an impossible task. As mentioned earlier, short films made during the early days of cinema by pioneers such as Georges Méliès, Victorin Jasset, and others who followed in their footsteps, were often genre films. Listing all these separately here would be confusing.

Also—and this became particularly true from the mid-1970s onward—film festivals, state subsidies, and a very real demand from television channels such as M6 or Canal-Plus encouraged young filmmakers to make an increasingly larger number of short features. There is, sadly, very little material available on these, and what exists is often very cursory, rendering any research extremely difficult.

We have, however, made a few exceptions for significant works that have attracted a degree of fame and deserve special recognition.

2019 Après la Chute de New York [*2019 After New York Fell*] (col., 91 min., 1983)
Dir: Sergio Martino; *Wri*: Ernesto Gastaldi, Sergio Martino, Gabriel Rossini.
Cast: Michael Sopkiw, Valentine Monnier, Anna Kanakis.
Story: After a nuclear war, the Federation sends an agent into New York to get the last fertile woman out.
Note: French-Italian co-production.

À la Conquête du Pôle [*The Conquest of the Pole*] (B&W., 300 M., 1913)
Dir/Wri: Georges Méliès.
Cast: Georges Méliès.
Story: Explorers at the North Pole battle a Snow Giant.
Note: A classic Méliès and one of his last productions. The special effect Snow Giant was particularly remarkable.

À ton image [*According to your Image*] (col., 94 min., 2004)
Dir: Aruna Villiers; *Wri*: Guillaume Laurant, Franck Philippon, Aruna Villiers, based on the novel by Louise L. Lambrichs.
Cast: Nastassja Kinski, Christophe Lambert, Audrey DeWilder.
Story: Haunted by painful memories and a terrible feeling of guilt a sterile young woman (Kinski) uses extreme cloning methods to give birth to a daughter (DeWilder), while comforted by her obstetrician husband (Lambert).

L'Abîme des Morts-Vivants [*The Abyss of the Living Dead*, transl. as *Oasis of the Zombies, Tomb of the Blind Dead*] (col., 95 min., 1981)
Dir: A. M. Franck (pseudonym of Daniel Lesoeur); *Wri*: Daniel Lesoeur.
Cast: Manuel Gélin, France Jordan, Jeff Montgomery, Henri Lambert.
Story: Nazi cannibal zombies protect a treasure hidden in a Moroccan oasis.

Note: A Spanish version of the same film exists, directed by Jess Franco, with a different cast.

Ada dans la Jungle [*Ada in the Jungle*] (col., 90 min., 1988)
Dir/Wri: Gérard Zingg, based on the eponymous Italian comic book series by Francesco Altan.
Cast: Marie Louisa (Ada), Richard Bohringer (Pilic), Bernard Blier (Collins), Philippe Léotard, Isaach de Bankolé, Victoria Abril, Charley Boorman, Katerine Boorman, Robert Stephens.
Story: A British Lord dispatches young Ada to Africa to search for a child he once abandoned in the jungle.
Note: This film is an adaptation of a popular Italian comic book series spoofing African adventures *à la Tim Tyler's Luck*.

ADN, l'Âme de la Terre [*DNA, The Soul of Earth*] (col., 94 min., 2014)
Dir/Wri: Thierry Obadia.
Cast: Pascal J. Jardel (Akim), Thierry Obadia, Alexia Barlier.
Story: Akim, a young boy, is endowed with the ability to heal. A pharmaceutical laboratory covets his unique DNA. He has no choice but to defend himself, helped by his friends.
Note: French-Tunisian co-production.

Adrénaline - Le Film (80 min., 1990)
Compilation of 13 short features listed here in order of appearance:

    1. *Les Aveugles* [*The Blind*] (col., 8 min, 1990)
    Dir/Wri/Cast: Anita Assal, John Hudson.
    Story: Blind people go to the movies.

    2. *Métrovision* (col., 4 min., 1986)
    Dir/Wri/Cast: Yann Piquer.
    Story: The Paris subway suddenly goes insane.

    3. *Revestriction* [*Dream Restriction*] (b&w., 6 min., 1989)
    Dir/Wri: Barthélémy Bompard.

Cast: Bernadette Coqueret.
Story: The walls and ceiling of a room start closing in on its occupant.

4. *Graffiti* (col., 3 min., 1990)
Dir/Wri: Barthélémy Bompard.
Cast: Marie-Christine Munchery.
Story: An old woman draws graffiti with a dead cat.

5. *Cimetière des Éléphants* [*Graveyard of the Elephants*] (col., 6 min., 1989)
Dir/Wri: Philippe Dorison.
Cast: Alain Aithnard.
Story: Cars go to a junkyard to die by themselves, taking their drivers with them.

6. *Embouteillage* [*Traffic Jam*] (b&w., 5 min., 1986)
Dir/Wri: Barthélémy Bompard.
Cast: Franck Baruk.
Story: A new solution to get rid of traffic jams.

7. *Corridor* (col., 7 min., 1989)
Dir: Alain Robak; *Wri*: Alain Robak, Jean-Marc Toussaint.
Cast: Jean-François Gallotte.
Story: To be allowed to buy a house, people must first take a cruel exam.

8. *Interrogatoire* [*Interrogation*] (col., 7 min., 1989)
Dir/Wri: Yann Piquer, Jean-Marie Madeddu.
Cast: Jean-Marie Madeddu, Arnaud Chevrier, Carla Teillot.
Story: Love makes a man agree to submit to a horrible torture.

9. *Urgence* [*Emergency*] (col., 3 min., 1987)
Dir/Wri: Yann Piquer, Jean-Marie Madeddu.
Cast: Jean-Marie Madeddu, Gilbert Duprez.

Story: A man asking for directions in the countryside unwittingly causes a catatrophe.

10. *La Dernière Mouche* [*The Last Fly*] (b&w., 4 min., 1987)
Dir/Wri: Yann Piquer, Jean-Marie Madeddu.
Cast: Jean-Marie Madeddu, Anne-Marie Pisani.
Story: A lunatic covers the walls of his room with dead insects.

11. *TV Buster* (col., 14 min., 1987)
Dir/Wri: Anita Assal, John Hudson.
Cast: Clémentine Célarié, Ged Marlon, Jean-Marie Madeddu, Barthélémy Bompard.
Story: A television set is possessed by the devil.

12. *Cyclope* [*Cyclops*] (col., 5 min., 1989)
Dir: Anita Assal, John Hudson; *Wri*: Jean-Marie Madeddu.
Cast: Jean-Marie Madeddu.
Story: The revolt of a surveillance camera.

13. *Sculpture Physique* [*Physical Sculpture*] (col., 4 min., 1987)
Dir/Wri: Yann Piquer, Jean-Marie Madeddu.
Cast: Jean-Marie Madeddu.
Story: Beating up someone creates a work of art.

L'Affaire des Divisions Morituri [*The Case of the Morituri Department*] (B&W., 75 min., 1985)
Dir/Wri: Frédéric-Jacques Ossang.
Cast: Gina Lola Benzina, Philippe Sfez, Lionel Tua, Frankie Tavezzano.
Story: An underground network of modern gladiators.

After Blue (Paradis sale) [*Dirty Paradise*] (col., 127 min., 2021)
Dir/Wri: Bertrand Mandico.

Cast: Elina Löwensohn (Zora), Paula Luna (Roxy), Vimala Pons, Agata Buzek (Kate).
Story: In the future, Roxy is a teenage girl living with her mother, Zora, on the planet After Blue. One day, she meets a criminal named Kate with hairy arms and a third eye. Roxy helps her but she and her mother are then held responsible for Kate's crimes.

L'Age d'Or [*The Golden Age*] (B&W., 67 min., 1930)
Dir: Luis Buñuel; Wri: Luis Buñuel, Salvador Dali.
Cast: Lya Lys, Gaston Modot, Pierre Prévert, Lionel Salem.
Story: Surreal story and imagery.

Aimez-Vous les Femmes ? [*Do You Like Women?*] (B&W., 100 min., 1964)
Dir: Jean Léon; *Wri*: Gérard Brach, based on a novel by Georges Bardawil.
Cast: Sophie Daumier (Violette), Guy Bedos (Jerome), Guido Alberti, Edwige Feuillère, Grégoire Aslan, Gérard Séty, Roger Blin.
Story: Black comedy about cannibalism.
Note: French-Italian co-production.

Aladin ou la Lampe merveilleuse [*Aladin and the Magic Lamp*] (B&W., 12 min., 1906)
Dir/Wri: Albert Capellani.
Cast: Georges Vinter.
Story: Adapted from the *Thousand and One Nights*.

Alerte au Sud [*Alert in the South*] (color, 110 min., 1953)
Dir: Jean Devaivre; *Wri*: Jean-Paul Le Chanois, Jean Devaivre.
Cast: Jean-Claude Pascal (Pasquier), Erich Von Stroheim (Nagel), Gianna-Maria Canale (Nathalie), Peter Van Eyck, Daniel Sorano, Thomy Bourdelle.

Story: In the Southern Moroccan desert, Captain Nagel uses a green death ray to blast planes out of the sky. A brave French Officer (Pascal) thwarts his nefarious schemes.

Ali Baba et les Quarante Voleurs [*Ali Baba and the Forty Thieves*] (col., 92 min., 1954)
Dir: Jacques Becker; *Wri*: Césare Zavattini, Jacques Becker, Marc Maurette, Maurice Griffe.
Cast: Fernandel (Ali Baba), Samia Gamal (Morgiane), Dieter Borsche (Abdul), Henri Vilbert (Cassim), Édouard Delmont, Edmond Ardisson, Manuel Gary, Julien Maffre, Gaston Orbal.
Story: The legendary tale of Ali Baba retold with famous French comic actor Fernandel in the leading role.

Alice, ou La Dernière Fugue [*Alice, or The Last Escapade*] (col., 93 min., 1976)
Dir/Wri: Claude Chabrol.
Cast: Sylvia Kristel (Alice), Charles Vanel (Vergennes), André Dussolier, Fernand Ledoux, Jean Carmet.
Story: After a car accident at night on a lonely road, Alice (played by *Emmanuelle* title actress Sylvia Kristel) finds herself in a mysterious mansion where she experiences a series of surreal encounters. In reality, she died in the accident.

Alice chez les Satyres [*Alice Among the Satyrs*] (col., 85 min., 1971)
Dir/Wri: Francis Dubois.
Cast: Diane Dubois, Thierry de Brem, Dominique Cale.
Story: X-rated version of *Alice in Wonderland*.

Alien Crystal Palace (col., 97 min., 2019)
Dir/Wri: Arielle Dombasle.
Cast: Arielle Dombasle, Nicolas Ker, Michel Fau.
Story: A preacher manipulator of souls seeks to recreate the ideal couple according to the Greco-Egyptian gnosis.

L'Alliance [*The Alliance*] (col., 90 min., 1970)

Dir: Christian de Chalonge; *Wri*: Christian de Chalonge, Jean-Claude Carrière, based on his novel.
Cast: Jean-Claude Carrière (Hughes), Anna Karina (Jeanne), Isabelle Sadoyan, Jean-Pierre Darras, Tsilla Chelton, Rufus.
Story: Hughes, a reclusive veterinarian, who conducts ESP experiments, and Jeanne, a mysterious young woman, eventually fall in love after a long courtship, but a final cataclysm upsets their world.

Alone aka *Don't Grow Up* (col., 81 min., 2015)
Dir: Thierry Poiraud; *Wri*: Marie Garel-Weiss.
Cast: Fergus Riordan, Darren Evans, McKell David, Madeleine Kelly, Natifa Mai, Dominique Baute.
Story: Teenage delinquents living in an island youth center wake up to find themselves alone. All the adults on the island have been infected by a mysterious epidemic.

Alphaville - Une Étrange Aventure de Lemmy Caution [*Alphaville - A Strange Adventure of Lemmy Caution*] (B&W., 100 min., 1965)
Dir/Wri: Jean-Luc Godard.
Cast: Eddie Constantine (Lemmy Caution), Anna Karina (Natacha), Akim Tamiroff, Howard Vernon (Von Braun), Laszlo Szabo.
Story: Tough private eye Lemmy Caution is sent to Alphaville to convince Professor Von Braun to return. After destroying Alpha-60, the computer which rules the city, he leaves with Von Braun's daughter, Natacha, who has fallen in love with him.
Note: The character of Lemmy Caution was created by British thriller writer Peter Cheyney, and was the subject of several French films, all starring expatriate American actor Constantine.

Les Amazones du Temple d'Or [*The Golden Temple Amazons*] (col., 85 min., 1984)

Dir: James Gartner (pseudonym of Jess Franco), Alain Payet; *Wri*: A. L. Mariaux, George Freeland, based on the story *Akagu, Forbidden Temple* by Jeff Manner.
Cast: Stanley Kapoul, William Berger, Robert Foster, Joan Virly, Françoise Blanchard, Claire Marchal.
Story: B-movie about a Jungle Queen's revenge on the tribe of amazons who killed her parents.
Note: This is a French/Spanish co-production.

L'Amour à Mort [*Love Unto Death*] (col., 92 min., 1984)
Dir: Alain Resnais; *Wri*: Jean Gruault.
Cast: Sabine Azéma (Elisabeth), Pierre Arditi (Simon), Fanny Ardant (Judith), André Dussolier (Jérôme), Jean Dasté.
Story: Elisabeth and Simon are in love. Simon dies but comes back to life a changed man. When he decides to die again, Elisabeth chooses to join him.

Un Amour de Poche [*A Pocket Love*, transl. as *Girl in His Pocket, Nude in His Pocket*] (B&W., 88 min., 1957)
Dir: Pierre Kast; *Wri*: Pierre Kast, France Roche, based on the story *The Diminishing Draft* (1918) by Waldemar Kaempfert.
Cast: Jean Marais (Prof. Nordmann), Geneviève Page, (Édith), Agnès Laurent (Simone), France Roche, Amédée.
Story: Professor Nordmann discovers a way to shrink human beings and uses it to thwart his fiancée's jealousy.

Un Amour de Sorcière [*A Witch's Love*] (col., 100 min., 1997)
Dir/Wri: René Manzor.
Cast: Jeanne Moreau (Eglantine), Vanessa Paradis (Morgane), Jean Reno (Molok).
Story: Morgane is a good fairy and the mother of an 11-month-old baby. Her grand-mother Eglantine helps her defeat the villainous Molok.

L'Ampélopède (col., 83 min., 1974)
Dir/Wri: Rachel Winberg.

Cast: Patrizia Pierangeli, Isabelle Huppert, Jean-Marie Marguet, Philippe Lehembre, Louise Dhour.
Story: A young woman, tired of seeing her beloved countryside ravaged by pollution and home builders, invents a story about a fantastic creature which lives in the woods.

L'An 01 [*The Year 01*] (B&W., 90 min., 1972)
Dir: Jacques Doillon; *Wri*: Gébé (Georges Blondeaux), based on his novel.
Cast: Romain Bouteille, Cabu, Cavanna, Henri Guybet, Jacques Higelin.
Story: One day, men stop working and take time to enjoy life, thus beginning a new era.
Note: This post-1968, utopian sketch film was made by a number of famous French cartoonists from *Charlie-Hebdo*. Alain Resnais allegedly directed the Wall Street scene.

L'Âne Qui A Bu La Lune [*The Ass Which Drank the Moon*] (col., 95 min., 1986)
Dir/Wri: Marie-Claude Treilhou.
Cast: José Pech (Storyteller), Charles Serres, Marie-Thérèse Rocalve, Francis Serres, Magali Arnaud.
Story: An Old Man tells five stories adapted from folk tales:

1. *Les Trois Jeunes Gens* [*The Three Young Men*]
Story: Three young peasants go to Paris and are framed for murder.

2. *Le Cochon Élu Maire* [*The Pig Who Was Elected Mayor*]
Story: In a feud-torn village, a pig is elected mayor.

3. *Le Moine Changé en Âne* [*The Monk Who Was Turned into an Ass*]
Story: A cursed monk turns into an ass.

4. *L'Âne Qui A Bu la Lune* [*The Ass Which Drank the Moon*]

Story: A credulous young farmer believes his donkey has magical powers.

5. *Le Carnaval* [*Carnival*]
Story: A young man meets the ghost of a woman he once loved.

L'Ange [*The Angel*] (col., 70 min., 1982)
Wri/Dir: Patrick Bokanowski.
Cast: Maurice Baquet, Jean-Marie Bon, Martine Couture, Jacques Faure.
Story: A series of symbolic scenes linked together by the thematic image of a man climbing a staircase.
Note: This plotless film, which took five years to make, is mostly a technical achievement in weird special effects and image manipulation.

L'Ange et la Femme [*The Angel and the Woman*] (Col., 90 min., 1977)
Dir/Wri: Gilles Carle.
Cast: Carole Laure, Lewis Furey, Jean Comtois.
Story: An angel saves a woman from death and falls in love with her.
Note: This is a French-Canadian production, shot in French.

Angel-A (B&W., 90 min., 2005)
Dir/Wri: Luc Besson.
Cast: Jamel Debbouze (André), Rie Rasmussen (Angel), Gilbert Melki.
Story: A young man who tries to commit suicide is saved by an Angel.

Les Anges Gardiens [*The Guardian Angels*] (col., 110 min., 1995)
Dir: Jean-Marie Poiré; *Wri*: J.-M. Poiré, Christian Clavier.

Cast: Gérard Depardieu, Christian Clavier, Eva Grimaldi, Yves Rénier, Alexandre Eskimo, Jennifer Herrera, Zouzou, Fabienne Chaudat, Françoise Bertin, François Morel.
Story: A French gangster (Depardieu) and a priest (Clavier) face the task of rapatriating a Hong Kong orphan (Eskimo). Their guardian angels (Depardieu, Clavier), acting as their moral opposites, complicate matters.

L'Angle Mort [*Blind Spot*] (col. 104 min., 2019)
Dir/Wri: Patrick Mario Bernard, Pierre Trividic.
Cast: Jean-Christophe Folly (Dominick), Isabelle Carré.
Story: Dominick has the power to make himself invisible, until the day he loses his power.

Animal (col., 103 min., 2005)
Dir/Wri: Roselyne Bosch
Cast: Andreas Wilson, Emma Griffiths Malin.
Story: In the near future, an idealistic and ambitious young geneticist discovers the genes of aggression. He tries to modify a serial killer, before being himself tempted to increase his animalistic part.

Anna Oz (color, 98 min., 1996)
Dir: Eric Rochant; *Wri*: Gérard Brach, Eric Rochant.
Cast: Charlotte Gainsbourg (Anna Oz), Gerard Lanvin, Sami Bouajila, Gregori Derangère.
Story: In Venice, Anna Oz meets an art thief (Lanvin). But it may be the dream of a woman who lives in Paris.

L'Année Dernière à Marienbad [*Last Year in Marienbad*] (B&W., 93 min., 1961)
Dir: Alain Resnais; *Wri*: Alain Robbe-Grillet.
Cast: Delphine Seyrig, Giorgio Albertazzi, Sacha Pitoëff.
Story: In a strange hotel seemingly located outside of time, a man (Albertazzi) and a woman (Seyrig) meet, perhaps not for the first time...

Note: Robbe-Grillet's story was reportedly inspired by genre novel *La Invencion de Morel* by Argentinian writer Adolfo Bioy Casares. The novel deals with the protagonist's search for immortality through the recreation of time-looped holograms. It was filmed as a telefilm in 1967 (see next section).

Les Années Lumière [*Light Years Away*] (col., 90 min., 1981)
Dir/Wri: Alain Tanner, based on the novel *La Voie Sauvage* [*The Savage Way*] by Daniel Odier.
Cast: Trevor Howard, Mick Ford, Bernice Stegers.
Story: In Ireland, in the year 2000, a bartender learns the secret of flying from an old eccentric.
Note: French-Swiss co-production.

À Nous la Liberté ! [*Freedom Is Ours*] (B&W., 104 min., 1931)
Dir/Wri: René Clair.
Cast: Raymond Cordy (Louis), Henri Marchand (Émile), Paul Ollivier, Rolla France.
Story: Louis and Émile escape from jail. Later, Louis becomes a businessman, but eventually ends up giving away all his wealth to join Émile on the roads.
Note: Socialist utopia which inspired Charlie Chaplin. Its motto "work is freedom" became famous.

À Pied, à Cheval et en Spoutnik [*On Foot, on Horseback and in a Sputnik*, transl. as *A Dog, a Mouse and a Sputnik, Hold Tight for the Satellite*] (B&W., 100 min., 1958)
Dir: Jean Dréville; *Wri*: Jean-Jacques Vital, Jacques Grello, Robert Rocca, Noël-Noël.
Cast: Noël-Noël (Léon Martin), Denise Grey (Marguerite), Noël Roquevert, Darry Cowl, Pauline Carton, Misha Auer, Francis Blanche, Nathalie Nerval, Serge Nadaud, Sophie Daumier.
Story: Léon, a peace-loving Frenchman, finds in his garden a lost Russian satellite and the dog it contains.

Les Aquariens (col., 15 min., 2021)
Dir/Wri: Alice Barsby.
Cast: Jean-Michel Balthazar, Julie Maes, Finnegan Oldfield.
Story In the future gigantic tides cover the coasts of the littoral. However, in a deserted seaside town, a couple of rebels refuse to leave.

L'Araignée d'Eau [*The Water Spider*] (B&W., 95 min., 1968)
Dir: Jean-Daniel Verhaeghe; *Wri*: Marcel Béalu, based on his novel.
Cast: Marie-Ange Dutheil, Elisabeth Wiener, Marc Eyraud.
Story: A water spider turns into a beautiful girl to better doom the man who captured her.

Arako (col., 77 min., 2009)
Dir/Wri: Alexandre Laugier
Cast: Chris Tomneer, Gilles Azzopardi, Chantal Lechalier
Story: In the middle of the World War II, a soldier sees his brother killed on the battlefield. His general shows him a machine that can send him into the past to save his brother.

L'Arbre Sous La Mer [*The Underwater Tree*] (col., 95 min., 1984)
Dir/Wri: Philippe Muyl, based on the novel *A Naked Young Girl* by Nikos Athanassiadis.
Cast: Christophe Malavoy (Mathieu), Eleni Dragoumi, Julien Guiomar.
Story: In the Greek islands, Mathieu, a young geologist, falls in love with a beautiful "sea girl" (Dragoumi) but eventually discovers that their love cannot be.

Les Arcanes du Jeu [*The Arcanas of the Game*] (col., 26 min., 1982)
Dir/Wri: Chantal Picault.

Cast: Anne Morello, Zazie, Max Vialle, Jacques Rispal, Yves Carlevaris, Bernard Szajner.
Story: A young girl travels back in time to prevent her friend's death.

L'Arche de Noé [*Noah's Ark*] (B&W., 95 min., 1946)
Dir: Henri Jacques; *Wri*: Jacques Prévert, Pierre Laroche, based on a novel by Albert Paraz.
Cast: Pierre Brasseur (Bitru), Claude Larue, Jacqueline Pierreux, Jane Marken, Georges Rollin, Armand Bernard, Yves Deniaud, André Alerme.
Story: The mysterious Bitru leads a series of fantasy sketches illustrating that money does not make happiness, and that great inventions cause more harm than good.

Les Ardentes [*The Fiery Ones*] (col., 85 min., 1973)
Dir/Wri: Henri Sala.
Cast: Anne Libert, Sherry Parker, Monique Vila, Yann Keredec.
Story: X-rated story about a colony of women who live isolated in a strange medieval society.

Arès (col., 80 min., 2016)
Dir: Jean-Patrick Benes; *Wri*: Jean-Patrick Benes, Benjamin Dupas, Allan Mauduit.
Cast: Ola Rapace, Micha Lescot, Thierry Hancisse, Hélène Fillières.
Story: A boxer (Rapace) who is forced into testing a dangerous new performance-enhancing drug for one of the corporations that now controls France.

Armaguedon (col., 96 min., 1977)
Dir: Alain Jessua; *Wri*: Alain Jessua, based on a novel by David Lippincott.
Cast: Alain Delon (Dr. Ambrose), Jean Yanne (Armaguedon), Renato Salvatori.

Story: Dr. Ambrose is charged by the Government to locate a mysterious terrorist code-named "Armaguedon".

Arsène Lupin

Based on the famous gentleman burglar created in 1905 by popular writer Maurice Leblanc. Genre elements are few and far between, but Lupin being the French equivalent of *Sherlock Holmes*, its inclusion here seems warranted.

Arsène Lupin (B&W., 1914)
Dir/Wri: Émile Chautard.
Cast: Georges Tréville (Lupin).

Arsène Lupin, Détective (B&W., 98 min., 1937)
Dir/Wri: Henri Diamant-Berger.
Cast: Jules Berry (Lupin), Gabriel Signoter (Béchoux), Suzy Prim, Rosine Deréan, Mady Berry, Thomy Bourdelle.
Story: Lupin in his identity of private eye Jim Barnett matches wits with with Inspector Béchoux.

Les Aventures d'Arsène Lupin [*The Adventures Of Arsène Lupin*] (B&W., 104 min., 1956)
Dir: Jacques Becker; *Wri*: Albert Simonin, Jacques Becker.
Cast: Robert Lamoureux (Lupin), O. E. Hasse, Liselotte Pulver, Georges Chamarat.
Story: Original story about an elaborate series of robberies.

Signé Arsène Lupin [*Signed: Arsène Lupin*] (B&W., 100 min., 1959)
Dir: Yves Robert; Wri: Jean-Paul Rappeneau, Yves Robert, François Chavane, Robert Lamoureux.
Cast: Robert Lamoureux (Lupin), Alida Valli, Jacques Dufilho, Roger Dumas, Yves Robert, Robert Dalban.
Story: Original story in which Lupin seeks the legendary Golden Fleece.

Arsène Lupin contre Arsène Lupin [*Arsène Lupin vs. Arsène Lupin*] (B&W., 106 min., 1962)
Dir: Édouard Molinaro; *Wri*: Georges Neveux.
Cast: Jean-Pierre Cassel (Lupin), Jean-Claude Brialy (Lupin), Françoise Dorléac, Geneviève Grad, Michel Vitold, Jean Le Poulain, Henri Virlojeux.
Story: Original story in which Lupin's two sons compete against each other.

Arsène Lupin (col., 125 min., 2004)
Dir: Jean-Paul Salomé; Wri: Jean-Paul Salomé, Laurent Vachaud.
Cast: Romain Duris (Lupin), Kristin Scott Thomas (Joséphine Balsamo), Pascal Greggory, Eva Green, Robin Renucci, Patrick Toomey, Mathieu Carrière, Philippe Magnan, Philippe Lemaire.
Story: Free adaptation of *Countess Cagliostro*.

Atarrabi et Mikelats (col., 122 min., 2020)
Dir/Wri: Eugène Green
Cast: Saia Hiriart (Atarrabi), Lukas Hiriart (Mikelats), Ainara Leemans, Thierry Biscary.
Story: Two brothers, Atarrabi and Mikelats, sons of the goddess Mari and a mortal, are entrusted to the Devil for their education. Having become adults, Mikelats chooses to stay with the Master, while Atarrabi wants to flee. But when he leaves, the Devil holds back his shadow.
Note: Belgian production shot in the Basque language.

L'Atlantide [*Atlantis*]
Based on the classic novel by Pierre Benoît (1919) in which two French officers lost in the Sahara come across the last city of Atlantis, ruled by the cruel Queen Antinéa.
L'Atlantide (B&W., 90 min., 1921)
Dir/Wri: Jacques Feyder.

Cast: Stacia Napierkowska (Antinéa), Jean Angelo (Morhange), Georges Melchior (Saint-Avit), Marie-Louise Iribe.

L'Atlantide (B&W., 110 min., 1932)
Dir: Georg Wilhelm Pabst; *Wri*: Ladislao Vajda, Alexandre Arnoux & Jacques Deval.
Cast: Brigitte Helm (Antinéa), Jean Angelo (Morhange), Pierre Blanchar (Saint-Avit).
Note: French-German co-production.

L'Atlantide (B&W., 110 min., 1961)
Dir: Edgar G. Ulmer & Giuseppe Masini; *Wri*: Edgar G. Ulmer, Edmond Gréville, Ugo Liberatore, André Tabet, Remigio Del Grosso & Amadeo Nazzari.
Cast: Haya Harareet (Antinéa), Rad Fulton (Robert / Morhange), Jean-Louis Trintignant (Pierre / Saint-Avit).
Note: French-Italian co-production. The film ends with an atomic explosion.

L'Atlantide (col., 110 min., 1991)
Dir/Wri: Bob Swaim.
Cast: Victoria Mahoney (Antinéa), Tchéky Karyo (Morhange), Christopher Thompson (Saint-Avit).

Atomik Circus, le retour de James Bataille [*Atomik Circus, The Return of James Bataille*] (col., 91 min., 2004)
Dir: Didier Poiraud, Thierry Poiraud; *Wri*: Jean-Philippe Dugand, Marie Garel-Weiss, Didier Poiraud, Thierry Poiraud, Vincent Tavier.
Cast: Vanessa Paradis (Concia), Jean-Pierre Marielle, Benoît Poelvoorde, Jason Flemyng (James), Venantino Venantini.
Story: Skotlett City is still traumatized by the disastrous Big Cow Pie Party. James Bataille ended up in prison and escapes, determined to find Concia, his fiancée, who wants to become a country singer. But starfish from another planet attack and Concia's future impresario turns into a monster.

Attack of Serial Killers from Outer Space (col., 90 min., 1993)
Dir/Wri: Richard J. Thomson.
Cast: Blaise Michel R., Richard J. Thomson, Héléna Halat, Axel Vyridar, Stanley Théophane.
Story: Two murderous aliens escape from the clutches of French security.
Note: Low-budget feature shot on video.

Au Coeur de la Vie [*In the Midst of Life*] (B&W., 90 min., 1962)
Dir/Wri: Robert Enrico, based on three stories by Ambrose Bierce.

1. *Chickamauga*
Story: A little deaf boy plays with the ghosts of the soldiers who died during the famous Civil War battle.
Cast: Pierre Boffety (Johnny), Frédérique Ruchaud (Mother), Jean Mauvais, Pierre de Roubaix, Fred Lissou, Richard Glanz, Pierre Lobreau (Soldiers).

2. *L'Oiseau Moqueur* [*Mockingbird*]
Story: A soldier shoots his own twin brother by mistake.
Cast: Éric Frankiel (William Grteyrock), François Frankiel (John Greyrock), Micheline Caty, Georgette Larson.

3. *La Rivière du Hibou* [*Owl River*, transl. as *An Occurrence at Owl Creek Bridge*] (27 min.)
Cast: Roger Jacquet (Peyton Farquhar), Anne Cornaly (Abby Farquhar), Anker Larsen, Stéphane Fey, Jean-François Zeller, Pierre 7Danny, Louis Adelin (Union Soldiers).
Story: During the Civil War, a Confederate spy who is about to be hung miraculously escapes and manages to return home. But the whole thing was only a dream, and he dies on the gallows.

Note: In order to save money, *The Twilight Zone* producer William Froug purchased the rights to the third short feature, which had won a prize at the 1962 Cannes Film Festival. A new introduction was recorded by Rod Serling and it was incorporated as episode 22 of Season 5 of *The Twilight Zone* and originally broadcast on 28 February 1964. This reedited version went on to win an Oscar.

Au-delà du sang [*Beyond the Blood*] (col., 82 min., 2012)
Dir/Wri: Guillaume Tauveron.
Cast: Takahiro Ono (Shinji), Mari Yoshida (Tomoko), Omocha Chiba, Keisaku Kimura.
Story: A year after the murder of his wife, Shinji receives a mysterious message. Haunted by his memories and the ghost of his wife, he will then sink into the darkness of Tokyo where he meets a young runaway, Tomoko.
Note: French-Japanese co-production.

Au Rendez-Vous de la Mort Joyeuse [*Rendezvous with Joyous Death*] (col., 90 min., 1972)
Dir: Juan Luis Buñuel; *Wri*: Pierre-Jean Maintigneux, Juan Luis Buñuel.
Cast: Yasmine Dahm (Sophie), Jean-Marc Bory, Françoise Fabian, Jean-Pierre Darras, Michel Creton, Claude Dauphin, Gérard Depardieu.
Story: A family moves into a haunted house which succeeds in making all of them, except their daughter, Sophie, leave.

Au Service du Diable [*In The Devil's Service*]
See *La Plus Longue Nuit du Diable*.

L'Autre Sang [*The Other Blood*] (col., 19 mion., 2012)
Dir/Wri: François Tchernia & François Vacarisas.
Cast: Xavier Gallais, Juana Acosta, Karina Testa, Thomas Chabrol.
Story: Paul finally gives himself the gift of his dreams: a 30 centimeter-high avatar.

L'Autre Vie de Richard Kemp [*Richard Kemp's Other Life*, transl. as *Back in Crime*] (col., 102 min., 2013)
Dir: Germinal Alvarez; *Wri*: Germinal Alvarez, Nathalie Saugeon.
Cast: Jean-Hugues Anglade (Kemp), Mélanie Thierry (Hélène), Philippe Berodot.
Story: A murder victim is found near a river by Hélène (Mélanie Thierry), a psychiatrist. Police Captain Richard Kemp investigates and discovers it is similar to an old serial-killer case he worked on. Kemp is attacked by an unknown assailant, thrown into the river, and finds himself twenty years in the past, just before the murders begin.

L'Avant-Dernier [*The Penultimate*]
See *Le Dernier Combat*.

Les Aventures d'Eddie Turley [*The Adventures of Eddie Turley*] (B&W., 85 min., 1987)
Dir/Wri: Gérard Courant.
Cast: Philip Dubuquoy (Eddie Turley), Françoise Michaud (Lola), Joël Barbouth, Mariola San Martin, Lucia Fioravanti, Joseph Morder, Gérard Tallet.
Story: *La Jetée* meets *Alphaville*. In this feature made of 2400 stills, galactic agent Eddie Turley arrives in Modern City, which he eventually discovers is ruled by a giant computer. He leaves with his new-found love, Lola.

Les Aventures Extraordinaires d'Adèle Blanc-Sec [*The Extraordinary Adventures of Adèle Blanc-Sec*] (col., 107 min., 2010)
Dir/Wri: Luc Besson, based on the comic book series by Jacques Tardi.
Cast: Louise Bourgoin (Adèle), Mathieu Amalric, Gilles Lellouche, Jean-Paul Rouve, Jacky Nercessian
Story: The adventures of the eponymous female writer in 1910s Paris; this episode, the first in the series, revolves

around a pterodactyl, a group of parapsychologist and advanced Ancient Egyptian technology.
Note: Tardi's popular comic book series is a pastiche of French science fiction of the times.

L'Avion [*The Plane*] (col., 100 min., 2005)
Dir: Cédric Kahn; *Wri*: Ismaël Ferroukhi, Cédric Kahn, Denis Lapière, Gilles Marchand, Raphaëlle Valbrune.
Cast: Roméo Botzaris (Charly), Isabelle Carré, Vincent Lindon, Nicolas Briançon.
Story: Charly, an eight-year-old boy, receives a model airplane at Christmas, His father dies shortly thereafter and the boy realizes that the plane is "alive". He manages to tame it and leaves to search for his father with its help.
Note: French-German co-production.

Babel (color, 95 min., 1998)
Dir: Gérard Pullicino; *Wri*: Vincent Lambert, Serge Richez & Gérard Pullicino.
Cast: Maria de Medeiros, Michel Jonasz, Tchéky Karyo, Mitchell David Rothpan.
Story: Since the beginning of time, the Babels have watched over the Earth. Now they need human help to save the world.

Baby Blood [transl. as *The Evil Within*] (col., 89 min., 1989)
Dir: Alain Robak; *Wri*: Alain Robak, Serge Cukier.
Cast: Emmanuelle Escourrou (Yanka), Jean-François Gallotte, Roselyn Geslot, Christian Sinniger, Alain Chabat, Anne Singer, Jean-Claude Romer.
Story: Yanka is a circus woman whose womb is taken over by a creature and later protects the life of the blood-sucking monster to which she eventually gives birth.
Note: French critic Jean-Claude Romer has a small role in this unusualy gory French horror film. Gary Oldman provided the voice of the creature in the U.S. version.

Babylon A.D. (col., 101 min., 2008)

Dir: Mathieu Kassovitz; *Wri*: Mathieu Kassovitz, Éric Besnard, Joseph Simas, based on the novel by Maurice G. Dantec,
Cast: Vin Diesel, Mélanie Thierry, Michelle Yeoh, Lambert Wilson, Charlotte Rampling, Gérard Depardieu.
Story: In a dystopian near-future, Russian mobster Gorsky (Depardieu) hires the mercenary Toorop (Diesel) to bring a young woman known only as Aurora (Thierry) from Europe to New York City.

Balaoo, ou Des Pas Au Plafond [*Balaoo, or Footprints on the Ceiling*] (B&W., 652 M., 1913)
Dir: Victorin Jasset, based on the novel by Gaston Leroux.
Cast: Lucien Bataille (Balaoo), Camille Bardou, Henri Gouget.
Story: The story of a murderous man-ape.
Note: An American film version was produced under the title *The Wizard* in 1927, directed by Richard Rosson with Gustav von Seyfferlitz, Edmund Lowe and Leila Hyams, and again in 1942 as *Dr. Renault's Secret*, directed by Harry Lachman, with J. Carrol Naish, George Zucco and Lynne Roberts.

Le Bal des Folles [*The Mad Woman's Ball*] (col., 122 min., 2021)
Dir: Mélanie Laurent; *Wri*: Mélanie Laurent, Christophe Deslandes, based on the novel by Victoria Mas.
Cast: Mélanie Laurent, Lou de Laâge (Eugénie), Emmanuelle Bercot, Benjamin Voisin, Martine Chevallier.
Story: In the 1880s, Eugénie, a woman who has the gift to hear and see the dead, is unfairly institutionalized at a Paris asylum and plots to escape with the help of one of her nurses.

Ballade de la Féconductrice [*Ballad of the Feconductrix*] (col., 85 min., 1979)
Dir/Wri: Laurent Boutonnat.
Cast: Orit Mizrahi, Gilles Mathé.
Story: The tale of an evil fairy.

Le Ballon Sorcier [*The Enchanted Balloon*] (col., 90 min., 1999)
Dir: Danny Deprez; *Wri*: Danny Deprez, Jean-Claude Van Rijckeghem.
Cast: Martje Ceulemans (Sophia), Jonas De Ro, Matthias Meersmans.
Story: Sophia, 11, is lonely and is bothered by a gang of kids who have taken over a vacant lot where her only friend, a stray dog, lives. She then meets a gypsy who offers her a balloon with mysterious powers.
Note: Belgian production.

Banlieue 13 [*Suburb 13*] (col., 84 min., 2004)
Dir: Pierre Morel; *Wri*: Luc Besson, Bibi Naceri.
Cast: David Belle (Leïto), Cyril Raffaelli (Damien), Tony D'Amario, Dany Verissimo.
Story: A WMD having been stolen by the most powerful gang in the suburbs, policeman Damien is tasked with infiltrating the area to either defuse or recover it.

Banlieue 13 : Ultimatum [*Suburb 13: Ultimatum*] (col., 101 min., 2009)
Dir: Patrick Alessandrin; *Wri*: Luc Besson.
Cast: David Belle, Cyril Raffaelli, Philippe Torreton, Daniel Duval, Élodie Yung
Story: Three years later, Damien and Leïto team up again to save the city from chaos.

Barbarella (col., 98 min., 1967)
Dir: Roger Vadim; *Wri*: Terry Southern, Jean-Claude Forest, Roger Vadim, Vittorio Bonicelli, Brian Degas, Claude Brulé, Tudor Gates, Clement Biddle Wood; based on the graphic novel by Jean-Claude Forest.
Cast: Jane Fonda (Barbarella), John Philip Law (Pygar), Anita Pallenberg (Black Queen), Milo O'shea, Marcel Marceau, Ugo Tognazzi, David Hemmings, Claude Dauphin

Story: Barbarella is sent by Earth to planet Sogo to bring back a missing scientist. There, she encounters Pygar, a blind angel, and a lesbian queen.
Note: French-Italian co-production.

Barbe-Bleue [*Bluebeard*] (B&W., 90 min., 1951)
Dir: Christian-Jaque; *Wri*: André-Paul Antoine, Henri Jeanson, Christian-Jaque, based on the fairy tale by Charles Perrault.
Cast: Pierre Brasseur (Amédée de Salfère), Cécile Aubry (Aline), Jacques Semas, Jean Debucourt, Robert Arnoux, Georges Chamarat.
Story: Variation on the famous legend. Aline, the sixth wife of the Count of Salfere, discovers that her husband's previous wives are still alive.

Barbe-Bleue [*Bluebeard*] (col., 80 min., 2009)
Dir/Wri: Catherine Breillat, based on the fairy tale by Charles Perrault.
Cast: Dominique Thomas (Barbe-Bleue), Lola Créton, Daphné Baiwir.
Story: Same as above.

Le Baron Fantôme [*The Ghostly Baron*] (B&W., 99 Min, 1942)
Dir: Serge de Poligny; *Wri*: Serge de Poligny, Louis Chavance, Jean Cocteau.
Cast: Odette Joyeux (Elfy), Jany Holt (Anne), Alain Cuny (Hervé), Gabrielle Dorziat (Countess), Claude Sainval, André Lefaur, Aimé Clariond, Jean Cocteau.
Story: The Countess of Saint-Hélié and her two daughters, Elfy and Anne, move into a castle reputedly haunted by their late uncle, baron Carol (Cocteau, in a small role). They eventually find the Baron's body in a secret chamber, and the daughters find their true loves.

Baxter (col., 82 min., 1988)

Dir: Jérôme Boivin; *Wri*: Jacques Audiard, Jérôme Boivin, based on the novel by Ken Greenhall.
Cast: Maxime Leroux (voice of Baxter), Lise Delamare, Jean Mercure, Jacques Spiesser, Catherine Ferran, Jean-Paul Roussillon, Sabrina Leurquin, Daniel Rialet, Evelyne Didi.
Story: A thinking, talking dog, Baxter, narrates the grim story of his life.

La Beauté du Diable [*The Beauty and the Devil*] (B&W., 92 min., 1949)
Dir: René Clair; *Wri*: Armand Salacrou, René Clair.
Cast: Michel Simon (Mephistopheles), Gérard Philipe (Henri), Simone Valère, Nicole Besnard, Gaston Modot, Paolo Stoppa.
Story: A remake of the classic *Faust* story, recast in modern times.
Note: French-Italian co-production.

Belle (col., 93 Min, 1972)
Dir/Wri: André Delvaux.
Cast: Jean-Luc Bideau (Mathieu), Adriana Bogdan (Belle), Danièle Delorme (Jeanne), Roger Coggio.
Story: Mathieu, a writer, falls in love with a mysterious woman who lives in the woods and never speaks. She drives him to commit murder, but it may all have been a dream.
Note: This is a French-language Belgian production.

La Belle et la Bête [*The Beauty and the Beast*] (B&W., 100 min., 1945)
Dir/Wri: Jean Cocteau, based on the classic fairy tale by Mesdames Gabrielle-Suzanne Barbot de Villeneuve & Jeanne-Marie Leprince de Beaumont.
Cast: Josette Day (Belle), Jean Marais (Beast/Prince), Marcel André, Michel Auclair, Mila Parély.
Story: To save her father's life, a beautiful young woman agrees to spend her life in the castle of a magical beast. Her love will turn the Beast back into a Prince Charming.

La Belle et la Bête [*The Beauty and the Beast*] (col., 112 min., 2014)
Dir: Christophe Gans; Wri: Christophe Gans, Sandra Vo-Anh, based on the classic fairy tale by Mesdames Gabrielle-Suzanne Barbot de Villeneuve & Jeanne-Marie Leprince de Beaumont.
Cast: Léa Seydoux (Belle), Vincent Cassel (Beast/Prince), André Dussollier, Eduardo Noriega, Audrey Lamy
Story: Same as above.

La Belle Captive [*The Beautiful Prisoner*] (col., 88 min., 1983)
Dir/Wri: Alain Robbe-Grillet.
Cast: Daniel Mesguich (Walter), Gabrielle Lazure (Marie-Ange), Cyrille Claire (Sara), Daniel Emilfork, Roland Dubillard, François Chaumette.
Story: Sara entrusts her boyfriend Walter with a mysterious mission. He then encounters the beautiful, vampire-like Marie-Ange, who takes him on a series of surreal adventures.

La Belle Histoire [*A Beautiful Story*] (col., 210 min., 1991)
Dir: Claude Lelouch; *Wri*: Claude Lelouch, Marilyne Dupoux.
Cast: Gérard Lanvin, Béatrice Dalle, Patrick Chesnais, Constantin Alexandrov, Vincent Lindon, Paul Préboist, Anémone, Charles Gérard.
Story: A gypsy (Lanvin) and a young female thief (Dalle) are the reincarnations of a couple who lived at the time of Jesus and are fated to fall in love.

La Belle Image [*The Beautiful Image*] (B&W., 90 min., 1950)
Dir: Claude Heymann; *Wri*: Jean Ferry, Claude Heymann, based on the story by Marcel Aymé.
Cast: Franck Villard (Raoul), Françoise Christophe (Renée), Pierre Larquey, Junie Astor, Suzanne Flon.
Story: Raoul, a man with a plain face, magically finds himself transformed into a very handsome man.

Les Belles de Nuit [*Beauties of the Night*] (col., 89 min., 1952)
Dir: René Clair; *Wri*: René Clair, Pierre Barillet, Jean-Pierre Grédy.
Cast: Martine Carol, Gina Lollobrigida, Gérard Philipe.
Story: A frustrated pianist (Philipe) has vivid dreams in which he is pursued by beautiful women in different historical eras.
Note: French-Italian co-production.

Belphegor (B&W., Serial in four episodes, 1926)
Dir: Henri Desfontaines; *Wri*: Arthur Bernède.
Cast: René Navarre (Chantecoq), Lucien Dalsace (Bellegarde), Elmire Vautier (Simone Desroches/Belphégor), Georges Paulais (Commissioner Ménardier), Jeanne Brindeau (Elsa).
Story: A ghostly presence is haunting the Louvre. The villains are unmasked by journalist Bellegarde and detective Chantecoq. Belphegor is revealed to be Bellegarde's mistress, Simone.
Note: Arthur Bernède also created the character of *Judex* (see below). *Belphegor* was later remade as a television series (see next section).

Belphégor, le Fantôme du Louvre [*Belphegor, the Phantom of the Louvre*] (col., 97 min., 2001)
Dir: Jean-Paul Salomé, *Wri*: Jean-Paul Salomé, Danièle Thompson, Jérôme Tonnerre, based on the story by Arthur Bernède.
Cast: Sophie Marceau (Lisa/Belphégor), Frédéric Diefenthal, Michel Serrault, Julie Christie
Story: Mediocre remake in which a mummy's spirit that possesses a woman.

La Bête [*The Beast*] (col., 104 min., 1975)
Dir/Wri: Walerian Borowczyk.

Cast: Sirpa Lane, Lisbeth Hummel, Pierre Benedetti, Guy Tréjean, Marcel Dalio, Roland Armontel, Jean Martinelli, Pascale Rivault.
Story: A strange, erotic variation on *La Belle et la Bête*, in which the Beast turns out to be an over-endowed wild boy.

Bien Profond dans ton Âme [*Deep Into Your Soul*] (col., 86 min., 2013)
Dir/Wri: Jean Adrien Espiasse.
Cast: Gunther Van Severen (Jacques), Colin Deleau, Sophie Lewish.
Story: Jacques accidentally stumbles into a manhole that turns out to be the portal to a fantasy world.

Big Bug (col., 111 min., 2022)
Dir: Jean-Pierre Jeunet; *Wri*: Jean-Pierre Jeunet, Guillaume Laurant.
Cast: Elsa Zylberstein (Alice), Isabelle Nanty, Stéphane de Groodt, Claude Perron.
Story: In the year 2045, everyone uses domestic robots. Alice's house is equipped only with old models. After a party, as her guests prepare to leave, the robots revolt.

Black Moon (Col., 100 Min, 1975)
Dir/Wri: Louis Malle.
Cast: Cathryn Harrison (Lily), Thérèse Giehse, Alexandra Stewart, Joe Dallesandro
Story: During a war between the sexes, Lily finds refuge in a forest cabin inhabited by an Old Woman who talks to rats (Giehse), a strange brother-sister couple (Dallesandro, Stewart), a discursive unicorn and a piano-playing cat.

Une Blonde Comme Ça [*A Blonde Like That*] a.k.a. **Miss Shumay Jette un Sort** [*Miss Shumway Casts a Spell*] (color, 91 min., 1962)
Dir: Jean Jabély; *Wri*: Félicien Marceau, Jean Jabély, Jacques Robert, based on the 1944 novel *Miss Shumay Waves a Hand*

by "Raymond Marshall" (a pseudonym of James Hadley Chase).
Cast: Taïna Beryl (Myra Shumway), Harold Kay, Jess Hahn, Robert Manuel, René Lefèvre.
Story: Miss Shumway is a witch who possesses supernatural powers.

Blondie Maxwell Ne Perd Jamais [*Blondie Maxwell Never Loses*] (col., 87 min., 2020)
Dir/Wri: Julien Ivanowich.
Cast: Léonie Langlart, Stéphane Dufourcq, Vincent Terrier.
Story: Blondie Maxwell is a future anticipation thriller. It explores the consequences of unreasonable use of technology and artificial intelligence while addressing concepts of the ultra uberisation of society and the privatization of justice.

Blondine (B&W., 61 min., 1943)
Dir: Henri Mahé; *Wri*: Paule Hutzler.
Cast: Nicole Maurey (Blondine), Michele Philippe (Brune), Guita Karen, Lolita de Sylva, Michele Grimoin, Georges Marchal, Pierre Piéral (Moncheri).
Story: In this fairy tale, the daughter of a fisherman, Blondine, marries a Prince and then rescues him from the clutches of an Ogre.
Note: The only time where the "simplifilm" process (use of painted backgrounds instead of real sets) was used for a feature-length production.

Blood Machines (col., 50 min., 2019)
Dir: Seth Ickerman; *Wri*: Seth Ickerman, Paul La Farge.
Cast: Elisa Lasowski, Anders Heinrichsen, Christian Erickson.
Story: A crew sets off in pursuit of an artificial intelligence that has escaped from their spaceship.

Blueberry, L'Expérience Secrète [*Blueberry, The Secret Experience*, transl. as *Renegade*] (col., 124 min., 2004)

Dir: Jan Kounen; *Wri*: Matthieu Le Naour, Alexandre Coquelle, Gérard Brach, Louis Mellis, Jan Kounen, Cassidy Pope, inspired by the comic-book series by Jean-Michel Charlier & Moebius.

Cast: Vincent Cassel (Mike Donovan), Juliette Lewis, Michael Madsen (Blount), Ernest Borgnine, Djimon Honsou, Eddie Izzard, Tchéky Karyo, Colm Meaney.

Story: U.S. Marshal Mike Donovan (referred to as "Broken Nose" by the aboriginal tribe; unlike the comic his nickname is not Blueberry) has dark memories of the death of his first love. He keeps peace between the whites and the aborigines who had temporarily adopted and taken care of him. The evil actions of Blount, a "white sorcerer," lead him to confront the villain in the Sacred Mountains, and, through shamanic rites involving an entheogenic brew, conquer his fears and uncover a suppressed memory he would much rather deny.

Note: "Acid western" which has little in common with the source material. The Estate of Jean-Michel Charlier had his name removed from the credits.

Le Boucher [*The Butcher*] (col., 95 min., 1969)
Dir/Wri: Claude Chabrol.
Cast: Jean Yanne (Popaul), Stéphane Audran, Roger Rudel, William Guerault, Mario Beccaria, Antonio Passalia, Pascal Ferone.
Story: Popaul, the butcher of a small regional village, is suspected of being a serial killer by the new schoolteacher

Boulevard de l'Étrange [*Boulevard of the Weird*] (117 min., 1986)
Compilation of 8 short features (listed in order of appearance):
1. *Le Mauvais Oeil* [*The Evil Eye*] (col., 15 min, 1985)
Dir/Wri: Jean-Louis Cros.
Cast: Georges Claisse, Catherine Wilkening, François Capelier.
Story: A 19th century photographer discovers he has magical powers.

2. *Je Reviens De Suite* [*I'll Be Right Back*] (col., 15 min, 1982)
Dir/Wri: Henri Gruvman.
Cast: Henri Gruvman, Florence Aguttes, Ulrika White.
Story: A stage magician enables people to enter the world of celluloid film.

3. *L'Abygène* (b&w., 9 min, 1985)
Dir/Wri: Anne Bocrie.
Cast: Anne Caudry, Samuel Malaval.
Story: An ordinary woman's breakfast turns into a nightmare.

4. *Le Ciel Saisi* [*The Captured Sky*] (col., 23 min, 1983)
Dir/Wri: Henri Herré.
Cast: Marie Vayssière, Philippe Marbot.
Story: Omnipresent surveillance cameras spy on an ordinary couple.

5. *Le Réacteur Vernet* [*The Vernet Reactor*] (col., 11 min, 1985)
Dir: Laurent Dussaux; *Wri*: Laurent Dussaux, Laurent Zerah, based on a story by Lion Miller.
Cast: Claude Klotz, Gérard Grobman, Philippe Mareuil.
Story: A retarded man invents a wonderful machine.

6. *La Fonte de Barlaeus* [*The Melting of Barlaeus*] (col., 15 min, 1983)
Dir/Wri: Pierre-Henri Salfati.
Cast: Roland Dubillard, Sylvie Flepp, Rachel Salik, Michel Caccia.
Story: A man believes he is made of butter.

7. *Game Over* (col., 8 min, 1984)
Dir/Wri: Bernard Villiot.
Cast: Roger Mirmont, Marc Mazza, Roxanne Nouban.

Story: A killer, his victim and a witness are trapped in a deadly game.

8. *La Consultation* (b&w., 21 min, 1985)
Dir/Wri: Radovan Tadic.
Cast: Isabelle Weingarten, Dominique Marcas, Sébastien Floche.
Story: A troubled mother visits a psychiatrist who turns out to be a monkey.

Buffet Froid [*Cold Cuts*] (col., 95 min., 1979)
Dir/Wri: Bertrand Blier.
Cast: Gérard Depardieu (Alphonse Tram), Bernard Blier (The Inspector), Jean Carmet (The Killer), Michel Serrault, Carole Bouquet.
Story: Alphonse Tram, a police inspector, and a serial killer embark on a murder spree.

Le Bunker de la Dernière Rafale [*The Bunker of the Last Gale*] (B&W., 27 min., 1981)
Dir: Jean-Pierre Jeunet & Marc Caro; *Wri*: Jean-Pierre Jeunet, Marc Caro, Gilles Adrien.
Cast: Marc Caro, Jean-Pierre Jeunet, Jean-Marie de Busscher, Bruno Richard.
Story: In a bunker where the survivors of a future war hide, a countdown begins and destroys the precarious social fabric.

Bunker Palace Hotel (col., 95 min., 1989)
Dir: Enki Bilal; *Wri*: Enki Bilal, Pierre Christin.
Cast: Jean-Louis Trintignant (Holm), Carole Bouquet (Klara), Maria Schneider (Muriel), Roger Dumas, Yann Collette, Jean-Pierre Léaud, Hans Meyer.
Story: In an unidentified Eastern European country torn by civil war, the former political elite has found refuge in a vast underground bunker. A young rebel, Klara, manages to infiltrate the bunker, but things begin to fall apart.

Note: Enki Bilal and Pierre Christin are two renowned French graphic novelists.

La Cage [*The Cage*] (col., 83 min., 1963)
Dir: Robert Darène; *Wri*: Christine Garnier, Alain Bouvette, Pierre Tristan, Marc Boureau, Georges de la Grandière, Robert Darène.
Cast: Marina Vlady, Jean Servais, Philippe Maury, Myriel David, Colette Duval, Alain Bouvette.
Story: An African spell causes a man to see apparitions of his dead wife.

Calmos [*Quiet Please!*] (col., 107 min., 1976)
Dir: Bertrand Blier; *Wri*: Bertrand Blier, Philippe Dumarçay.
Cast: Jean-Pierre Marielle (Paul), Jean Rochefort (Albert), Bernard Blier (Priest), Pierre Bertin, Brigitte Fossey.
Story: A group of men who are tired of women decide to retire to the countryside and live in peace.

Camille redouble [*Camille Rewinds*] (col., 115 min., 2012)
Dir: Noémie Lvovsky; *Wri*: Noémie Lvovsky, Florence Seyvos, Pierre-Olivier Mattei, Maud Ameline.
Cast: Noémie Lvovsky (Camille), Yolande Moreau, Michel Vuillermoz, Denis Podalydès, Samir Guesmi.
Story: On her way to a party Camille consults a quirky clockmaker because she needs to have her watch fixed. The watch has sentimental value for her because she got it as a present for her 16th birthday. Next morning Camille realises it is the year 1985 and she is again a teenager.

Cartes sur Table [*Cards on the Table*, transl. as *Attack of the Robots*] (B&W., 93 min., 1966)
Dir: Jess Franco; *Wri*: Jean-Claude Carrière.
Cast: Eddie Constantine, Sophie Hardy, Fernando Rey, Alfredo Mayo.
Story: Men are turned into killer robots.
Note: French-Spanish co-production.

Cauchemar Blanc [*White Nightmare*] (B&W., 8 min., 1991)
Dir/Wri: Mathieu Kassovitz, based on a comic-book story by Moebius.
Cast: Yvan Attal, François Toumarkine, Roger Souza, Jean-Pierre Darroussin, Abder El Kebir, Émile Abossolo M'Bo, Laurent Goldstein.
Story: A gang of racists who sets out to beat up an innocent Arab worker experiences a nightmarish adventure.

La Cavalcade des Heures [*The Cavalcade of the Hours*] (B&W., 99 min., 1943)
Dir/Wri: Yvan Noé.
Cast: Pierrette Caillol (Hora), Fernandel (Antonin), Charles Trenet, Tramel, Gaby Morlay, Jeanne Fusier-Gir, Jean Chevrier, Jules Ladoumègue.
Story: In this sketch film, the Incarnation of Time (Caillol) helps a series of characters to take control of their destiny.

Le Cerf-Volant du Bout du Monde [*The Kite from the End of the World*, transl. as *The Magic of the Kite*] (color, 80 min., 1958)
Dir: Roger Pigault, Wang Kia-Yi; *Wri*: Roger Pigault, Antoine Tudal.
Cast: Patrick de Bardine (Pierrot), Jacques Faburel, Sylviane Rozenberg, Charles Vissieres.
Story: Young Pierrot is transported to China by a magic kite.
Note: Rare French-Chinese co-production.

C'est Arrivé Près De Chez Vous [*It Happened Near You*, transl. as *Man Bites Dog*] (B&W., 95 min., 1992)
Dir: Rémy Belvaux, André Bonzel, Benoît Poelvoorde; *Wri*: Rémy Belvaux, André Bonzel, Benoît Poelvoorde, Vincent Tavier.
Cast: Benoît Poelvoorde (Ben), André Bonzel, Rémy Belvaux, Jacqueline Poelvoorde Pappaert, Nelly Pappaert, Hector Pappaert, Valérie Parent, Jenny Drye, Malou Madou.

Story: A television crew follows and interviews Ben, a serial killer, and eventually becomes involved in his insane life.
Note: French-language Belgian production with no specific genre elements, but an incredibly surreal and violent ambiance.

La Chambre Ardente [*The Burning Court*] (B&W., 111 min., 1963)
Dir: Julien Duvivier; *Wri*: Julien Duvivier, Charles Spaak, based on the novel by John Dickson Carr.
Cast: Jean-Claude Brialy, Nadja Tiller, Balpêtré, Walter Giller, Helena Manson.
Story: A woman who seems possessed by her ancestor, a famous poisoner, commits a murder.
Note: Despite a rational explanation at the end, the entire film operates on the basis that possession by a spirit is real.

La Chambre Verte [*The Green Room*] (col., 94 min., 1978)
Dir: François Truffaut; *Wri*: François Truffaut, Jean Gruault, based on the novel by Henry James.
Cast: François Truffaut (Davenne), Nathalie Baye (Cécilia), Jean Dasté, Jean-Pierre Moulin, Antoine Vitez, Jane Lobre, Jean-Pierre Ducos.
Story: Davenne, a man who literally worships the dead, falls in love with Cécilia, a woman who shares his obssession.

Les Charlots contre Dracula [*The Charlots vs. Dracula*] (col., 85 min., 1980)
Dir: Jean-Pierre Desagnat; *Wri*: Les Charlots (Gérard Rinaldi, Gérard Filippelli, Jean Sarrus, Jean-Guy Fechner, Luis Rego et Richard Bonnot), Jean-Pierre Desagnat, Olivier Mergault, Fernand Pluot, based on an idea by Vera Belmont and Jacques Dorfmann.
Cast: Les Charlots, Amélie Prévost, Andréas Voutsinas (Dracula), Gérard Jugnot.

Story: A famous French comedy team (*à la* Three Stooges) fights the notorious undead Count, who is looking for a magic bottle, in this slapstick farce.

Le Charme Discret de la Bourgeoisie [*The Discreet Charm of the Bourgeoisie*] (col., 105 min., 1972)
Dir: Luis Buñuel; *Wri*: Luis Buñuel, Jean-Claude Carrière.
Cast: Fernando Rey (Ambassador), Paul Frankeur (Thévenot), Delphine Seyrig (Mrs. Thévenot), Bulle Ogier (Florence), Jean-Pierre Cassel, Stéphane Audran, Michel Piccoli, Claude Piéplu, Julien Bertheau, François Maistre.
Story: A series of surreal, satirical sketches (often dealing with death and dreams) assembled around the theme of a dinner party held by the same cast of bourgeois characters. Perhaps they are all dead and this is their afterlife?

La Charrette Fantôme [*The Ghost Cart*] (B&W., 93 min., 1939)
Dir/Wri: Julien Duvivier, based on the book by Selma Lagerlöf.
Cast: Pierre Fresnay (David), Louis Jouvet (Georges), Micheline Francey (Edith), Valentine Tessier, Mila Parély, Pierre Palau.
Story: Edith, a Salvation Army worker, tries to save the soul of David, whose nights are haunted by the shade of his late friend Georges, condemned to drive the Ghost Cart because of his evil deeds.

La Chasse au Nuage [*The Hunt for the Cloud*]
See *Le Petit Nuage*.

Le Château de la Dernière Chance [The Castle of Last Chance] (B&W., 85 min., 1946)
Dir: Jean-Paul Paulin; *Wri*: Jean-Paul Paulin, Henri Troyat.
Cast: Pierre Bertin (Prof. Patureau-Duparc), Nathalie Nattier, Corinne Calvet, Robert Dhéry, Jean Marchat, Julien Carette.

Story: Professor Patureau-Duparc offers a personality-altering serum to people who want to commit suicide.

Le Château des Messes Noires [*The Castle of Black Masses*, transl. as *The Devil's Plaything*] (col., 100 min., 1972)
Dir/Wri: Joseph Sarno.
Cast: Nadia Henkowa, Anke Syring.
Story: A couple finds refuge in a castle inhabited by vampires.
Note: Swiss production.

Le Château de la Mort Lente [*The Castle of Slow Death*] (B&W., 90 min., 1925)
Dir: Donatien; *Wri*: André de Lorde, based on his play co-written with Henri Bauche.
Cast: Donatien (Hermann), Lucienne Legrand (Lola), Pierre Etchepare (Enrique), Rachel Devirys (Maud Hammersley), Viguier.
Story: A castle houses a community of lepers. Any intruder is given the leper's kiss and made into a leper himself.
Note: This is based on a popular *Grand-Guignol* play.

Le Château du Passé [*The Castle of the Past*] (B&W., 20 min., 1959)
Dir/Wri: Marc de Gastyne.
Cast: Gaston Modot.
Story: Ghosts make two shepherdesses' wishes come true.

Le Château du Vice [*The Castle of Vice*]
See *La Plus Longue Nuit du Diable*.

Le Chemin d'Azatoth [*Azatoth's Path*] (col., 13 min., 1987)
Dir/Wri: Clément Delage.
Cast: Jean Bouise, Jean-Marie Marion, Valérie Steffen, Robert Enrico.
Story: A gangster on the lam in the countryside meets a strange sect.

Les Chemins de la Violence [*The Paths of Violence*]
See *Perversions Sexuelles*.

Cherchez l'Erreur [*Find the Mistake*] (col., 92 min., 1980)
Dir: Serge Korber; *Wri*: Roland Magdane.
Cast: Roland Magdane (Paul), Roland Dubillard, Henri Virlojeux, Caroline Grimaldi, Micheline Luccioni, Tania Lopert, Marthe Villalonga, Béatrice Lord.
Story: Paul, an eccentric scientist, discovers a miracle formula that might save the world, or destroy it. After the formula kills his dog, he destroys it.

Chéri-Bibi
The adventures of a former convict gifted with extraordinary strength created by Gaston Leroux. After being unjustly incarcerated, Cheri-Bibi and La Ficelle are sent to Devil's Island. They take over the prison ship and later rescue some shipwrecked people, including the beautiful Cecily who is fianced to the evil Maxime du Touchais. Dr. Kanak kills Maxime and grafts his face on Cheri-Bibi who hopes to start a new life.

Chéri-Bibi (B&W., 1913)
Dir: Gérard Bourgeois; *Wri*: Gaston Leroux.
Cast: René Navarre (Chéri-Bibi), Josette Andriot (Cécily), Camille Bardou, Gilbert Dalleu.

Chéri-Bibi (B&W., 1330 meters, 1914)
Dir/Wri: Charles Krauss.
Cast: Émile Keppens (Chéri-Bibi), Marise Dauvray, Charles Krauss.

Chéri-Bibi : **La Nouvelle Aurore** [*The New Dawn*] (B&W., 16 episodes, 1919)
1: *Palas au Bagne* (*Palas at the Penitentiary*); 2: *L'Evasion* (*The Escape*); 3: *Vers la Lumière* (*Towards the Light*) ; 4: *Le Combat du Jour et de la Nuit* (*The Battle of Day and Night*) ; 5: *Le Jugement de Dieu* (*The Judgment of God*) ; 6: *La Lune de Miel* (*The Honeymoon*) ; 7: *Les Cau-*

chemars de Palas (*Palas' Nightmares*) ; 8: *Le Héros et le Bandit* (*The Hero and the Bandit*) ; 9: *Les Voiles Se Déchirent* (*The Veils Are Torn*) ; 10: *La Vengeance de Gorbio* (*Gorbio's Revenge*) ; 11: *Deux Douleurs* (*Two Pains*) ; 12: *Le Calvaire* (*The Calvary*) ; 13: *Gisèle ;* 14: *La Tullia ;* 15: *Fatalitas!;* 16: *Le Calice* (*The Chalice*).
Dir: Edouard E. Violet; *Wri*: Gaston Leroux.
Cast: José Davert (Chéri-Bibi), René Navarre (Palas), Manuel Caméré, Suzanne Linker, Rachel Devirys, Jacqueline Arly.

Chéri-Bibi (B&W., 120 min., 1937)
Dir: Léon Mathot; *Wri*: Jacques Constant.
Cast: Pierre Fresnay (Chéri-Bibi), Suzet Maïs (Ginette), Jean-Pierre Aumont (Palas), Marcel Dalio, Thomy Bourdelle.
Note: Remake of the 1919 serial.

Chéri-Bibi (col., 84 min., 1954)
Dir: Marcello Pagliero; *Wri*: Paul Mesnier.
Cast: Jean Richard (Chéri-Bibi), Danielle Godet (Cécily), Raymond Bussières, Albert Préjean.
Note: French-Italian co-production

Le Chevalier de la Nuit [*The Knight of the Night*] (B&W., 90 min., 1953)
Dir: Robert Darène; *Wri*: Jean Anouilh, Robert Darène.
Cast: Jean-Claude Pascal, Renée Saint-Cyr, Grégoire Aslan, Max Dalban, Louis de Funès.
Story: In this *Dr. Jekyll & Mr. Hyde* variation, a man is haunted by two personalities, one good, the other evil.

Les Chevaliers de la Table Ronde [*The Knights of the Round Table*] (col., 230 min., 1989)
Dir: Denis Llorca; *Wri*: Denis Llorca, Philippe Vialèles, based on the classic stories by Chrétien de Troyes.

Cast: Alain Cuny (Merlin), Alain Macé (Arthur), Maria Casarès (Viviane), Michel Vitold (Fisher King), Mireille Delcroix (Amythe), Nadine Darmon (Morgaine), Gilles Geisweiller (Perceval), Denis Llorca (Lancelot), Valérie Durin (Guinevere), François Berreur (Galaad), Benoist Brione (Gauvain).
Story: Faithful, if somewhat static, translation of the saga of King Arthur and the Quest for the Holy Grail.
Note: This was based on an 11-hour-long stage play.

La Chevelure [*The Hair*] (col., 19 min., 1960)
Dir/Wri: Ado Kyrou, based on a story by Guy de Maupassant.
Cast: Michel Piccoli
Story: A madman has come into possession of some feminine hair of great beauty. He becomes obsessed with it, until he believes that the dead woman has appeared to him, and become his mistress.

Les Chiens [*The Dogs*] (col., 99 min., 1979)
Dir: Alain Jessua; *Wri*: Alain Jessua, André Ruellan.
Cast: Gérard Depardieu (Morel), Victor Lanoux (Dr. Féret), Nicole Calfan (Elisabeth), Pierre Vernier, Gérard Séty, Fanny Ardant.
Story: Morel, a trainer of aggressive guard dogs, uses fear of crime to gain control of the minds of the inhabitants of a suburban town, until the pent-up violence he has fostered eventually turns against him.
Note: André Ruellan is the noted science fiction writer Kurt Steiner. He also wrote the film's novelization.

Les Chinois à Paris [*The Chinese In Paris*] (col., 95 min., 1974)
Dir: Jean Yanne; *Wri*: Jean Yanne, Gérard Sire, Robert Beauvais, based on his novel.
Cast: Jean Yanne (Régis), Michel Serrault (Grégoire), Nicole Calfan (Stéphanie), Bernard Blier, Paul Préboist, Jacques François, Georges Wilson, Daniel Prévost, Macha Méril, Fernand Ledoux.

Story: Thinly veiled political satire about a Chinese invasion of France.

Christina, Princesse de l'Erotisme [*Christina, Princess of Erotism*]
See *Une Vierge chez les Morts Vivants*.

Chrysalis (col., 93 min., 2007)
Dir: Julien Leclercq; *Wri*: Julien Leclercq, Franck Philippon.
Cast: Albert Dupontel, Marie Guillard, Marthe Keller (Brügen), Mélanie Thierry.
Story: In the near future, the army has developed an experimental machine, Chrysalis, capable of creating a digital copy of the brain and implanting it in a human body. Professor Brügen hopes to create a "copy" of his daughter in a coma following a car accident and has young girls abducted and implanted in them with his daughter's memories.

La Chute de la Maison Usher [*The Fall of the House of Usher*] (B&W., 55 min., 1928)
Dir/Wri: Jean Epstein, based on the story by Edgar Allan Poe.
Cast: Marguerite Gance (Lady Usher), Jean Debucourt (Roderick Usher), Charles Lamy.
Story: Much praised silent adaptation of the classic story about an evil house inhabited by a cursed family.
Note: Luis Buñuel assisted Jean Epstein on this film. The same year, another version of this classic story was made in Rochester, New York, by James Sibley Watson & Melville Webber.

Le Ciel sur la Tête [*The Sky Over My Head*] (col., 107 min., 1964)
Dir: Yves Ciampi; *Wri*: Yves Ciampi, Alain Satou & Jean Chapot.
Cast: André Smagghe, Jacques Monod, Marcel Bozzuffi, Yves Brainville, Guy Tréjean, Henri Piegay, Bernard Fresson, Béatrice Cenci.

Story: The crew of a French aircraft carrier must solve the mystery of an unidentified satellite. Is it American, Russian, or extraterrestrial?

Le Cinquième Élément [*The Fifth Element*] (col., 127 min., 1997)
Dir: Luc Besson; *Wri*: Robert Mark Kanen, Luc Besson.
Cast: Bruce Willis (Korben), Gary Oldman (Zorg), Ian Holm (Cornelius), Milla Jovovich (Leeloo), Chris Tucker.
Story: In a futuristic world, cab driver Korben Dallas and alien clone Leeloo team up to search for the elusive "Fifth Element" and defeat the forces of darkness.
Note: French-American co-production. Visual designs were provided by renowed comic book artists Moebius and Jean-Claude Mézières.

La Cité des Enfants Perdus [*The City of Lost Children*] (col., 111 min., 1995)
Dir: Jean-Pierre Jeunet & Marc Caro; *Wri*: J.-P. Jeunet, M. Caro, Gilles Adrien, Guillaume Laurent.
Cast: Ron Perlman, Daniel Emilfork (Krank), Judith Vittet, Dominique Pinon, Jean-Claude Dreyfus, Geneviève Brunet, Odile Mallet, Mireille Mosse, François Hadji-Lazaro, Joseph Lucien.
Story: Crazed inventor Krank is aging because he can't dream. To counter this, his cyclopean henchmen kidnap children from the local port. A circus strongman (Perlman) teams up with a band of ragamuffins to stop him.

La Cité Foudroyée [*The City Struck by Lightning*] (B&W., 60 min., 1924)
Dir: Luitz-Morat; *Wri*: Jean-Louis Bouquet.
Cast: Daniel Mendaille, Jeanne Maguenat, Armand Morins.
Story: A mad scientist (Mendaille) who has found the way to control lightning threatens to destroy Paris, but it all turns out to be events in a novel.

La Cité de l'Indicible Peur [*The City of Unspeakable Fear*] (aka *La Grande Frousse* [*The Great Fear*]) (B&W., 90 min., 1964)
Dir: Jean-Pierre Mocky; *Wri*: Jean-Pierre Mocky, Gérard Klein, based on the novel by Jean Ray.
Cast: Bourvil (Triquet), Jean-Louis Barrault (Douve), Francis Blanche (Franqui), Jean Poiret, Victor Francen, Raymond Rouleau, Jacques Dufilho, René-Louis Lafforgue, Véronique Nordey.
Story: Triquet, a charming but hapless police inspector, unmasks several murderers in a small provincial town whose residents harbor dark secrets.
Note: The Gérard Klein who co-wrote the script is not the homonymous French science fiction writer/editor.

La Cité de la Peur [*The City of Fear*] (col., 90 min., 1994)
Dir: Alain Berberian; *Wri*: Les Nuls (Alain Chabat, Chantal Lauby et Dominique Farrugia).
Cast: Chantal Lauby, Alain Chabat, Dominique Farrugia, Gérard Darmon, Valérie Lemercier.
Story: During the Cannes Film Festival, a serial killer duplicates the murders of a low-budget horror film ("Red is Dead") being promoted there.
Note: Les Nuls are a famous French troupe of television comics.

Clash (col., 100 min., 1983)
Dir/Wri: Raphaël Delpard.
Cast: Catherine Alric (Martine), Pierre Clémenti (Stranger), Bernard Fresson (Bé), Jean-Claude Benhamou, Igor Galo.
Story: Martine helps Bé commit a robbery; later, they meet a mysterious Stranger, who turns into a monster. It was all a dream. She is killed by the gangsters, but the Stranger returns to take her away.
Note: French-Yugoslavian co-production.

Clérambard (Col., 100 min., 1969)

Dir: Yves Robert; *Wri*: Yves Robert, Jean-Loup Dabadie, based on a novel by Marcel Aymé.
Cast: Philippe Noiret (Clérambard), Dany Carrel, Lise Delamare, Roger Carel, Claude Piéplu.
Story: Clérambard is an odious country squire who becomes a saintly prophet after seeing a vision of St. Francis of Assisi.

Club Extinction
See *Docteur M*.

Coeur de Coq [*Rooster Heart*] (B&W., 75 min., 1946)
Dir: Maurice Cloche; *Wri*: Raymond Vinci, Jean-Pierre Feydeau, Jean Manse.
Cast: Fernandel (Tulipe), Mireille Perrey (Vera), Gisèle Alcée (Loulou), Paul Azaïs, Jean Temerson.
Story: The shy Tulipe is in love with Loulou, his boss' daughter. A mad scientist (Temerson) transplants the heart of a rooster who gives him the courage to pursue his love. But it was all a dream.

Coincidences (B&W., 95 min., 1946)
Dir: Serge Debecque; *Wri*: Pierre Laroche, Serge Debecque.
Cast: Serge Reggiani (Menetrier), Pierre Renoir (Badolas), Andrée Clément (Françoise), Françoise Deillie (Michèle), Louise Sylvie (Amélie), Jean Parédès, Robert Le Béal, Denise Grey, Suzanne Bara.
Story: Three cursed magic balls destroy the life of a man.

Coma (col., 85 min., 1994)
Dir: Denys Granier-Deferre; *Wri*: Jacqueline Carot, based on a novel by Frédéric Dard.
Cast: Richard Anconina, Anna Kanakis, Isabelle Candelier.
Story: A crippled man is the prisoner of two beautiful women in a Portuguese mansion. But it may all be an illusion.
Note: Frédéric Dard is a famous thriller writer, known for his popular satirical detective character, Police Commissioner San Antonio.

Le Coma des Mortels [*Deadly Coma*, transl. as *Perpetual Present*] (col., 42 min., 2004)
Dir/Wri: Philippe Sisbane
Cast: Alexandre Cross, Roger Carel, Alexandre Zeff, Marie Riva.
Story: A biologist manages to keep alive the brain of his twin brother, who has just been guillotined. But it takes possession of the scientist's mind and threatens vengeance.

Combat contre l'amour en songe [*Love Torn in a Dream*] (col., 122 min., 2000)
Dir/Wri: Raoul Ruiz.
Cast: Melvil Poupaud, Elsa Zylberstein, Lambert Wilson, Christian Vadim.
Story: Ghosts, heroes, nuns, dead, philosophers, pirates, etc. come to express themselves in the present.

Comédie de l'Innocence [*Comedy of Innocence*] (col., 100 min., 2000)
Dir: Raoul Ruiz; *Wri*: Raoul Ruiz, François Dumas, adapted from Massimo Bontempelli novella *Il Figilio del Due Madri* (The Child of Two Mothers).
Cast: Isabelle Huppert (Ariane), Jeanne Balibar (Isabella), Charles Berling (Serge), Denis Podalydès (Pierre), Nils Hugon (Camille), Laure de Clermont-Tonnerre (Hélène), Chantal Bronner (Martine), Bruno Marengo (Alexandre).
Story: Camille frightens his mother, Ariane, during his ninth birthday party when he proclaims that she's not his real parent. The next day, he leads her to the home of violin teacher Isabella, whose son died by drowning two years ago and would now be the same age as Camille. Isabella, a mentally unstable patient of Camille's psychiatrist uncle, Serge, claims the boy is her dead son reincarnated and moves in with the family.

La Comète [*The Comet*] (col., 22 min., 1981)
Dir/Wri: Catherine Cohen.

Cast: Christine Fersen, Romain Trembleau.
Story: A mother and a child fight while a comet threatens to destroy Earth.

Comment je suis devenu super-héros [*How I Became a Superhero*] (col., 101 mion., 2020)
Dir: Douglas Attal; *Wri*: Douglas Attal, Mélisa Godet, Charlotte Sanson, Cédric Anger, Gérald Bronner, bsased on his novel.
Cast: Pio Marmaï (Moreau), Vimala Pons (Cécile), Benoît Poelvoorde, Leïla Bekhti.
Story: In Paris 2020, superheroes are now fully integrated into society. Lieutenant Moreau investigates incidents caused by a mysterious substance giving superpowers to those who did not have them. He teams up with Cécile, a new recruit.

La Comtesse Noire [*The Dark Countess*, transl. as *The Bare-Breasted Countess*] (col., 85 min., 1973)
Dir/Wri: Jess Franco.
Cast: Lina Romay, Jack Taylor.
Story: X-rated vampires.
Note: French-Belgian co-production.

La Concentration (col., 94 min., 1968)
Dir/Wri: Philippe Garrel.
Cast: Jean-Pierre Léaud, Zouzou.
Story: In a surrealistic prison, a man and a woman live and fight, until he eventually kills her.

Le Concile de Pierre [*The Stone Council*] (col., 102 min., 2006)
Dir: Guillaume Nicloux; *Wri*: Guillaume Nicloux, Stéphane Cabel, based on a novel by Jean-Christophe Grangé.
Cast: Monica Bellucci (Laura), Catherine Deneuve (Sybille), Moritz Bleibtreu, Sami Bouajila, Elsa Zylberstein.
Story: Laura adopts a Mongolian child with the help of her friend Sybille. Years later, a bruise appears on the boy's chest,

and the two women suffer nightmares. The child begins speaking in an unknown tongue. Mysterious murders began occurring. The women discover the boy comes from an ancient, mystic Mongolian tribe who want him returned to fulfill a religious prophecy.

Confessions d'un Barjo [*Confessions of a Crap Artist*, transl. as *Barjo*] (col., 85 min., 1991)
Dir: Jérôme Boivin; *Wri*: Jacques Audiard, Jérôme Boivin, based upon a novel by Philip K. Dick.
Cast: Hippolyte Girardeau (le Barjo), Richard Bohringer (Charles), Anne Brochet (Fanfan), Consuelo de Haviland.
Story: Fanfan just married Charles; unfortunately, his crazy, head-in-the-clouds brother lives with them.
Note: Virtually no fantasy elements, but the film is based on a novel by SF master Philip K. Dick.

Coplan FX-18
The adventures of Francis Coplan, Agent FX-18, are the French equivalent of *James Bond*. The novels were published by Editions Fleuve Noir, and written by Paul Kenny, a pseudonym of writers Jean Libert & Gaston Vandenpanhuyse. These two authors also wrote a number of noted science fiction novels under the pseudonym of Jean-Gaston Vandel.

Action Immédiate [*Immediate Action*] (B&W., 105 mon., 1957)
Dir: Maurice Labro; *Wri*: Yvan Audouard, Frédéric Dard & Jean Redon.
Cast: Henri Vidal (Coplan), Barbara Laage, Jacques Dacqmine, Nicole Maurey, Lino Ventura.
Story: Coplan is sent to Geneva to track down the head of an international spy ring.

Coplan, Agent Secret FX-18 [*Copan, Secret Agent Fx-18*, transl. as *Coplan Tries His Luck*] (col., 97 min., 1964)
Dir: Maurice Cloche; Wri: Christian Plume, Joaquin Bollo, Maurice Cloche.

Cast: Ken Clark (Coplan), Jany Clair, Guy Delorme, Jacques Dacqmine.
Story: A spy satellite must be destroyed.

Coplan prend des risques [*Coplan Takes Risks*] (col., 89 min., 1964)
Dir: Maurice Labro; *Wri*: François Chavane, Pascal Jardin, Jean Marsan, Jean-Louis Roncoroni.
Cast: Dominique Paturel (Coplan), Virna Lisi, Jacques Balutin, André Weber.
Story: Coplan must find a stolen protype.

Coplan FX-18 Casse Tout [*Coplan Fx-18 Destroys Everything*; transl. as *The Exterminators*] (col., 95 min., 1965)
Dir: Ricardo Freda; *Wri*: Claude Marcel Richard.
Cast: Richard Wyler (Coplan), Robert Manuel, Gil Delamare, Jany Clair, Valeria Ciangottini.
Story: Coplan helps Israeli agents thwart the plans of a neo-nazi tycoon (Manuel) who plots to destroy New York with a nuclear rocket assembled in a secret underground base.

Coplan Ouvre le Feu à Mexico [*Coplan Opens Fire in Mexico*, transl. as *Coplan Between the Nets*] (col., 93 min., 1966)
Dir: Ricardo Freda; *Wri*: José Antonio de la Loma.
Cast: Lang Jeffries (Coplan), Sabine Sun, Silvia Solar, Frank Oliveras, Ida Galli, Antonio Orengo.
Story: A Mexican tycoon is building atom bombs to take over the world.

Coplan Sauve Sa Peau [*Coplan Saves His Skin*] (col., 90 min., 1967)
Dir: Yves Boisset; *Wri*: Claude Veillot, Yves Boisset.
Cast: Claudio Brook (Coplan), Margaret Lee, Jean Servais, Bernard Blier, Jean Topart, Klaus Kinski.

Story: In Istanbul, Coplan thwarts the plans of a Count Zaroff-like mad scientist (Servais).

Cosmodrama (col., 112 min., 2015)
Dir/Wri: Philippe Fernandez.
Cast: Jackie Berroyer, Bernard Blancan, Émilia Dérou-Bernal, Ortès Holz, Serge Larivière, Sascha Ley, Emmanuel Moynot, Stefanie Schüler.
Story: A spaceship lost in the universe is carrying a small team of explorers who, after too long a cryogenization, no longer know where they are, where they are going, or where they come from.

Les Couleurs du Diable [*The Devil's Colors*] (col., 90 min., 1996)
Dir/Wri: Alain Jessua.
Cast: Ruggero Raimondi (Bellisle), Wadeck Stanczak (Nicolas), Isabelle Pasco (Valérie), Bettina Giavannini (Hélène).
Story: Young artist Nicolas produces macabre paintings that have no success until the mysterious and charismatic Bellisle offers to help him.

Coup de Jeune [*Getting Young*] (col., 88 min., 1992)
Dir: Xavier Gélin; *Wri*: Philippe Setbon, Xavier Gélin.
Cast: Martin Lamotte, Ludmila Mikaël, Jean Carmet, Daniel Gélin (Gaudéamus), Antonin Lebas-Joly, Jean-Pierre Castaldi, Anémone, Patrick Chesnais, Manuel Gélin.
Story: The 70 years-old Professor Gaudéamus finds a serum which turns him into a 6 years-old, while retaining all his memories and personality. His son (Carmet) helps him reach a more satisfying middle age, before eventually reverting to his natural age, having learned that age is a thing of the mind.
Note: This film is obviously inspired by Howard Hawks' *Monkey Business* (1952), as well as René Goscinny & Coq's comic strip, *Docteur Gaudéamus*.

Le Couple Idéal [*The Ideal Couple*] (B&W., 92 min., 1945)

Dir: Bernard Roland; *Wri*: Pierre Léaud, André Cayatte, Michel Duran.
Cast: Raymond Rouleau (Diavolo), Hélène Perdrière (Diane), Denise Grey, Annette Poivre, Simone Signoret, Jean Lanier, Yves Deniaud, Marcel Vallée.
Story: Romantic comedy involving the two stars of a 1912 *Judex*-like serial entitled *Justex*.

Les Créatures [*The Creatures*] (B&W., 90 min., 1966)
Dir/Wri: Agnès Varda.
Cast: Michel Piccoli, Catherine Deneuve, Éva Dahlbeck, Britta Petterson, Jacques Charrier, Ursula Kubler, Marie-France Mignal.
Story: A novelist (Piccoli) on holiday with with his pregnant wife (Deneuve), who lost her voice in a car accident, plots his next book by using real people and twisting their lives through the prism of his imagination.

Le Cri du Hibou [*The Cry of the Owl*] (col., 112 min., 1987)
Dir: Claude Chabrol; *Wri*: Claude Chabrol, Odile Barski, based on a novel by Patricia Highsmith.
Cast: Christophe Malavoy (Robert), Mathilda May (Juliette), Jacques Penot, Jean-Pierre Kalfon.
Story: Gory thriller in which two jilted lovers plot a bloody revenge.

Du Crime Considéré Comme Un Des Beaux Arts [*Of Crime Considered as One of the Fine Arts*] (col., 15 min., 1980)
Dir: Frédéric Compain; *Wri*: Frédéric Compain, Gilles Taurand.
Cast: Michel Piccoli, Dominique Farro, Rebecca Pauly, Pat Andréa.
Story: In the future, a detective (Piccoli) investigates a crime.

Le Crime du Dr. Chardin [*Dr. Chardin's Crime*])
See *Les Hommes Veulent Vivre !*

Croisières Sidérales [*Star Cruises*] (B&W., 95 min., 1941)
Dir: André Zwobada; *Wri*: Pierre Guerlais.
Cast: Madeleine Sologne (Françoise), Julien Carette (Lucien), Suzanne Dehelly, Robert Arnoux, Jean Marchat.
Story: Two astronauts, Lucien and Françoise, explore outer space in a hot-air balloon (!) and return to Earth to discover that they've aged only two weeks while twenty-five years have elapsed. This leads to holiday cruises in space.

Crying Freeman (Col., 100 min., 1995)
Dir: Christophe Gans; *Wri*: Christophe Gans, Thierry Cazals, based on the comic book by Kazuo Koike & Ryoichi Ikegami.
Cast: Julie Condra, Mark Dacascos, Masaya Kato, Tchéky Karyo.
Story: An Asian hit man who cries when he kills people falls in love with his intended target.
Note: French-Canadian co-production.

La Dame de Pique [*The Queen of Spades*] (B&W., 92 min., 1964)
Dir: Léonard Kiegel; *Wri*: Julien Green, Eric Jourdan, based on the novel by Alexander Pushkin.
Cast: Dita Parlo (Anna), Michel Subor (Hermann), Jean Negroni (Saint-Germain), Simone Bach, Philippe Lemaire.
Story: The mysterious Count Saint-Germain teaches Countess Anna the secret of winning at cards. Many years later, Hermann, a young officer eventually learns the secret from her ghost. But when he draws the Queen of Spades, he kills himself.

Le Danger vient de l'Espace [*Danger from Outer Space*] (B&W., 82 min., 1958)
Dir: Paolo Heusch, Mario Bava; *Wri*: Marcello Coscia, Sandro Continenza, based on a story by Virgilio Sabel.
Cast: Paul Hubschmid, Fiorella Mari, Madeleine Fischer, Ivo Garranl, Giacomo Rossi-Stuart, Dario Michaelis, Peter Meersman, Jean-Jacques Delbo.

Story: A large asteroid is diverted from its path and is heading straight for Earth. All nations join forces to send a barrage of nuclear missiles to destroy the object.
Note: French-Italian co-production.

Dans la Brume [*In the Mist*] (Col., 89 min., 2018)
Dir: Daniel Roby; *Wri*: Jimmy Bemon, Mathieu Delozier, Guillaume Lemans.
Cast: Romain Duris (Mathieu), Olga Kurylenko (Anna), Fantine Harduin, Michel Robin, Anna Gaylor, Réphaël Ghrenassia, Erja Malatier.
Story: A couple lives peacefully in Paris with their daughter. One day, a strange mist coming from the sewers kills people and floods the entire capital, forcing the survivors onto the rooftops.

Dans les Griffes du Maniaque [*In the Clutches of the Maniac*, aka, *The Diabolical Dr. Z, Miss Death and Dr. Z, Miss Death*] (B&W., 86 min., 1965)
Dir: Jess Franco; *Wri*: Jean-Claude Carrière, based on the novel by David Kuhne.
Cast: Mabel Karr, Fernando Montes, Estella Blain.
Story: Men are turned into killer robots.
Note: French-Spanish co-production. This is the third in the *Dr. Orloff* series.

Dans le Ventre du Dragon [*In the Belly of the Dragon*] (col., 100 min., 1988)
Dir: Yves Simoneau; *Wri*: Pierre Revelin, Marcel Beaulieu.
Cast: Rémy Girard (Steve), Michel Côté (Bozo), David La Haye (Lou), Marie Tifo, Monique Mercure, Andrée Lachapelle.
Story: A scientist working for a Quebec-based pharmaceutical company conducts research into the power of the brain, but her human guinea pigs start aging at an accelerated pace.
Note: French-Canadian production

Dante 01 (col., 88 min. 2008)
Dir: Marc Caro; *Wri*: Marc Caro, Pierre Bordage.
Cast: Lambert Wilson, Linh-Dan Pham, Simona Maicanescu, Dominique Pinon.
Story: In the future, a biologist and a prisoner arrive at a secure psychiatric station, Dante 01, where the most dangerous criminals of the galaxy are incarcerated.
Note: Pierre Bordage is a renowned science fiction writer.

Dead Shadows (col., 75 min., 2015)
Dir/Wri: David Cholewa.
Cast: Fabian Wolfrom, Gilles Barret, Laurie Cholewa.
Story: Eleven years ago, Chris' parents were brutally murdered during the passage of Haley's Comet. Today, the comet is back and people are turning into monsters...

Le Déclic [*Click*] (col., 90 min., 1984)
Dir/Wri: Jean-Louis Richard, based on the graphic novel by Milo Manara.
Cast: Jean-Pierre Kalfon (Fez), Florence Guérin (Claudia), Bernard Kuby, Jasmine Maimone, Lisa Marks.
Story: Fez, a lovesick scientist, uses an electronic gadget to trigger Claudia's erotic behavior; but her husband becomes jealous.

Delicatessen (col., 95 min., 1992)
Dir: Jean-Pierre Jeunet & Marc Caro; *Wri:* J.-P. Jeunet, M. Caro, Adrien Gilles.
Cast: Marie-Laure Dougnac, Dominique Pinon, Karin Viard, Jean-Claude Dreyfus, Ticky Holgado, Anne-Marie Pisani, Edith Ker, Patrick Paroux, Jean-Luc Caron.
Story: In a surreal near-future, a butcher murders to provide the building's other tenants with fresh meat.

Demain la Veille [*Tomorrow Yesterday*] (col., 15 min., 2006)
Dir: Julien Lecat & Sylvain Pioutaz; *Wri*: Julien Lecat, Sylvain Pioutaz, Laurent Caillaud.

Cast: Stéphane Metzger, Julie de Bona, François Levantal, Frédéric Pierrot, Nicky Naudé.
Story: People live in a backwards bizarro universe.

Demain les Mômes [*Tomorrow, The Kids*] (col., 100 min., 1975)
Dir: Jean Pourtalé; *Wri*: Jean Pourtalé, Franck Vialle, Raymond Lepoutre.
Cast: Niels Arestrup (Philippe), Brigitte Rouan, Emmanuelle Béart.
Story: After a mysterious cataclysm, a lone survivor, Philippe, encounters a tribe of children who obstinately refuse all contact with him.

Le Démon dans l'Île [*The Demon on the Island*] (col., 102 min., 1982)
Dir: Francis Leroi; *Wri*: Francis Leroi, Owen T. Rozmann.
Cast: Jean-Claude Brialy (Dr. Marshall), Anny Duperey (Gabrielle) Pierre Santini, Cerise, Gabriel Cattand.
Story: Gabrielle, a young doctor newly arrived on an island, eventually discovers that a series of deadly accidents have been caused by a psychokinetic child controlled by the evil Dr. Marshall.

Les Démoniaques [*Demoniacs*] (aka *Les Diablesses* [*The She-Devils*], *Deux Vierges Pour Satan* [*Two Virgins For Satan*]) (col., 84 min., 1973)
Dir/Wri: Jean Rollin.
Cast: Joëlle Coeur, Live Lone, John Rico.
Story: Three men and a woman draw passing ships to their doom on a lonely coast.

Les Démons [*The Demons*] (col., 114 min., 1973)
Dir/Wri: Jess Franco.
Cast: Anne Libert, Britt Nichols.
Story: Dermonic possession.

Le Dernier Chaperon Rouge [*The Last of the Red Riding Hoods*] (col., 26 min., 1996)
Dir: Jan Kounen; Wri: Jan Kounen, Carlo de Boutiny, based on the fairy tale by Charles Perrault.
Cast: Emmanuelle Béart (Red Riding Hood), Gérald Weingand (The WEolf).
Story: Sci-fi version of the classic fairy tale.

Le Dernier Combat [*The Last Combat*] (B&W., 90 min., 1982)
Dir: Luc Besson; Wri: Luc Besson, Pierre Jolivet.
Cast: Pierre Jolivet, Jean Bouise, Jean Reno, Fritz Wepper, Christiane Kruger.
Story: In a post-apocalyptic world where men have lost their voices, a survivor (Jolivet) is taken in by a doctor (Bouise) who has managed to save the last woman on Earth and fights a savage warrior (Reno) to the death.
Note: Expanded version of a 1981 short entitled *L'Avant-Dernier* [*The Penultimate*].

Le Dernier Homme [*The Last Man*] (col., 82 min., 1969)
Dir/Wri: Charles Bitsch.
Cast: Jean-Claude Bouillon, Corinne Brill, Sophia Torkelli.
Story: Three spelunkers—one man and two women—are the only survivors after an atomic war.

Le Dernier Voyage [*The Last Journey*] (col., 87 min., 2020)
Dir: Romain Quirot; *Wri*: Romain Quirot, Antoine Jaunin, Laurent Turner.
Cast: Hugo Becker (Paul), Paul Hamy, Lya Oussadit-Lessert, Jean Reno.
Story: In a post-apocalyptic future, a strange red star is over-exploited for its energy. As its trajectory changes and it hurtles straight towards Earth, Paul is the only astronaut capable of destroying it.
Note: Based on a short feature entitled *Le Dernier voyage de l'énigmatique Paul W.R.* (2015) also by Romain Quirot.

La Dernière Vie de Simon [*Simon's Last Life*] (col., 103 min., 2019)
Dir: Léo Karmann; *Wri*: Léo Karmann, Sabrina B. Karine.
Cast: Benjamin Voisin (Simon), Martin Karmann, Camille Claris.
Story: Eight year-old Simon is an orphan who wants to find a foster family; he has the power to take on the appearance of the people he touches.

Les Derniers Jours [*The Last Days*] (col., 100 min., 2013)
Dir/Wri: David Pastor, Alex Pastor.
Cast: Quim Gutiérrez, José Coronado, Marta Etura.
Story: Since the spread of a strange virus, the world has become terrifying: people are condemned to live cloistered and must fight for their survival.
Note: French-Spanish co-production.

Les Derniers Jours du Monde [*The Last Days of the World*] (col., 130 min., 2009)
Dir: Arnaud & Jean-Marie Larrieu; *Wri*: Arnaud & Jean-Marie Larrieu, Dominique Noguez.
Cast: Mathieu Amalric, Catherine Frot, Sergi López.
Story: The end of the world is approaching. Robinson (Mathieu Amalric) embarks on a quest to flee disaster and find a woman he once loved.

Les Deux Mondes [*The Two Worlds*] (col., 105 min., 2007)
Dir: Daniel Cohen; *Wri*: Daniel Cohen, Jean-Marc Culiersi.
Cast: Benoît Poelvoorde (Rémy), Augustin Legrand (Zotan), Natacha Lindinger, Michel Duchaussoy.
Story: In a parallel world with three Suns, a small tribe lives under the oppression of a tyrant named Zotan. Then comes a savior from another world, Rémy, a simple art restorer.

Les Deux Orphelines Vampires [*The Two Vampire Orphan Girls*] (col., 108 min., 1995)

Dir/Wri: Jean Rollin.
Cast: Alexandra Pic, Brigitte Lahaie, Isabelle Teboul, Tina Aumont.
Story: The melodramatic adventures of two female vampires.

Deux Vierges pour Satan [*Two Virgins For Satan*]
See *Les Démoniaques*.

Devil Story
See *Il était une fois le Diable*.

Le Diable et les Dix Commandements [*The Devil and the Ten Commandements*] (B&W., 80 min., 1962)
Dir: Julien Duvivier; *Wri*: Julien Duvivier, Maurice Bessy, René Barjavel, Henri Jeanson, Michel Audiard.
Cast: Fernandel, Gaston Modot, Jean-Claude Brialy, Charles Aznavour, Danielle Darrieux, Alain Delon, Claude Dauphin, Germaine Kerjean, Françoise Arnoul, Mel Ferrer, Louis de Funès, Lino Ventura, Georges Wilson.
Story: This often amusing, sometimes sad, star-studded sketch film, narrated by the Devil (as a snake), illustrates God's Ten Commandements, and how to twist them.
Note: "Thou Shalt Not Kill" was based on a story by David Alexander; "Thou Shalt Not Steal" was based on a story by William Link & Richard Levinson, the creators of *Columbo*. René Barjavel is a famous science fiction writer. Henri Jeanson is a famous historian.

Les Diablesses [*The She-Devils*]
See *Les Démoniaques*.

Les Diaboliques [*Diabolique*] (B&W., 110 min., 1954)
Dir: Henri-Georges Clouzot; *Wri*: H.-G. Clouzot, Jérôme Geromini, René Masson, Frédéric Grendel, based on the novel by Boileau-Narcejac.
Cast: Simone Signoret (Nicole), Véra Clouzot (Christina), Paul Meurisse (Michel), Charles Vanel (Inspector Fichet),

Jean Brochard, Michel Serrault, Pierre Larquey, Noël Roquevert.

Story: Christina (his wife) and Simone (his mistress) join forces to murder Michel, the director of a private school. But in reality, it is a diabolical plot conceived by Michel and Simone to get rid of weak-hearted Christina.

Note: Pierre Boileau and Thomas Narcejac are a famous team of mystery writers. They later provided the story for Alfred Hitchcock's *Vertigo*. The police inspector played by Vanel was reportedly the basis for the popular *Columbo* character. The film was remade in the U.S. in 1996 as *Diabolique*, starring Sharon Stone in the role played by Simone Signoret and Isabelle Adjani in the role played by Véra Clouzot.

Didier (col., 105 min., 1996)
Dir/Wri: Alain Chabat.
Cast: Alain Chabat (Didier), Isabelle Gelinas, Jean-Pierre Bacri, Lionel Abelanski.
Story: A man (Chabat) behaves like a dog.

Diesel (col., 79 min., 1985)
Dir: Robert Kramer; *Wri*: Richard Morgiève.
Cast: Gérard Klein, Agnès Soral (Anna).
Story: In a post-apocalyptic futuristic society, Anna witnesses a murder in the underground city. She struggles to escape the killers chasing her.

Dinosaurs from the Deep (col., 90 mion., 1994)
Dir/Wri: Norbert Moutier.
Cast: Jean Rollin, Norbert Moutier, Quélou Parente.
Story: A criminal sentenced to death is sent back to the Jurassic Era.
Note: Direct to video.

Dites-le avec des Fleurs [*Say It with Flowers*] (col., 100 min., 1974)

Dir: Pierre Grimblat, *Wri*: Lucile Laks, Tonino Guerra, Pierre Grimblat, based on the novel by Christian Charrière.
Cast: Delphine Seyrig, John Moulder Brown, Francis Blanche, Fernando Rey, Frédéric Mitterand, Julien Guiomar.
Story: A German maid (Seyrig) joins a stange family who are hiding a secret linked to World War II.

Djinns (col., 103 min., 2010)
Dir/Wri: Hugues & Sandra Martin.
Cast: Grégoire Leprince-Ringuet, Thierry Frémont, Aurélien Wiik, Saïd Taghmaoui, Stéphane Debac.
Story: A group of French soldiers is attacked by a Djinn during a rescue mission in Algeria.
Note: French-Moroccan co-production.

Docteur Jekyll et les Femmes [*Doctor Jekyll and Women*, transl. as *Doctor Jekyll and Miss Osborne*] (col., 95 min., 1981)
Dir/Wri: Walerian Borowczyk.
Cast: Udo Kier (Jekyll), Marina Pierro, Howard Vernon, Patrick Magee.
Story: In this low-budget, mildly pornographic version of Dr. Jekyll & Mr. Hyde, Jekyll chooses to remain Hyde.

Docteur M (aka *Club Extinction*) (col., 116 min., 1990)
Dir: Claude Chabrol; *Wri*: Solace Mitchell, Claude Chabrol, based on the novel by Norbert Jacques.
Cast: Alan Bates (Dr. M), Jan Niklas (Hartmann), Jennifer Beals, Hanns Zischler, Benoît Régent, Alexander Radszun, Peter Fitz, Daniela Poggi, William Berger, Michael Degen, Andrew McCarthy.
Story: French-German co-production, loosely inspired by Fritz Lang's *Docteur Mabuse*, in which a mad scientist uses advanced brainwashing techniques to gain power and create death and destruction.

Docteur Petiot (col., 102 min., 1989)

Dir: Christian de Chalonge; *Wri*: Christian de Chalonge, Dominique Garnier.
Cast: Michel Serrault (Petiot), Pierre Romans, Bérangère Bonvoisin, Nita Klein.
Story: The story of a notorious French serial killer of the 1940s.

Documents Interdits [*Forbidden Files*] (B&W/Col., 92 min., 1991)
Dir/Wri: Jean-Teddy Filippe.
Cast: N/A.
Story: Pseudo-documentaries made to look like amateur/found footage of unexplained paranormal phenomenon. Includes: Pilot. *La Barque* (*The Embarkation*), 1. *Les Plongeurs* (*The Divers*), 2. *L'Enfant* (*The Child*), 3. *Les Fantômes* (*The Ghosts*), 4. *Le Naufrage* (*The Shipwreck*), 5. *Le Pique-nique* (*The Picnic*), 6. *L'Extra-terrestre* (*The Alien*), 7. *Le Cas Ferguson* (*The Ferguson Case*), 8. *Le Soldat* (*The Soldier*), 9. *Les Crown filment les Young* (*The Crowns film the Youngs*), 10. *Le Fou du carrefour* (*The Madman at the Crossroad*), 11. *La Sorcière* (*The Witch*), 12. *La Sibérie* (*Siberia*), 13. *L'Examen* (*The Exam*), 14. *La découverte de 110 bobines Super 8 ayant pour objet la surveillance d'une famille est-allemande* (*The Discovery of 110 Super-8mm Reels on the Surveillance of an East German Family*).

Documents Secrets [*Secret Documents*] (B&W., 100 min., 1940)
Dir: Léo Joannon; *Wri*: Jacques Companez, Léopold Marchand.
Cast: Hugo Haas (Morenius), Raymond Rouleau, Marie Déa, Marcelle Monthil.
Story: Spy thriller in which two rival camps fight for a process that can extract fuel out of sea water.

Le Don d'Adèle [*Adèle's Gift*] (B&W., 93 min., 1950)

Dir: Émile Couzinet; *Wri*: Robert Eyquem, Pierre Barillet, based on his play co-written with Jean-Pierre Grédy.
Cast: Lilo (Adele), Marguerite Pierry, Charles Dechamps, Jacques Bénétin, Marcel Vallée, Hélène Bellanger, Robert Lamoureux.
Story: Adele is gifted with second sight, which creates much trouble for the rich family for whom she works as a maid.

Don't Grow Up
See *Alone*.

Dora, ou La Lanterne Magique [*Dora, or The Magic Lantern*] (col., 89 min., 1976)
Dir: Pascal Kane; *Wri*: Pascal Kane, Raoul Ruiz.
Cast: Valérie Mairesse, Nathalie Manet, Rita Maiden, Gérard Boucaron.
Story: The fairy tale-like adventures of an innocent young woman in a surreal Paris.

Dracula Père et Fils [*Dracula, Father and Son*, transl. as *Dracula & Son*] (col., 100 min., 1976)
Dir: Édouard Molinaro; *Wri*: Alain Godard, Jean-Marie Poiré, based on the novel *Paris Vampire* by Claude Klotz.
Cast: Christopher Lee (Dracula), Bernard Menez (His Son), Marie-Hélène Breillat, Raymond Bussières, Gérard Jugnot.
Story: Dracula is forced to leave Romania and become a horror film star. His son, who is a failure as a vampire, becomes a minimum wage worker. He eventually defies his father to save his fiancée.
Note: The U.S. version of this film was mutilated by an English adaptation which destroyed the light-hearted and often moving nature of the original. This is the last film in which Lee played Dracula. He was re-dubbed in the U.S. version.

Duelle (col., 118 min., 1976)
Dir: Jacques Rivette; *Wri*: Eduardo de Gregorio, Marilu Parolini, Jacques Rivette.

Cast: Bulle Ogier (Viva), Juliet Berto (Leni), Jean Babilée, Hermine Karagheuz, Nicole Garcia, Claire Nadeau.
Story: Two sorceresses, blonde Leni and brunette Viva, battle to recover a magic jewel.

Dying God (col., 85 min., 2008)
Dir: Fabrice Lambot; *Wri*: Jean Depelley, Fabrice Lambot, Nicanor Loreti, Germán Val.
Cast: Samuel Arena, Louis Ballester, Agathe de La Boulaye, Hugo Halbrich, Lance Henriksen.
Story: To stop his girls from being slaughtered by a mythological monster, a South American crimelord teams up with a local corrupt policeman.

L'Éclaireur [*The Scout*] (col., 85 min., 2006)
Dir: Djibril Glissant; *Wri*: Céline Bozon, Djibril Glissant, Gilles Marchand.
Cast: Grégoire Colin (Aton), Romane Bohringer (Nina), Jackie Berroyer.
Story: A young man is possessed by a panther spirit.

Eclipse sur un Ancien Chemin vers Compostelle [*Eclipse on an Old Road Towards Compostelle*] (col., 90 min., 1977)
Dir/Wri: Bernard Férié.
Cast: Jean Martin, Martine Chevallier, Bruno Pradal.
Story: During a traditional village celebration honoring two local saints, a young witch unearths the memories of old crimes.

Écoute Voir [*Hear See*] (col., 105 min., 1978)
Dir: Hugo Santiago; *Wri*: Claude Ollier.
Cast: Catherine Deneuve (Claude), Sami Frey, Florence Delay, Anne Parillaud, Jean-François Stévenin.
Story: Claude, a woman detective, investigates a mysterious religious sect which uses a paralyzing ray.

L'Écume des Jours [*Froth on the Daydream*] (col., 115 min., 1968)
Dir: Charles Belmont; *Wri*: Pierre Pelegri, Philippe Dumarçay, Charles Belmont, based on the novel by Boris Vian.
Cast: Annie Buron (Chloé), Jacques Perrin (Colin), Marie-France Pisier, Alexandra Stewart, Sacha Pitoëff, Bernard Fresson, Claude Piéplu.
Story: Colin falls in love with Chloé, but a water lily growing inside her eventually kills her. He steals her coffin and runs away.

L'Écume des Jours [*Froth on the Daydream*, transl. as *Mood Indigo*] (col., 125 min., 2013)
Dir: Michel Gondry; *Wri*: Luc Bossi, Michel Gondry, based on the novel by Boris Vian.
Cast: Romain Duris (Colin), Audrey Tautou (Cholé), Gad Elmaleh, Omar Sy.
Story: Same as above.

L'Éden et Après [*Eden and Afterwards*] (col., 100 min., 1971)
Dir/Wri: Alain Robbe-Grillet.
Cast: Catherine Jourdan, Pierre Zimmer, Lorraine Rainer, Sylvain Corthay, Richard Leduc.
Story: A Tunisian stranger initiates a young woman (Jourdan) in a surreal game of love and death.

Eden Log (col., 95 min., 2007)
Dir: Franck Vestiel; *Wri*: Franck Vestiel, Pierre Bordage.
Cast: Clovis Cornillac (Tolbiac), Vimala Pons.
Story: Tolbiac wakes up with amnesia in a cave. He then goes through a series of underground levels while escaping pursuers and trying to understand the reason for his presence in this place.

Elle Voit Des Nains Partout [*She Sees Dwarves Everywhere*] (col., 85 min., 1981)

Dir: Jean-Claude Sussfeld; *Wri*: Jean-Claude Sussfeld, Philippe Bruneau, based on his play.
Cast: Philippe Bruneau (Albert), Marilyn Canto, Christian Clavier, Agnès Daems, Roland Giraud, Martin Lamotte, Gaëlle Legrand, Thierry Lhermitte, Zabou, Jacques Monnet, Renaud, Louis Navarre, Valentine Monnier, Coluche, Josiane Lévêque.
Story: Parody of Disney's animated films, *The Three Musketeers*, *Les Misérables*, Robin Hood and *Tarzan*, all centered around Snow White's quest for Prince Charming.

En êtes-vous bien sûr ? [*Are You So Sure?*] (B&W., 90 min., 1946)
Dir: Jacques Houssin; *Wri*: Jean Féline, Jacques Houssin, Michel Duran.
Cast: Martine Carol, Robert Dhéry, Colette Brosset, Sylviane Rambaux, Raymonde Sartène, Coco Aslan.
Story: An old professor experiments a personality-altering machine on a shy bank clerk.
Note: French-Belgian co-production.

Les Enfants [*The Children*] (col., 94 min., 1984)
<u>*Dir*</u>: Marguerite Duras; <u>*Wri*</u>: Marguerite Duras, Jean Mascolo, Jean-Marc Turine.
<u>*Cast*</u>: Alexander Bougosslavsky (Ernesto), Daniel Gélin, Tatiana Moukhine, Martine Chevallier, Pierre Arditi, André Dussolier.
Story: In this allegoric fable, Ernesto, a seven-year-old child who looks like a thirty-year-old man, is a mental prodigy, but chooses a simple life over the sum of all knowledge.

L'Ennemi sans Visage [*The Enemy Without a Face*] (B&W., 105 min., 1946)
Dirs: Maurice Cammage, completed by Robert-Paul Dagan; *Wri*: René Wheeler, based on a novel by Stanislas-André Steeman.

Cast: Jean Tissier, Franck Villard, André Fouché, Louise Carletti, Huguette Montréal, Denise Réal, Colette Ripert.
Story: A scientist has developed a process to transfer life into an automaton's body. He decides to experiment on a prisoner condemned to death.

Entr'acte [*Intermission*] (B&W., 22 min., 1924)
Dir: René Clair; *Wri*: Francis Picabia.
Cast: Jean Borlin (Magician), Man Ray, Marcel Duchamp, Inge Fries, Erik Satie, Marcel Achard, Georges Auric.
Story: A series of surreal scenes ending with a funeral. A magician comes out of the coffin and causes everyone to disappear.

Un Escargot dans la Tête [*A Snail in the Head*] (col., 90 min., 1980)
Dir/Wri: Jean-Étienne Siry.
Cast: Florence Giorgetti, Renaud Verley, Jean-Claude Bouillon.
Story: A novelist (Giorgetti) in a hospital for a nervous breakdown meets a strange artist. She then experiences a series of surreal nightmares featuring snails.

L'Eternel Retour [*The Eternal Return*] (B&W., 115 min., 1943)
Dir: Jean Delannoy; *Wri*: Jean Cocteau.
Cast: Jan Marais (Patrice), Madeleine Sologne (Nathalie), Jean Murat, Yvonne de Bray, Jean d'Yd, Pierre Piéral.
Story: Modern version of the Tristan & Yseult story with Marais as Tristan and Sologne as Yseult.

...Et Mourir de Plaisir [*...And To Die From Pleasure*, transl. as *Blood and Roses*] (col., 80 min., 1960)
Dir: Roger Vadim; *Wri*: Roger Vadim, Roger Vailland, Claude Brulé, Claude Martin, based on the story by Sheridan Le Fanu.

Cast: Annette Vadim (Carmilla), Elsa Martinelli, Mel Ferrer, Jacques-René Chauffard, Serge Marquand, Marc Allégret.
Story: Modern version of Le Fanu's classic vampire tale, *Carmilla*. Vampire Carmilla interferes with her cousin's wedding with a nobleman (Ferrer).

L'Étrange Fiancée [*The Strange Fiancée*] (B&W., 80 min., 1931)
Dir: Georges Pallu; *Wri*: Dimitri Fexis, Georges Pallu, based on the story by Edgar Allan Poe.
Cast: Henri Baudin (The Doctor), Lilian Constantini, Frédéric Mariotti.
Story: Two young people on a hike meet a beautiful woman whose driver has a sinister appearance. They accompany her to her castle. In reality, it is a lunatic asylum whose doctor has lost his mind.

L'Étrangleur [*The Strangler*] (col., 93 min., 1970)
Dir/Wri: Paul Vecchiali.
Cast: Jacques Perrin (Émile), Julien Guiomar, Eve Simonet, Paul Barge, Nicole Courcel, Jacqueline Danno, Hélène Surgère.
Story: Emile strangles women because he can't stand to see them unhappy. A scavenger nicknamed the "Jackal" (Barge) robs his victims' bodies. A policeman (Guiomar) undertakes a surreal investigation.

L'Éveillé du Pont de l'Alma [*The Insomniac on the Bridge of Alma*] (col., 85 min., 1985)
Dir/Wri: Raoul Ruiz.
Cast: Michael Lonsdale, Jean-Bernard Guillard, Olimpia Carlisi, Jean Badin.
Story: A peeping Tom and a prizefighter decide to rape a pregnant woman, who then kills herself. The men are tormented when she returns regularly in new and horrifying forms with the specter of her son.

L'Évènement Le Plus Important Depuis Que l'Homme A Marché Sur La Lune [*The Most Important Event Since Man Walked on the Moon*, transl. as *A Slightly Pregnant Man*] (col., 94 min., 1973)
Dir/Wri: Jacques Demy.
Cast: Catherine Deneuve (Irène), Marcello Mastroianni (Mario), Micheline Presle, Marisa Pavan, Mireille Matthieu, Claude Melki, André Falcon, Maurice Biraud, Alice Sapritch, Raymond Gérôme.
Story: Mario lives with Irène. When he learns that *he* is pregnant, he marries her, but eventually discovers it was only a nervous pregnancy. Irène has the baby.
Note: The theme of this film was recycled in *Junior* (1994), starring Arnold Schwarzenegger.

Évolution (col., 81 min., 2015)
Dir: Lucile Hadzihalilovic; *Wri*: Lucile Hadzihalilovic, Alanté Kavaïté.
Cast: Max Brebant (Nicolas), Roxane Duran, Julie-Marie Parmentier.
Story: The only residents of young Nicholas' sea-side town are women and boys. When he sees a corpse in the ocean one day, he begins to question his existence and surroundings. The women are creating a new breed of humans capable of breathing underwater.

Exit (col., 110 min. 2000)
Dir/Wri: Olivier Megaton.
Cast: Patrick Fontana (Stan), Féodor Atkine.
Story: Stan, an alleged psychopathic killer and recidivist, is released after 5 years of imprisonment.

Exorcisme [*Exorcism*]
See *Sexorcismes*.

Exorcisme et Messes Noires [*Exorcism and Black Masses*]
See *Sexorcismes*.

Les Expériences Érotiques de Frankenstein [*Frankenstein's Erotic Experiments*] (col., 90 min., 1972)
Dir/Wri: Jess Franco.
Cast: Britt Nichols, Howard Vernon.
Story: Cagliostro uses the Frankenstein Monster to kidnap girls whose body parts he needs to build the perfect woman.
Note: French-Spanish co-production.

Expériences Sexuelles au Château des Jouisseuses [*Sexual Experiences at the Castle of Pleasure*]
See *Sexorcismes*.

Extinction (col., 112 min., 2016)
Dir/Wri: Miguel Angel Vivas.
Cast: Matthew Fox, Jeffrey Donovan, Quinn McColgan.
Story: Jack, his 12-year-old daughter, and their neighbor Patrick try to survive in an apocalyptic future with infected zombies.
Note: French-Hungarian co-production.

Extraneus (98 min., 1981)
Compilation of eight short features (listed in order of appearance):

1. *La Voix du Large* [*A Voice from the Sea*] (col., 9 min., 1972)
Dir/Wri: François Porcile, Philippe de Poix.
Cast: Anne Dimitriadis.
Story: A young woman is threatened by a flooding river.

2. *Nuit de Noce* [*Wedding Night*] (col., 15 min., 1974)
Dir/Wri: Bernard Férié.
Cast: Jean Barney, Mireille Férié.
Story: A newlywed groom is struck by lightning while playing piano.

3. *L'Inconnu* [*The Unknown Man*] (col., 15 min., 1978)

Dir/Wri: Claude Monrond.
Cast: Béatrice Lord, Daniel Peigné.
Story: A mysterious stranger follows an old woman.

4. *La Tache* [*The Blot*] (col., 19 min., 1976)
Dir/Wri: Nicolas Brachlianoff.
Cast: Muse Dalbray, Bernard Malaterre, Monique Fabre.
Story: The ghost of a former tenant haunts an apartment.

5. *Casse-Tête* [*Mind-Bender*] (col., 7 min., 1978)
Dir/Wri: Daniel Chevalier.
Cast: Jacques Ebner.
Story: A man asks a filmmaker to film his suicide.

6. *L'Empreinte* (col., 8 min, 1975)
Dir/Wri: Jacques Cardon.
Story: A baby grows up with a prosthetic device shaped like a footprint already provided for the convenience of his future oppressor.

7. *Le Motard de l'Apocalypse* [*The Apocalypse Biker*] (col., 10 min., 1978)
Dir/Wri: Richard Olivier.
Cast: Roland Mahauden, Serge Degroot, Yannick Degroot, Alain Delforge, Michel Lederman, Roland Vanberg.
Story: In a post-apocalyptic landscape, a German zombie biker fights mutant Hell's Angels.

8. *Fracture* [*Break*] (col., 18 min, 1977)
Dir/Wri: Paul & Gaëtan Brizzi.
Story: Mankind's last survivor fights in a plant world.

L'Extraterrestre [*The Extra-Terrestrial*] (col., 93 min., 2000)
Dir: Didier Bourdon; *Wri*: Didier Bourdon, Valentine Albin.
Cast: Didier Bourdon (Zerf), Bernard Campan, Pascale Arbillot, Antoine du Merle, Danièle Lebrun, Olivier Rabourdin.

Story: As Zerf the alien arrives on Earth, two robots programmed for murder are sent to kill him. He will have to rely on humans to help him.

Faeryland (col., 93 min., 2016)
Dir/Wri: Magà Ettori.
Cast: Yves Duteil, Janine Piguet, Ariakina Ettori, Souad Amidou, Mylène Demongeot.
Story: In 2050, a virus threatens to kill all life in Faeryland. To be able to save the planet, the god-druid Cathbad must find the grail, chalice linked to the curse.
Note: French-Irish co-production.

Fahrenheit 451 (col., 113 min., 1966)
Dir: François Truffaut; *Wri*: François Truffaut, Jean-Louis Richard, based on the novel by Ray Bradbury.
Cast: Julie Christie, Oskar Werner, Cyril Cusak, Anton Diffring.
Story: Masterful adaptation of Bradbury's classic novel describing a furure when books are routinely burned, and rebels learn to memorize them to preserve culture.
Note: French-British co-production.

Fantômas
A series of films based on the popular novels by Marcel Allain & Pierre Souvestre published between 1911 and 1913.
    Fantômas (B&W., 1146 M, 1913)
    Juve Contre Fantômas [*Juve vs. Fantômas*] (B&W., 1913)
    Le Mort Qui Tue [*The Dead Man Who Kills*] (B&W., 1913)
    Fantômas contre Fantômas [*Fantomas vs. Fantomas*] (B&W., 1914)
    Le Faux Magistrat [*The Phony Magistrate*] (B&W., 1914)
    Dir/Wri: Louis Feuillade.

Cast: René Navarre (Fantômas), Bréon (Juve), Georges Melchior (Fandor), Renée Carl (Lady Beltham).
Story: Master criminal Fantômas outwits police commissioner Juve and journalist Jerôme Fandor.
Note: The original silent serial series is faithful to the early novels and displays considerable poetic charm.

Fantômas (B&W., 91 min., 1932)
Dir/Wri: Paul Féjos.
Cast: Jean Galland (Fantômas), Thomy Bourdelle (Juve), Tania Fedor (Lady Beltham), Marie-Laure, Gaston Modot, Georges Rigaud.
Story: Fantômas murders a rich lady, but is unmasked by Juve.

Mr. Fantômas (B&W., 20 min., 1937)
Dir/Wri: Ernst Moerman.
Cast: Jean Michel, Trudi Ventonderen, Françoise Bert, Jacqueline Arpé, Susan Samuel, Léa Dumont.
Note: Belgian short feature.

Fantômas (B&W., 95 min., 1946)
Dir: Jean Sacha; *Wri*: Jean-Louis Bouquet.
Cast: Marcel Herrand (Fantômas), Alexandre Rignault (Juve), André Le Gall (Fandor), Lucienne Le Marchand (Lady Beltham), Simone Signoret (Hélène), Yves Deniaud, Georges Gosset.
Story: Fantômas tries to prevent Fandor from marrying the arch-villain's daughter, Hélène, but Juve saves the day.

Fantômas contre Fantômas [*Fantomas vs. Fantomas*] (B&W., 95 min., 1948)
Dir: Robert Vernay; *Wri*: Solange Térac.
Cast: Maurice Teynac (Fantômas), Alexandre Rignault (Juve), Yves Furet (Fandor), Aimé Clariond, Balpêtré, Marcelle Chantal.

Story: Fantômas teams up with a mad surgeon (Clariond) who turns people into assassins.

Fantômas (col., 95 min., 1964)
Fantômas Se Déchaîne [*Fantomas Strikes Back*] (col., 94 min., 1965)
Fantômas contre Scotland Yard [*Fantomas vs. Scotland Yard*] (col., 92 min., 1966)
Dir: André Hunebelle; *Wri*: Jean Halain, Pierre Foucaud.
Cast: Jean Marais (Fantômas/Fandor), Louis de Funès (Juve), Mylène Demongeot.
Story: Fantômas now borrows gadgets from James Bond's panoply (a pocket submarine in the first installment, a flying car in the second). De Funès plays the role of Juve for laughs. Jean Marais plays the double role of Fantômas (wearing a very effective green mask) and his nemesis, journalist Fandor.

Le Fantôme de la Liberté [*The Phantom of Liberty*] (col., 103 min., 1974)
Dir: Luis Buñuel; *Wri*: Luis Buñuel, Jean-Claude Carrière.
Cast: Julien Bertheau, Adriana Asti, Michel Lonsdale, Michel Piccoli, Claude Piéplu, Jean-Claude Brialy, Monica Vitti, Paul Frankeur, Adolfo Celi.
Story: A series of surreal sketches, often satirical in nature, some dealing with dreams and death.

Le Fantôme de Longstaff [*Longstaff's Ghodt*] (col., 20 min., 1996)
Dir/Wri: Luc Moullet, based on *Longstaff's Marriage* by Henry James.
Cast: Iliana Lolic, Geoffrey Carey (Longstaff), Hélène Lapiower.
Story: In 1880, James Longstaff, a wealthy, consumptive and moribund Englishman, meets a pretty young American woman. He falls in love with her, but she turns him away. Two years later, Longstaff reappears. Is it him, or a ghost?

Le Fantôme du Moulin-Rouge [*The Ghost of the Moulin-Rouge*] (B&W., 90 min., 1924)
Dir/Wri: René Clair.
Cast: Georges Vaultier (Julien), Sandra Milowanoff (Yvonne), Madeleine Rodrigue, Albert Préjean, Paul Ollivier.
Story: In order to marry Yvonne, Julien's astral body helps her father to get rid of a blackmailer.

Fascination (col., 82 min., 1979)
Dir/Wri: Jean Rollin.
Cast: Franka Maï, Brigitte Lahaie, Jean-Marie Lemaire, Fanny Magier.
Story: A young burglar (Lemaire) finds refuge in a castle inhabited by two vampires.

Le Faucheur [*The Reaper*] (B&W., 20 min., 1968)
Dir/Wri: Alain Gassener, based on a story by Claude Seignolle.
Cast: André Faure, Adrien Nicati, Stanley White (The Reaper), Lali Holm, Alain Véron.
Story: A careless driver (Faure) picks up Death as a hitchhiker.

La Femme aux Bottes Rouges [*The Woman with Red Boots*] (col., 95 min., 1974)
Dir: Juan Luis Buñuel; *Wri*: Juan Luis Buñuel, Jean-Claude Carrière.
Cast: Catherine Deneuve (Françoise), Fernando Rey (Pérou), Adalberto Marias Merli, Jacques Weber.
Story: Pérou, a rich but aging art collector, meets Françoise, a beautiful enchantress.

La Femme Objet [*The Woman Thing*] (col., 90 min., 1981)
Dir/Wri: Frédéric Lansac.
Cast: Richard Allan, Helen Shirley, Laura Clair, Marilyn Jess.

Story: X-rated (and satirical) adventures of a science-fiction writer who is the victim of satyriasis. Having run out of willing women, he ends up building female androids.

La Fiancée de Dracula [*The Bride of Dracula*] (col., 91 min., 2002)
Dir/Wri: Jean Rollin,
Cast: Cyrille Iste (Isabelle), Jacques Orth (the Professor), Thomas Smith, Sandrine Thoquet, Brigitte Lahaie (The Wolf-Woman), Thomas Desfossé (Dracula).
Story: Having set off in search of the remains of Dracula, the Professor and his young assistant find themselves in a parallel universe populated by monstrous and phantasmagorical creatures. Their quest leads them to Isabelle, a mysterious young woman guarded by the nuns of the Order of the White Virgin.

La Fiancée des Ténèbres [*The Fiancée of Darkness*] (B&W., 100 min., 1944)
Dir: Serge de Poligny; *Wri*: Serge de Poligny, Gaston Bonheur.
Cast: Jany Holt (Sylvie), Pierre Richard-Willm (Roland), Simone Valère, Edouard Delmont, Fernand Charpin, Line Noro.
Story: Two lovers discover a secret, underground cathedral leading to a fairyland where they'll live a wonderful day of love.

Fifi la Plume [*Fifi Feather*] (color, 80 min., 1965)
Dir/Wri: Albert Lamorisse.
Cast: Philippe Avron (Fifi), Mireille Nègre, Henri Lambert.
Story: Fifi, a thief, is forced to find refuge in a circus. There he becomes a bird-man, learns how to fly and impersonates an angel.

Figures de cire [*Waxworks*] (B&W., 11 min., 1914)
Dir: Maurice Tourneur; *Wri*: André de Lorde
Cast: Henry Roussel, Émile Tramont.
Story: Gruesome murder in a wax museum.

Filles Traquées [*Hunted Girls*]
See *La Nuit des Traqués*.

La Fin du Monde [*The End of the World*, transl. as *Paris After Dark*] (B&W., 103 min., 1930)
Dir: Abel Gance; *Wri*: Camille Flammarion.
Cast: Colette Darfeuil, Abel Gance, Victor Francen, Samson Fainsilber, Jean d'Yd, Sylvie Grenade.
Story: A scientist announces that a comet will soon destroy the Earth. But it eventually spares the planet and helps bring about world unity.
Note: Camille Flammarion is a famous science fiction writer.

La Folie du Dr. Tube [*The Madness of Dr. Tube*] (B&W., 2 Reels, 1916)
Dir/Wri: Abel Gance.
Cast: Albert Dieudonné.
Story: Experimental film about a scientist who breaks light down into its basic components.

La Forêt Désenchantée [*The Disenchanted Forest*] (col., 28 min., 1981)
Dir/Wri: Jacques Robiolles.
Cast: Fabrice Luchini, Bojena Horackova, Colin Jorre, Jean-Luc Passereau, Pierre Atterand, Jean-Christophe Rosé.
Story: A love story among the fantastic inhabitants of a fairy wood threatened by the construction of a highway.

Le Fou du Labo 4 [*The Madman of Lab 4*] (col., 90 min., 1967)
Dir: Jacques Besnard; *Wri*: Jean Halain, Jacques Besnard, based on a story by Jacques Chambon.
Cast: Jean Lefèbvre (Eugène), Bernard Blier (Beauchard), Pierre Brasseur, Michel Serrault, Maria Latour.
Story: Eugène, a genial scientist, discovers a new, powerful, euphoric gas, and becomes the target of a spy ring.

France, Société Anonyme [*France, Inc.*] (col., 100 min., 1973)
Dir: Alain Corneau; *Wri*: Alain Corneau, Jean-Claude Carrière.
Cast: Michel Bouquet, Roland Dubillard, Allyn Ann Mac Lerie, Ann Zacharias, Michel Vitold, Yves Alfonso, Gérard Desarthe, Daniel Ceccaldi.
Story: In the year 2222, a former drug lord (Bouquet) comes out of hibernation and tells the story of how corporate power and the legalisation of drugs destroyed his empire.

François 1er [*Francis I*] (B&W., 100 min., 1936)
Dir: Christian-Jaque; *Wri*: Paul Fékété.
Cast: Fernandel (Honorin), Mona Goya, Alice Tissot, Henri Bosc.
Story: In this comedic French variation on *A Connecticut Yankee...*, Fernandel is hypnotized back to the days of King François I where, with the help of a pocket encyclopedia, he revolutionizes history.

Frankenstein 90 (col., 92 min., 1984)
Dir: Alain Jessua; *Wri*: Alain Jessua, Paul Gégauff.
Cast: Jean Rochefort (Victor Frankenstein), Eddy Mitchell (Creature), Fiona Gélin.
Story: Frankenstein's creature falls in love with his creator's fiancée, and vice-versa. The Monster ends up a millionaire.

Frankenstein: La Véritable Histoire [*Frankenstein: The True Story*] (col., 26 min., 1981)
Dir: Roland Portiche; *Wri*: Igor & Grichka Bogdanoff.
Cast: Gilles Guillot (Baron Frankenstein), Olivier Hémon (Monster), Gilbert Bahon.
Story: Satirical take on the Frankenstein story (Frankenstein becomes Einstein).

Les Frenchmen, les Premiers Super-Héros français [*The first French superheroes*] (col., 135 min., 2019)
Dir/Wri: Olivier Goujon.
Cast: Olivier Goujon, Julien Rochard, Jean-Michel Hautin, Virginie Goujon.
Story: In a small French village, two men accidentally become super-heroes.

Les Frères Pétard [*The Petard Brothers*] (col., 90 min., 1986)
Dir: Hervé Palud; *Wri*: Hervé Palud, Igor Aptekman.
Cast: Gérard Lanvin, Jacques Villeret, Josiane Balasko, Valérie Mairesse, Michel Galabru, Dominique Lavanant.
Story: French *Cheech & Chong*-type comedy, which takes place in a near future in which the sale of soft drugs has become legal.

Le Frisson des Vampires [*The Vampires' Shiver* transl. as *Sex and the Vampire, Terror of the Vampire*] (col., 89 min., 1970)
Dir/Wri: Jean Rollin.
Cast: Sandra Jullien, Nicole Nancel.
Story: The semi-parodic adventures of the owners of a castle which houses a female vampire cult.

Futur Antérieur [*Future Past*] (col., 81 min., 2016)
Dir/Wri: Franck Llopis.
Cast: Chris Imberdis, Louise De Fleury, Camille Lindskog.
Story: Paris, in the near future, Wilfried Max, director of a large advertising agency, acquires a smartphone application allowing one to travel in the past and in the future over 8 days.

Le Futur aux Trousses [*The Future in Pursuit*] (col., 100 min., 1974)
Dir/Wri: Dolorès Grassian.
Cast: Bernard Fresson, Michel Aumont, Andréa Ferréol.

Story: In a future when people only work three days a week, a corporation offers everyone the possibility of acquiring another identity to satisfy their fantasies.

Galaxie [*Galaxy*] (col., 82 min., 1971)
Dir: Mathias Mérigny; *Wri*: Mathias Mérigny, Roger Michel, Pierre Latzko.
Cast: Marika Green, Henri Serre, Reinhard Kolldehoff, Jean Gras.
Story: Five scientists investigate the concept of an "anti-universe." During an experiment, three die and one vanishes. A police inspector investigates.

Les Garçons Sauvages [*The Wild Boys*] (col., 110 min., 2017)
Dir/Wri: Bertrand Mandico, loosely based on William S. Burroughs novel.
Cast: Pauline Lorillard, Vimala Pons, Diane Rouxel, Anaël Snoek, Mathilde Warnier.
Story: Five adolescent boys from wealthy families commit a brutal crime and are taken in by a Dutch Captain for rehabilitation on his dilapidated sailboat, who sail for a tropical island on which they will secretly be changed into women.
Note: All five male protagonists are played by female actors.

Garou-Garou, Le Passe-Muraille [*Garou-Garou, The Walker Through the Walls*] (B&W., 85 min., 1950)
Dir: Jean Boyer; *Wri*: Michel Audiard, based on the story by Marcel Aymé.
Cast: Bourvil (Dutilleul), Joan Greenwood, Marcelle Arnold, Raymond Souplex, Gérard Oury, Frédéric O'Brady.
Story: Dutilleul, a modest civil servant, discovers that he has the power to walk through walls and uses it to become a master burglar.

Les Gaspards (col., 94 min., 1973)
Dir: Pierre Tchernia; *Wri*: Pierre Tchernia, René Goscinny.

Cast: Michel Serrault (Rondin), Philippe Noiret (Gaspard), Chantal Goya, Charles Denner, Michel Galabru.
Story: Rondin, a meek bookseller, discovers a secret Parisian underground society led by the colorful Gaspard de Montfermeil.
Note: René Goscinny is better known as the writer of the *Astérix* comic-book series,

Gawin (col., 95 min., 1990)
Dir: Arnaud Sélignac; *Wri*: Arnaud Sélignac, Alexandre Jardin.
Cast: Jean-Hugues Anglade (Nicolas), Wojtek Pszoniak (Pierre), Bruno (Félix), Catherine Samie.
Story: Nicolas' son, Félix, is dying from leukemia. Knowing that his son's fondest dream is to meet an extraterrestrial, Nicolas impersonates the alien Gawin, and takes the boy to a glacier which passes as Saturn. Eventually, they meet an old man, who may be a real alien, and who cures Felix.

Le Gendarme et les Extra-Terrestres [*The Gendarme and the ETs*] (col., 95 min., 1978)
Dir: Jean Girault; *Wri*: Jacques Vilfrid.
Cast: Louis de Funès (Cruchot), Michel Galabru (Gerber), Maria Mauban, Maurice Risch, Jean-Pierre Rambal, Guy Grosso, Michel Modo, France Rumilly, Jean-Roger Caussimon, Mario David, Jacques François.
Story: The fifth in a series of slapstick comedies starring De Funès as a policeman from the French Riviera town of Saint-Tropez. Here, the bumbling *gendarme* is outwitted by ETs having taken human forms to study mankind.

Généalogies d'un Crime [*Genealogies of a Crime*] (col., 114 min., 1997)
Dir: Raoul Ruiz; *Wri*: Raoul Ruiz, Pascal Bonitzer.
Cast: Catherine Deneuve (Jeanne/Solange), Michel Piccoli (Georges), Bernadette Lafont, Melvil Poupaud (René), Andrzej Seweryn, Monique Mélinand.

Story: Jeanne, a psychiatrist, is killed by her sociopathic nephew, René. Solange, René's lawyer, arranges for the replay of the murder in René's mind with the help of another psychiatrist, Georges.

Giorgino (col., 177 min., 1994)
Dir: Laurent Boutonnat; *Wri*: Gilles Laurent, Laurent Boutonnat.
Cast: Mylène Farmer, Jeff Dahlgren, Louise Fletcher, Frances Barber, Jean-Pierre Aumont.
Story: After World War I, a young Doctor (Dahlgren) finds love in a village haunted by the ghosts of the men who died during the war.

Glissements Progressifs du Plaisir [*Progressive Slidings Into Pleasure*] (col., 104 min., 1974)
Dir/Wri: Alain Robbe-Grillet.
Cast: Anicée Alvina (Alice), Olga Georges-Picot (Nora), Jean-Louis Trintignant, Michael Lonsdale.
Story: The surreal interrogation of Alice, accused of having murdered Nora.

Goal of the Dead (col., 140 min., 2014)
Dir: Thierry Poiraud, Benjamin Rocher; *Wri*: Tristan Schulmann, Nicolas Peufaillit, Quoc Dang Tran.
Cast: Alban Lenoir, Charlie Bruneau, Tiphaine Daviot
Story: A professional football team arrives at their lowly rivals' stadium only to find a zombie apocalypse that has turned the hostile fans into rabid undead hooligans.

Le Golem [*The Legend of Prague*] (B&W., 100 min., 1935)
Dir: Julien Duvivier; *Wri*: Julien Duvivier, André-Paul Antoine, based on the novel by Gustav Meyrinck.
Cast: Harry Baur (The Emperor), Roger Karl, Germaine Aussey, Jany Holt.
Story: The Jews of Prague create a clay monster to destroy the Emperor who oppresses them.

Golem, L'Esprit de l'Exil [*Golem, The Spirit of Exile*] (col., 105 min., 1991)
Dir/Wri: Amos Gitaï.
Cast: Ophrah Shemesh, Hanna Schygulla (Golem), Samuel Fuller, Mireille Perrier, Vittorio Mezzogiorno, Fabienne Babe, Antonio Carallo, Bernard Levy, Sotigui Kouyaté.
Story: Modern transposition of the classic tale where the Golem helps those who are exiled from their native land.

Goto, L'Île d'Amour [*Goto, Island of Love*] (B&W/col., 93 min., 1968)
Dir/Wri: Walerian Borowczyk.
Cast: Pierre Brasseur (Goto), Ligia Branice (Glossia), Ginette Leclerc, René Dary.
Story: Surreal political fable about the imaginary island of Goto ruled by the dictator Goto and his wife Glossia.

La Goulve [*Erotic Witchcraft*] (col., 87 min., 1971)
Dir: Mario Mercier, Bepi Fontana; *Wri*: Mario Mercier.
Cast: Malka Simon (Goulve), Hervé Hendricks, César Torres, Anne Varèse, Marie-Ange Saint-Clair, Manuel Navo.
Story: The Goulve, an elemental snake goddess, possesses humans and drives them to suicide.

Les Gourmandes du Sexe [*Sex Gluttons*] (col., 85 min., 1978)
Dir/Wri: John Love.
Cast: Cathy Stewart, Dominique Aveline.
Story: X-rated tale of a revenge from beyond the grave.

Le Gout du Sang [*The Taste of Blood*]
See *Perversions Sexuelles*.

Grand Guignol (col., 90 min., 1986)
Dir/Wri: Jean Marboeuf.

Cast: Guy Marchand (Baptiste), Caroline Cellier (Sarah), Jean-Claude Brialy, Michel Galabru, Marie Dubois, Olivia Brunaux.
Story: Macabre vaudeville about a troupe of Grand Guignol actors.

Le Grand Tout [*The Big Everything*] (col., 130 min., 2015)
Dir: Nicolas Bazz; *Wri*: Nicolas Bazz, Yann Bazz.
Cast: Jauris Casanova (Niels), Hélène Seuzaret, Benjamin Boyer, Laure Gouget, Pierre-Alain de Garrigues.
Story: In exchange for a full pardon, Niels joins a group of scientists on a trip to a black hole 50 light years from earth. Because of time dilation, a hundred years will pass on Earth while they are away on their planned six-week journey. However, an accident pushes them even further into space, with no hope of ever returning to their former lives.

La Grande Frousse [*The Great Fear*]
See *La Cité de l'Indicible Peur*.

La Grande Trouille [*The Great Scare*] (aka *Tendre Dracula* [*Tender Dracula*]) (col., 100 min., 1974)
Dir: Pierre Grunstein; *Wri*: Justin Lenoir.
Cast: Peter Cushing (Mac Gregor), Alida Valli (Héloise), Miou-Miou (Marie), Nathalie Courval, Bernard Menez, Stéphane Shandor, Julien Guiomar.
Story: Film producers want to shoot a gothic movie in Dracula's castle.

Grave (col., 98 min., 2016)
Dir/Wri: Julia Ducournau.
Cast: Garance Marillier (Justine), Ella Rumpf, Rabah Naït Oufella, Joana Preiss, Laurent Lucas, Marion Vernoux, Bouli Lanners, Jean-Louis Sbille.
Story: Justine, 16, vegetarian, attends a veterinary school. During her hazing, she is forced to eat meat for the first time. The consequences are unexpected...

Le Grimoire d'Arkandias [*Arkandias' Grimoir*] (col., 92 min., 2014)
Dir/Wri: Alexandre Castagnetti, Julien Simonet, based on the book by Éric Boisset.
Cast: Christian Clavier (Arkandias), Ryan Brodie (Théo), Isabelle Nanty, Anémone.
Story: Young Théo unearths a book of magic that contains the secrets of making an invisibility ring, but he becomes the victim of three witches, and remains stuck in invisibility. Arkandias, a mysterious individual, may be the only one who can help him.

La Guerre du Feu [*Quest for Fire*] (col., 96 min., 1981)
Dir: Jean-Jacques Annaud; *Wri*: Gérard Brach, based on the novel by J.-H. Rosny Aîné.
Cast: Everett McGill, Rae Dawn Chong, Ron Perlman, Gari Schwartz, Brian Gill.
Story: Three cavemen go looking for fire. One of them finds love and eventually learns the secret of making fire.
Note: French-Ameruican co-production. J.-H. Rosny Aîné is one of the major science fiction writers of the 19th century.

Les Gueux au Paradis [*Two Funny Guys in Paradise*] (B&W., 85 min., 1945)
Dir: René Le Hénaff; *Wri*: André Obey, based on a story by G. M. Martens.
Cast: Fernandel, Raimu, Gaby Andreu, André Alerme, Armand Bernard.
Story: After being run over by a car, two funny guys visit Hell and Heaven before being sent back to Earth.

Gwendoline [*The Perils of Gwendoline in the Land of the Yik-Yak*] (col., 105 min., 1983)
Dir/Wri: Just Jaeckin, based on the British bondage comic book series by John Willie.

Cast: Tawny Kitaen (Gwendoline), Brent Huff (Willard), Zabou, Jean Rougerie, Bernadette Lafont.
Story: The exotic adventures of Gwendoline and Willard in an Asian fantasy world which includes the savage Kiops and an underground kingdom of Amazons, ruled by a cruel queen.

Hélas Pour Moi [*Woe Is Me!*] (col., 84 min., 1992)
Dir/Wri: Jean-Luc Godard.
Cast: Gérard Depardieu, Laurence Masliah, Bernard Verley, Jean-Louis Loca.
Story: A god borrows the body of a garage owner to seduce the man's wife.

Hémophilia (col., 15 min., 1985)
Dir/Wri: Norbert Moutier.
Cast: Eva Sinclair, Guy Penet, Jean-Marie Vauclin.
Story: In the future, private subways are heavily guarded; yet, mysterious murders occur.

Hibernatus (col., 80 min., 1969)
Dir: Édouard Molinaro; *Wri*: Jean Halain, Jacques Vilfrid, based on the play by Jean-Bernard Luc.
Cast: Louis de Funès (Hubert), Bernard Alane (Paul), Claude Gensac, Olivier de Funès, Paul Préboist, Claude Piéplu, Michel Lonsdale, Pascal Mazzotti, Jacques Legras.
Story: Hubert, a 19th century man trapped in the ice in Greenland, is brought back to life; his descendents must pretend to live in the past in order to not traumatize him.

High Life (col., 110 min., 2018)
Dir: Claire Denis; *Wri*: Claire Denis, Jean-Pol Fargeau, Geoff Cox.
Cast: Robert Pattinson, Mia Goth, Juliette Binoche, André Benjamin.
Story: A group of criminals serving death sentences are sent on a mission in space to extract alternative energy from a black hole.

Histoire de Chanter [*Just for a Song*] (B&W., 95 min., 1946)
Dir: Gilles Grangier; *Wri*: René Wheeler, Cami.
Cast: Noël Roquevert (Doctor Renault), Luis Mariano (Tenor Gino Fabretti), Arlette Merry, Jacqueline Roman.
Story: Jealous of a tenor, a surgeon transplants his vocal cords into a grocer.

Histoires Abominables [*Abominable Tales*] (80 min., 1979)
Compilation of six short features (listed here in order of appearance):

1. *Le Blanc des Yeux* [*The White of the Eyes*] (b&w, 11 min, 1977)
Dir/Wri: Henry Colomer.
Cast: Marcel Dalio, Sylvia Badesco, Robert Théophile, Régis Outin, Alain Petit.
Story: A mad scientist invents a machine that can paint portraits but sucks up the model's life.

2. *La Passion d'une Femme Sans Coeur* [*The Passion of a Heartless Woman*] (b&w, 15 min, 1975)
Dir/Wri: Moïse Maatouk, based on a story by Paul Deschelles.
Cast: Niels Arestrup, Catherine Gandois, Pierre Piéral.
Story: A showman exhibits a woman's living head, connected to an artificial life-support machine. The head falls in love with him and ends up killing him.

3. *Celui qui Venait d'Ailleurs* [*He Came From Beyond*] (col., 19 min, 1978)
Dir/Wri: Atahualpa Lichy, Jean-Paul Torok, based on a story by Claude Seignolle.
Cast: Gilles Chavassieux, Jean-Michel Goutier, Annick Michaud.
Story: The inhabitants of a lonely village believe that a stranger is a ghost.

4. *Pauvre Sonia* [*Poor Sonia*] (col., 13 min., 1975)
Dir/Wri: Dominique Maillet, based on a story by Claude Seignolle.
Cast: Anicée Alvina, Frank David, Eva Damien, Gérard Boucaron.
Story: A man follows a young prostitute and discovers that she belongs to the living dead.

5. *La Mémoire* [*The Memory*] (col., 10 min, 1975)
Dir/Wri: Gébé.
Cast: Philippe Léotard, Diane Kurys, Albert Augier, Philippe Moreau.
Story: A man forgets where he parked his car and panics.

6. *Le Déjeuner du Matin* [*The Morning Breakfast*] (col., 12 min, 1978)
Dir/Wri: Patrick Bokanowski.
Cast: n/a.
Story: Animated short about scenes of daily life.

Histoires Extraordinaires [*Extraordinary Tales*] (B&W., 90 min., 1949)
Dir: Jean Faurez; *Wri*: Jean Faurez, Guy Decomble, based on short stories by Edgar Allan Poe & Thomas de Quincey.
Cast: Fernand Ledoux, Suzy Carrier, Jules Berry, Paul Frankel, Olivier Hussenot, Marina de Berg, Roger Rafal, Roger Blin.
Story: Three gendarmes swap horror stories, including *The Tell-Tale Heart, The Cask of Amontillado* and *Thou Art the Man*.

Histoires Extraordinaires [*Extraordinary Tales*, transl. as *Spirits of the Dead*] (col., 120 min., 1968)
Film compised of three sketches based on short stories by Edgar Allan Poe, all narrated by Vincent Price.

1. *Metzengerstein*
Dir: Roger Vadim; *Wri*: Roger Vadim, Pascal Cousin.

Cast: Peter Fonda, Jane Fonda, Carla Marlier, Philippe Lemaire, James Robertson Justice, Andréas Voutsinas.
Story: A spurned woman who murdered her lover becomes attracted to a horse who may be his reincarnation.

2. *William Wilson*
Dir: Louis Malle; *Wri*: Daniel Boulanger.
Cast: Alain Delon, Brigitte Bardot, Katia Cristina, Umberto d'Orsini, Daniele Vargas.
Story: A man is stalked by his doppleganger.

3. *Toby Dammit*
Dir: Federico Fellini; *Wri*: Bernardino Zapponi.
Cast: Terence Stamp, Salvo Randone, Marina Yaru.
Story: A British actor meets the Devil in the guise of a little girl.
Note: French-Italian co-production.

Holy Motors (col., 115 min., 2012)
Dir/Wri: Leos Carax.
Cast: Denis Lavant (Oscar), Edith Scob, Eva Mendes, Michel Piccoli, Kylie Minogue.
Story: Oscar appears to have a job as an actor, as he is seen dressing up in different costumes and performing various roles in several locations around Paris over the course of a day, but no cameras or audiences are ever seen around him.

Home Sweet Home (col., 83 min., 1972)
Dir: Liliane de Kermadec; *Wri*: Liliane de Kermadec & Julien Guiomar.
Cast: Julien Guiomar, Coline Deble, Jacques Monory, Denis Gunzbourg, Patrick Dumont.
Story: People, chained and bloody, are kept in the attic of an old house; there are suggestions of ghosts.

Homicide By Night (col., 17 min., 1984)
Dir/Wri: Gérard Krawczyk, based on a story by Pierre Siniac.

Cast: Mado Maurin, Paul Crauchet, Claude Chabrol.
Story: Old people join forces to catch a serial killer.

L'Homme au Cerveau Greffé [*The Man with the Transplanted Brain*] (col., 90 min., 1971)
Dir/Wri: Jacques Doniol-Valcroze, based on a story by Victor Vicas & Alain Franck.
Cast: Jean-Pierre Aumont (Marcilly), Mathieu Carrière (Franz), Michel Duchaussoy (Degagnac), Nicoletta Machiavelli, Marianne Eggerickx, Martine Sarcey.
Story: Marcolly, a neurologist afflicted with with a deadly disease, asks one of his colleagues (Duchaussoy) to transplant his brain into the body of the young victim of a traffic accident (Carrière). His own daughter then falls in love with his new self.

L'Homme à l'Oreille Cassée [*The Man with the Broken Ear*] (B&W., 75 min., 1934)
Dir/Wri: Robert Boudrioz, based on the novel by Edmond About.
Cast: Thomy Bourdelle (Fougas), Jim Gérald, Jacqueline Daix, Alice Tissot.
Story: Fougas, a Napoleonic Army colonel, is placed in hibernation, then brought back to life. He dislikes the modern world and marries his granddaughter.

L'Homme qui Revient de Loin [*The Man Who Returned from Far Away*] (B&W., 1500 meters, 1916)
Dir: René Navarre; *Wri*: Gaston Leroux, based on his novel.
Cast: René Navarre, Garray, Marc Gérard, André Marnay, Andrée Pascal, Alice Beylat.
Story: A murder is revealed during a seance, and the victim appears to return to life.

L'Homme qui Revient de Loin [*The Man Who Returned from Far Away*] (B&W., 95 min., 1949)

Dir: Jean Castanier; *Wri*: Louis Chavance, based on the novel by Gaston Leroux.
Cast: Paul Bernard, Annabella, Maria Casarès.
Story: Same as above.

L'Homme Qui Vendit Son Âme au Diable] [*The Man Who Sold His Soul to the Devil*] (B&W., 1920)
Dir/Wri: Pierre Caron, based on the novel by Pierre Veber.
Cast: Charles Dullin.
Story: A banker sells his soul to the Devil in exchange for worldly riches, but he must then use the money to do evil.
Note: Lost silent film.

L'Homme Qui Vendit Son Âme [*The Man Who Sold His Soul*] (B&W., 90 min., 1943)
Dir: Jean-Paul Paulin; *Wri*: Charles Méré, based on the novel by Pierre Veber.
Cast: Robert Le Vigan (The Devil), Michèle Alfa, Mona Goya, André Luguet, Pierre Larquey, Huguette Saint-Arnaud, Renée Thorel.
Story: Same as above.

Les Hommes Veulent Vivre ! (aka *Le Crime du Dr. Chardin* [*Dr. Chardin's Crime*]) [*Men Want To Live!*] (B&W., 110 min., 1961)
Dir: Leonide Moguy; *Wri*: Leonide Moguy, Henri Torres.
Cast: Yves Massard (Chardin), Claudio Gora, John Justin, Jacqueline Huet.
Story: Professor Chardin, accused of murder, destroys his notes pertaining to a new deadly death ray.
Note: French-Italian co-production.

La Horde [*The Horde*] (Col., 90 min., 2009)
Dir: Yannick Dahan, Benjamin Rocher; *Wri*: Yannick Dahan, Benjamin Rocher, Stéphane Moïssakis, Arnaud Bordas.

Cast: Claude Perron (Aurore), Jean-Pierre Martins, Eriq Ebouaney, Yves Pignot, Doudou Masta, Jo Prestia, Antoine Oppenheim, Aurélien Recoing.
Story: Following the death of one of their own, murdered by a gang, a group of police officers raid a building to avenge their comrade. However, strange cries are heard in the building. The dead rise and attack. The gangsters and the police have to team up to face a horde of zombies.

L'Horrible Dr. Orloff [*The Awful Dr. Orloff*, aka *Cries In The Night*, *The Demon Doctor*] (B&W., 86 min., 1961)
Dir/Wri: Jess Franco, based on a novel by David Kuhne.
Cast: Howard Vernon, Conrado San Martin, Perla Cristal, Maria Silva.
Story: Unauthorized remake of Franju's *Les Yeux Sans Visage*, in which mad Dr. Orloff performs monstrous face transplants on disfigured people.
Note: This is a French-Spanish co-production by renowned Spanish B-movie director Jess Franco. It is the first in a Dr. Orloff series which includes *Les Maîtresses du Dr. Jekyll* aka *Dr. Orloff's Monster* (1964), *Dans les Griffes du Maniaque* (1965), *Les Orgies du Dr. Orloff* (1966), *Orloff et l'Homme Invisible* (1970), etc. It was remade as *Les Prédateurs de la Nuit* (see below).

Horsehead (col., 89 min., 2015)
Dir: Romain Basset; *Wri*: Romain Basset, Karim Chériguène.
Cast: Lilly-Fleur Pointeaux (Jessica), Catriona McCall, Murray Head, Gala Besson.
Story: Recurring nightmares in which she is chased by a mysterious horse-headed creature trouble Jessica, and they get worse after she attends her grandmother's funeral. As they intensify, she applies her knowledge of lucid dreaming to find the source of the horrible scenes.

Hostile (col., 83 min., 2017)
Dir/Wri: Mathieu Turi.

Cast: Brittany Ashworth (Juliette), Grégory Fitoussi, Javier Botet.
Story: Juliette, a survivor of the apocalypse, ventures from town to town to unearth food as survivors do in this ruined world.

House of Time (col., 86 min., 2015)
Dir: Jonathan Helpert; *Wri*: Jean Helpert, François Armanet.
Cast: David Atrakchi Laura Boujenah, Esther Comar, Maxime Dambrin (Robert).
Story: Video game creator and physicist Robert invites his friends to his castle to give them an incredible experience. According to his calculations, at 11:37 p.m., a time rift will open, allowing them to travel to 1944.

House of VHS [*Ghosts in the Machine*] (col., 83 min., 2016)
Dir/Wri: Gautier Cazenave.
Cast: Florie Auclerc, Delphine Lanniel, Isabel McCann, Morgan Lamorté, Pétur Sigurðsson.
Story: Six young people stumble upon a haunted VCR in an abandoned house in the French countryside.

Huis Clos [*No Exit*] (B&W., 95 min., 1954)
Dir: Jacqueline Audry; *Wri*: Pierre Laroche based on the play by Jean-Paul Sartre.
Cast: Arletty, Franck Villard, Gaby Sylvia, Yves Deniaud.
Story: Three persons who died from violent death are in hell, condemned to spend all eternity with each other.

Hu-Man (col., 90 min., 1974)
Dir: Jérôme Lapperousaz; *Wri*: André Ruellan.
Cast: Terence Stamp, Jeanne Moreau.
Story: An actor who lost his wife is enlisted by scientists who use him in a time travel experiment.

L'Ibis Rouge [*The Red Ibis*] (col., 90 min., 1975)

Dir: Jean-Pierre Mocky; *Wri*: Jean-Pierre Mocky, André Ruellan, based on a novel by Fredric Brown.
<u>*Cast*</u>: Michel Serrault (Jérémie), Michel Galabru (Raymond), Michel Simon, Jean Le Poulain.
Story: Jérémie is a serial killer who strangles women with a scarf embroidered with a red ibis. Raymond, who witnessed one of his crimes, tries to manipulate him into killing his wife.
Note: Fredric Brown is a renowned American science fiction writer.

I.F.1 Ne Répond Plus [*I.F.1 Does Not Answer*] (B&W., 100 min., 1932)
Dir: Karl Hartl; *Wri*: André Beucler, Walter Reisch, based on the novel by Curt Siodmak.
Cast: Charles Boyer, Jean Murst, Pierre Brasseur, Danièle Parola.
Story: Air transport companies fight against the building of a huge sea platform in the middle of the Atlantic.
Note: French version of a multinational co-production. Two other versions were shot simultaneously with different casts: a German version, *F.P.1 Antwortet Nicht*, with Hans Albers, Sybille Schmitz, Paul Hartman and Peter Lorre; and an English version, *F.P.1*, with Leslie Fenton, Conrad Veidt, Jill Esmond, and George Merritt. Curt Siodmak is the writer of *The Wolf Man* (1941).

Il Etait Une Fois Le Diable [*Once Upon A Time The Devil*, transl. as *Devil's Story*] (col., 100 min., 1982)
Dir/Wri: Bernard Launois.
Cast: Pascal Simon, Marcel Portier, Véronique Renaud.
Story: Nazi zombies attack a farm.

L'Île d'Épouvante [*The Island of Terror*] (B&W., 1930 ft., 1911/13)
Dir/Wri/Cast: Joe Hamman (reportedly loosely based on H. G. Wells' *The Island of Dr. Moreau*).

Story: Mad Dr. Wagner flees to an island to continue his skin grafts transplant research. The shipwrecked hero flees with the doctor's daughter when he discovers that he is to be his next subject.

L'Île de la Mort [*The Island of Death*] (B&W., 90 min., 1924)
Dir/Wri: Donatien.
Cast: Lucienne Legrand (Lucienne Garric), Donatien (Yves Kellec), Gaston Joncquet (Max Lannoë).
Story: On an island, a monkey steals capsules containing a deadly poison gas invented by a scientist and kills everyone.

L'Île Mystérieuse [*The Mysterious Island*] (col., 105 min., 1972)
Dir: Henri Colpi, Juan Antonio Bardem; *Wri*: Jacques Champreux, based on the novel by Jules Verne.
Note: Feature-length film version edited down from the eponymous television series. See next section.

Ils [*They*] (col., 100 min., 1970)
Dir: Jean-Daniel Simon; *Wri*: Jean-Daniel Simon, Jean Pierre Petrolacci, based on the novel *Le Seuil du Jardin* [*The Treshold of the Garden*] by André Hardellet.
Cast: Michel Duchaussoy, Charles Vanel, Alexandra Stewart, Vernon Potchess, Pierre Massimi.
Story: An old man has a machine which enables an artist to realize his unconscious dreams.

Ils Sont Fous, Ces Sorciers [*These Wizards Are Crazy*] (col., 95 min., 1978)
Dir: Georges Lautner; *Wri*: Norbert Carbonneaux, Albert Kantof, Georges Lautner, Claude Mulot.
Cast: Jean Lefèbvre, Daniel Ceccaldi, Henri Guybet, Julien Guiomar, Renée Saint-Cyr, Catherine Lachens.

Story: Having angered the native gods, two hapless French tourists (Lefèbvre, Ceccaldi) come back from a trip to the Islands with a curse on their heads.

Ils Sont Grands, Ces Petits [*The Kids Have Grown Up*] (col., 95 min., 1979)
Dir: Joël Santoni; *Wri*: Daniel Boulanger, Joël Santoni, Jean-Claude Carrière.
Cast: Claude Brasseur (Léo), Catherine Deneuve (Louise), Claude Piéplu, Eva Darlan, Jean-François Balmer, Roland Blanche, Yves Robert, Clément Harari.
Story: When Louise is expropriated by a real estate tycoon (Piéplu), her friend Léo, a gifted inventor, uses his knowledge of robotics to get her revenge.

L'Imprécateur [*The Imprecator*] (col., 100 min., 1977)
Dir: Jean-Louis Bertucelli; *Wri*: Jean-Louis Bertucelli, Stéphen Becker, René-Victor Pilhes, based on his novel.
Cast: Jean Yanne, Michel Piccoli, Jean-Pierre Marielle, Jean-Claude Brialy, Marlène Jobert, Michael Lonsdale.
Story: Surreal adventure in which a mysterious employee causes chaos and eventually destroys a large multinational corporation from within. Was it all a dream?

L'Inconnu de Shandigor [*The Unknown Man from Shandigor*] (col., 90 min., 1967)
Dir: Jean-Louis Roy; *Wri*: Jean-Louis Roy, Gabriel Arout.
Cast: Marie-France Boyer, Ben Carruthers, Daniel Emilfork, Howard Vernon, Jacques Dufilho.
Story: A villain discovers a way to make atomic weapons unworkable. He is devoured by his own sea monster at the climax.
Note: French-language Swiss production.

L'Invité de la 11ème Heure [*The 11th Hour Guest*] (B&W., 80 min., 1945)

Dir: Maurice Cloche; *Wri*: Maurice Cloche, Jean Ferry, Nino Franck.
Cast: Roger Pigault (Rémi), Jean Tissier (Berry), Blanchette Brunoy, Junie Astor.
Story: Young scientist Rémi tells his guests that he has invented a machine to read thoughts. He is murdered during the night and detective Berry investigates.

It Was on Earth That I Knew Joy (col., 35 min., 2009)
Dir/Wri: Jean-Baptiste de Laubier.
Cast: N/A.
Story: The story of a world ravaged by a pandemic, through a dialogue between two machines that trace the memories of a man from his archives in the year 20901.
Note: The film is a tribute to Chris Marker.

IXE-13 (col., 114 min, 1971)
Dir/Wri: Jacques Godbout, based on the novels of Pierre Saurel.
Cast: André Dubois (IXE-13), Louise Forestier, Serge Grenier, Marc Laurendeau, Marcel Saint-Germain, Diane Arcand, Little Brutus, Louisette Dussault, Luce Guilbeault, Suzanne Kay, Carole Laure.
Story: Musical parody of the adventures of the popular Canadian spy hero.
Note: Canadian production.

J'accuse [*I Accuse*] (B&W., 110 min., 1918)
Dir: Abel Gance; *Wri*: Blaise Cendrars, Abel Gance.
Cast: Séverin-Mars (François Laurin), Maryse Dauvray (Édith Laurin), Romuald Joubé (Jean Diaz).
Story: During World War I, the wife of a French soldier is raped by a German while her husband and a poet friend fight in the trenches.
Note: The film includes a striking ending where the war dead rise to get their revenge on those who stayed safely behind.

Blaise Cendrars (Frédéric Sauser, 1887-1961) is a famous poet and essayist.

J'accuse [*I Accuse*, (transl. as *They May Live*] (col., 125 min., 1937)
Dir: Abel Gance; *Wri*: Steve Passeur, Abel Gance.
Cast: Marcel Delaître (François Laurin), Line Noro (Édith Laurin), Victor Francen (Jean Diaz), Jean Max, Renée Devilliers.
Story: In this version, Diaz is a scientist who survived World War I. Desperately seeking to prevent another war, he invents a new indestructible glass. When he learns that another war is imminent, he raises the dead from the trenches and, this time, is heard. Peace prevails.

J'ai Rencontré le Père Noël [*I Have Met Santa Claus*, transl. as *Here Comes Santa Claus*] (col., 85 min., 1984)
Dir: Christian Gion; *Wri*: Christian Gion, Didier Kaminka.
Cast: Armand Meffre (Santa Claus), Karen Cheryl, Alexia Haudot, Eric Chapuis, Dominique Hulin, Hélène Zidi, Jean-Louis Foulquier.
Story: A little boy (Chapuis) is reunited with his missing parents thanks to Santa Claus.

James Bande 00 Sexe (col., 65 min., 1981)
Dir/Wri: Michel Baudricourt.
Cast: Guy Royer, Cathy Stewart, Helen Shirley, Dominique Trissou.
Story: X-rated *James Bond* parody.

Le Jardinier [*The Gardener*] (col., 94 min., 1980)
Dir/Wri: Jean-Pierre Sentier
Cast: Maurice Benichou (Gardener), Jean Bolo, Pierre Bolo, Michèle Marquais, Claude Faraldo.
Story: In a surreal future where water has become a precious commodity, a gardener revolts against two tyrannical brothers who run the factory where he works.

Je Ne Sais Pas [*I Don't Know*] (B&W., 315 M, 1966)
Dir/Wri: Gérard Pirès.
Cast: Bernadette Lafont, Jean-Pierre Kalfon.
Story: A man who broke-up with his girlfriend tries to commit suicide, but ends up stepping sideways in time.

Jessica Forever (col., 97 min., 2018)
Dir/Wri: Caroline Poggi & Jonathan Vinel.
Cast: Aomi Muyock (Jessica), Sebastian Urzendowsky, Augustin Raguenet, Lukas Ionesco.
Story: In a dystopian future world where violent misfits reign supreme, one woman and her makeshift family of rehabilitated marauders fight for peace and seek to create a new world.

Je t'aime, Je t'aime [*I Love You, I Love You*] (col., 91 min., 1968)
Dir: Alain Resnais; *Wri*: Jacques Sternberg.
Cast: Claude Rich, Olga Georges-Picot, Anouk Ferjac.
Story: A man (Rich) who tried to commit suicide is projected back into the past, where he can again live with his late wife (Georges-Picot). But the experiment goes wrong.
Note: Jacques Sternberg is a famous science fiction writer.

La Jetée [*The Pier*] (B&W., 29 min., 1964)
Dir/Wri: Chris Marker.
Cast: Davos Hanich, Hélène Chatelain, Jacques Ledoux, Jean Negroni.
Story: A time traveller (Hanich) tries to escape from a bleak, totalitarian future.
Note: This renowned short feature is the basis for Terry Gilliam's 1995 *Twelve Monkeys*.

Des Jeunes Gens Modernes [*Modern Youths*] (col., 97 min., 2012)
Dir: Jérôme de Missolz; *Wri*: Jean-François Sanz, Jérôme de Missolz.

Cast: Yves Adrien, Lio, Edwige Belmore.
Story: Rock fantasy.

Les Jeux de la Comtesse Dolingen de Gratz [*The Games of Countess Dolingen de Gratz*] (Col., 114 min., 1980)
Dir/Wri: Catherine Binet, based on story elements from Unica Zürn and Bram Stoker.
Cast: Michael Lonsdale (Bertrand), Carol Kane, Katia Watschenko, Marina Vlady, Roberto Plate.
Story: Bertrand, a wealthy art collector, brags about the horrible revenge he exacted on a thief who stole from him.

Les Jeux Sont Faits [*All Bets Are Off*] (B&W., 90 min., 1947)
Dir: Jean Delannoy; *Wri*: Jean-Paul Sartre, Jean Delannoy, Jacques-Laurent Bost.
Cast: Micheline Presle (Ève), Marcello Pagliero (Pierre), Colette Ripert, Marguerite Moreno, Fernand Fabre, Charles Dullin, Paul Ollivier, Marcel Mouloudji, Danièle Delorme.
Story: Pierre and Eve have died at the same exact second; she was poisoned by her husband; he was murdered by a fellow worker. Because they were fated to meet, they are returned to life for a day, but the difference in their respective social backgrounds proves too much for them, and they fail to fall in love.
Note: Novelist, playwright, and existentialist writer Jean-Paul Sartre (1905-1980) needs little introduction.

Je Vous Salue Marie [*Hail Mary*] (col., 65 min., 1984)
Dir: Jean-Luc Godard; *Wri*: Jean-Luc Godard, Anne-Marie Miéville.
Cast: Myriem Roussel (Mary), Thierry Rode, Philippe Lacoste, Juliette Binoche.
Story: The story of Gabriel, Mary, and Joseph recast in modern-day Switzerland.

J'irai comme un cheval fou [*I'll go like a crazy horse*] (col., 100 min., 1973)

Dir/Wri: Fernando Arrabal.
Cast: Emmanuelle Riva, George Shannon (Aden), Hachemi Marzouk (Marvel).
Story: Pursued by the police for the murder of his mother, Aden takes refuge in the desert where he meets Marvel, a strange man who mysteriously communicates with the Earth and all its creatures.

Jos Carbone (col., 75 min., 1975)
Dir/Wri: Hugues Tremblay, based on the novel by Jacques Benoît.
Cast: Yvon Barrette, Raymond Bélisle, Han Masson, Katerine Mousseau, Jean-Pierre Saulnier.
Story: Two couples try to survive in a post-cataclysmic world. A third man suddenly appears on the scene.
Note: French-Canadian production.

Le Joueur d'Échecs [*The Chess Player*] (B&W., 82 min., 1927)
Dir: Raymond Bernard; *Wri*: Henry Dupuy-Mazuel, based on the story of Johann Wolfgang Ritter von Kempelen's android chess player.
Cast: Edith Jehanne, Pierre Blanchar, Charles Dullin.
Story: A villain is killed by an android chess player.

Le Joueur d'Échecs [*The Chess Player*] (B&W., 90 min., 1938)
Dir: Jean Dréville; *Wri*: Albert Guyot, based on the famous story of Johann Wolfgang Ritter von Kempelen's android chess player.
Cast: Conrad Veidt (Kempelen), Françoise Rosay (Catherine II), Bernard Lancret, Micheline Francey, Paul Cambo, Jacques Grétillat, Gaston Modot.
Story: A romantic tale of young Polish patriots in love (Cambo and Francey) has been grafted onto the original Kempelen story.

Le Joueur de Flûte [*The Pied Piper of Hamelin*] (col., 90 min., 1971)
Dir: Jacques Demy; *Wri*: Jacques Demy, Andrew Birkin, Mark Peploe.
Cast: Donovan (the Piper), Jack Wild, Donald Pleasance, Cathryn Harrison, Peter Vaughan, John Hurt, Roy Kinnear.
Story: Faithful adaptation of the classic fairy tale.
Note: French- British co-production.

Le Joueur de Quilles [*The Bowler*] (col., 90 min., 1969)
Dir/Wri: Jean-Pierre Lajournade.
Cast: Fiammetta Ortega, Hugues Autexier, Tobias Engel.
Story: Surreal science fiction.

Le Jour de la Comète [*The Day of the Comet*] (col., 103 min., 2015)
Dir: Hervé Freiburger, Cédric Hachard, Sébastien Milhou; *Wri*: Hervé Freiburger, Cédric Hachard, Véronique Hauller, Sébastien Milhou.
Cast: Yves Arnault, Pascaline Ferrer, Béatrice de La Boulaye, Stéphane Roux, Aurélien Jegou, Alice Vial.
Story: As meteorite debris from Hallety's Comet disintegrate in Earth's atmosphere, Howard, Ana and Daryl, three inhabitants of the small town of Mont-Vallée, each wish for a better life, believing they've seen a shooting star...

Judex
Series of films featuring a crime-fighter created by Arthur Bernède, a popular pulp writer who also created *Belphegor*.
    Judex (B&W., 12 eps., 1916)
    La Nouvelle Mission de Judex [*Judex's New Mission*] (B&W., 12 eps., 1917)
Dir: Louis Feuillade; *Wri*: Arthur Bernède.
Cast: René Cresté (Judex), Louis Leubas (Favraux), Édouard Mathé, Yvonne Dario, Marcel Levesque, Musidora, André Brunelle.

Story: The original silent serial series introduces the character of avenging mystery man Judex, who is determined to bring corrupt banker Favraux to justice. Judex eventually falls in love with Favraux's daughter. In the second serial, Judex fights a spy ring controlled by a Dr. Mabuse-like villain.

Judex (B&W., 95 min., 1934)
Dir/Wri: Maurice Champreux.
Cast: René Ferté, Marcel Vallée, Mihalesco, Jean Lefèbvre, René Navarre, Constantini.
Story: Faithful remake of the Feuillade serial.

Judex (B&W., 100 min., 1963)
Dir: Georges Franju; *Wri*: Jacques Champreux, Francis Lacassin.
Cast: Channing Pollock (Judex), Michel Vitold (Favraux), Édith Scob (Jacqueline), Francine Bergé, Jacques Jouanneau, Théo Sarapo, Sylvia Koscina, René Genin.
Story: Inspired remake of the Feuillade serial; a moving and poetic homage to the original starring the renowned American magician in the title role.

Juliette, ou La Clé des Songes [*Juliette, or The Key to Dreams*] (B&W., 100 min., 1951)
Dir: Marcel Carné; *Wri*: Marcel Carné, Jacques Viot, Georges Neveux.
Cast: Gérard Philipe (Michel), Suzanne Cloutier (Juliette), Jean-Roger Caussimon, René Guénin, Yves Robert, Édouard Delmont, Roland Lesaffre, Gabrielle Fontan, Max Dejean, Arthur Devere, Marcelle Arnold, Fernand René, Martial Rebe, Marion Delbo.
Story: Michel is in prison because he stole from his employer at Juliette's behest. His experiences in a strange Land of Dream will change his life.

Kaamelott - Premier Volet [*Kaamelott - First Chapter*] (col. 120 min., 2021)
Dir/Wri: Alexandre Astier.
Cast: Alexandre Astier (Arthur), Thomas Cousseau (Lancelot), Lionnel Astier (Léodagan), Anne Girouard (Guenièvre), Frank Pitiot (Perceval), Jean-Christophe Hembert (Karadoc), Joëlle Sevilla (Séli), Audrey Fleurot (Viviane the Lady of the Lake), Jacques Chambon (Merlin), Alain Chabat, Antoine de Caunes, Christian Clavier, François Morel, Serge Papagalli, Clovis Cornillac, Guillaume Gallienne, Sting.
Story: The film takes place after the end of the TV series *Kaamelott* (see next section). Arthur, having fallen into crippling depression, vacated the throne of Camelot and returned Excalibur to the stone it came from. Meanwhile, his former friend and companion, Lancelot, under the influence of Maleagant, takes over Camelot and mercilessly hunts Arthur's friends and allies. Having spent an extended time on the verge of death at his mother's home in Tintagel after a suicide attempt, Arthur escapes the wrath of Lancelot, and progressively regains his health and will to live. Meanwhile, the Kingdom of Logres is resisting Lancelot, awaiting the moment when Arthur will return.

Kamikaze (col., 90 min., 1986)
Dir: Didier Grousset; *Wri*: Didier Grousset, Luc Besson, Michèle Halberstadt.
Cast: Michel Galabru (Albert), Richard Bohringer (Pascot), Dominique Lavanant, Riton Liebman, Jean-Paul Muel.
Story: Albert, an embittered, old scientist, builds a weapon which enables him to kill people who appear live on television. After a prodigious manhunt, police commissioner Pascot finds him, but for reasons of national security, the military kills the scientist.

Kandisha (col., 85 min., 2020)
Dir/Wri: Alexandre Bustillo & Julien Maury.
Cast: Mériem Sarolie, Walid Afkir, Suzy Bemba.

Story: Horror. A group of girls summon a nefarious spirit.

Le Lac des Morts-Vivants [*Zombie's Lake*] (col., 90 min., 1980)
Dir: Jean Rollin (credited as "J. R. Lazer"); *Wri*: Daniel Lesoeur (credited as Julian Estelim).
Cast: Howard Vernon, Pierre Escourrou, Anthony Mayans, Nadine Pascale.
Story: Nazi zombies emerge from a lake to eat their victims.

Lady Blood (col., 90 min., 2008)
Dir: Jean-Marc Vincent; *Wri*: Hubert Chardot, Jean-Marc Vincent.
Cast: Emmanuelle Escourrou, Matthias Van Khache, Serge Riaboukine.
Story: Sequel to *Baby Blood* (see above).

Landru [*Bluebeard*] (col., 155 min., 1962)
Dir: Claude Chabrol; *Wri*: Françoise Sagan.
Cast: Charles Denner (Landru), Michèle Morgan, Danielle Darrieux, Stéphane Audran, Juliette Mayniel, Catherine Rouvel.
Story: The story of the notorious French serial killer of the 1940s.

Léonor (col., 100 min., 1975)
Dir: Juan Luis Buñuel; *Wri*: Juan Luis Buñuel, Jean-Claude Carrière, Michel Nuridzani, Pierre Maintigneux, based on a story by Ludwig Tieck.
Cast: Michel Piccoli (Richard), Liv Ullman (Léonor), Ornella Muti (Catherine).
Story: During the Middle Ages, Richard marries Catherine after his wife Leonor's death. But ten years later, Léonor returns, possibly as a vampire.

Lèvres de Sang [*Bloody Lips*] (col., 92 min., 1975)
Dir: Jean Rollin; *Wri*: Jean Rollin, Jean-Lou Philippe.

Cast: Jean-Loup Philippe, Annie Briand, Natalie Perrey, Willy Braque, Paul Bisciglia.
Story: A child meets a beautiful woman. Twenty years later, he meets the same woman, who has not changed. because she is a vampire.

Les Lèvres Rouges [*Red Lips*, transl. as *Daughters of Darkness*] (col., 98 min., 1971)
Dir: Harry Kumel; *Wri*: Harry Kumel, Jean Ferry.
Cast: Delphine Seyrig (Countess Bathory), Danielle Ouimet, John Karlen, Andréa Rau.
Story: In Ostend, a newlywed couple (Karlen, Ouimet) runs afoul of the notorious vampire Countess Bathory.

Libra (col., 90 min., 1974)
Dir/Wri: Roland Moreau, Georges Perdriaud, Jean Talansier aka Groupe Pattern.
Cast: Pierre Sherley, Kris Frémont, Fabien Dutaillis, Jean-Pierre Pasquier.
Story: Upon their return to Earth, cosmonauts land on a mountain where a group of young people have dreamed a bucolic utopia.

Les Liens de Sang [*Blood Relatives*] (col., 100 min., 1977)
Dir: Claude Chabrol; *Wri*: Claude Chabrol, Sidney Banks, based on a novel by Ed McBain.
Cast: Donald Sutherland (Carella), Stéphane Audran, Aude Landry, Lise Langlois, David Hemmings, Donald Pleasance.
Story: *86th Precinct* story about a gory murder centered on an incest.
Note: French-Canadian co-production.

Liliom (B&W., 120 min., 1934)
Dir: Fritz Lang; *Wri*: Robert Liebmann, Bernard Zimmer, based on a story by Ferenc Molnar.
Cast: Charles Boyer (Liliom), Madeleine Ozeray, Roland Toutain, Alexandre Rignault, Antonin Artaud.

Story: A gambler and a drunk, Liliom kills himself. In Heaven, his Judges make him watch a film of his life and allow him to see his child again.
Note: Film made in France by Lang after he left Germany and before he emigrated to the United States.

Le Lit de la Vierge [*The Virgin's Bed*] (col., 100 min., 1969)
Dir/Wri: Philippe Garel.
Cast: Pierre Clémenti, Zazou, Jean-Pierre Kalfon.
Story: The surreal adventures of Mary and Jesus.

Litan (aka *La Cité des Spectres Verts* [*The City of the Green Spectres*]) (col., 88 min., 1981)
Dir: Jean-Pierre Mocky; *Wri*: Jean-Claude Romer, Jean-Pierre Mocky, Patrick Granier, Scott & Suzy Baker.
Cast: Jean-Pierre Mocky, Marie-José Nat, Nino Ferrer, Roger Lumont.
Story: In the atmospheric village of Litan, two lovers (Mocky and Nat) become involved in a plot by a mysterious doctor (Ferrer) to control the lifeforce of the dead.
Note: Scott Baker is an American science fiction writer living in France. Jean-Claude Romer is one of the foremost scholars on French fantastic cinema.

Livide [*Livid*] (col., 92 min., 2011)
Dir/Wri: Alexandre Bustillo & Julien Maury.
Cast: Chloé Coulloud, Félix Moati, Jérémy Kapone.
Story: In Brittany, on Halloween night, three friends decide to rob the house of a mysterious 100 years-old woman in a coma.

Le Locataire [*The Tenant*] (col., 125 min., 1976)
Dir: Roman Polanski; *Wri*: Gérard Brach, Roman Polanski, based on the novel by Roland Topor.
Cast: Roman Polanski (Trelkovsky), Isabelle Adjani (Stella), Melvyn Douglas, Shelley Winters, Héléna Manson, Bernard Fresson, Claude Piéplu, Rufus, Romain Bouteille, Jacques Monod.

Story: Trelkovsky, a meek bureaucrat, rents an apartment previously occupied by a woman who threw herself out of the window. He starts impersonating her, and eventually shares the same fate.

Note: Roland Topor is a renowned French writer/cartoonist who designed *La Planète Sauvage* [*Fantastic Planet*] (see Animation). He also acted in Werner Herzog's *Nosferatu*.

Lorna l'Exorciste [*Lorna the Exorcist*]
See *Les Possédés Du Diable*.

Le Loup-Garou [*The Werewolf*] (B&W., 90 min., 1923)
Dir/Wri: Jacques Roullet, Pierre Bressol, based on the novel by Alfred Machard.
Cast: Léon Bernard, Simone Jacquemin, Jeanne Delvair, Pierre Juvenet, Madeleine Guitty.
Story/Note: This film is listed here only because many reference works list it as the story of a priest's murderer who is cursed to turn into a werewolf. In reality, it is about an escaped convict who tries to escape from the police with his young son and tells the child that they are being pursued by a werewolf. It is *not* a fantasy film.

Le Loup des Malveneur [*The Wolf of Malveneur*] (B&W., 99 min., 1943)
Dir: Guillaume Radot; *Wri*: Francis Vincent-Bréchignac.
Cast: Pierre Renoir (Réginald), Madeleine Sologne (Monique), Michel Marsay, Gabrielle Dorziat, Yves Furet, Louis Salou.
Story: Réginald, the last descendant of the Malveneur family, is afraid of being struck by his ancestor's werewolf curse. Monique, a governess, solves the mystery.

Lucy (col., 89 min., 2014)
Dir/Wri: Luc Besson
Cast: Scarlett Johansson, Morgan Freeman, Choi Min-sik, Amr Waked, Pilou Asbæk.

Story: A woman who gains superhuman psychokinetic abilities when a nootropic, psychedelic drug is absorbed into her bloodstream.
Note: Multinational co-production.

La Lune dans le Caniveau [*The Moon in the Gutter*] (col., 137 min., 1983)
Dir: Jean-Jacques Beinex; *Wri*: Jean-Jacques Beinex, Olivier Mergault, based on the novel by David Goodis.
Cast: Gérard Depardieu (Gérard), Nastassja Kinski (Loretta), Victoria Abril (Bella), Vittorio Mezzogiorno, Dominique Pinon, Béatrice Reading.
Story: In a surreal, imaginary city, Gérard, a docker, searches for the man who raped his sister, driving her to kill herself. He then falls passionately in love with Loretta, a woman from the "high city," where rich people live.

La Machine (col., 94 min., 1994)
Dir/Wri: François Dupeyron, based on the novel by René Belletto.
Cast: Gérard Depardieu, Nathalie Baye, Didier Bourdon, Natalia Woerner, Erwan Baynaud.
Story: A neuropsychiatrist (Depardieu) invents a machine which switches his mind with that of a serial killer (Bourdon).

La Machine à Découdre [*The Killing Machine*] (col., 88 min., 1986)
Dir/Wri: Jean-Pierre Mocky.
Cast: Jean-Pierre Mocky (Dr. Enger), Patricia Barzyk, Peter Semler.
Story: A mad doctor embarks on a killing spree.

Madame Hyde (col., 95 min., 2017)
Dir: Serge Bozon; *Wri*: Serge Bozon, Axelle Ropert, based on the novel by Robert-Louis Stevenson.

Cast: Isabelle Huppert (Mme Géquil), Romain Duris, José Garcia, Patricia Barzyk, Guillaume Verdier, Pierre Léon, Karole Rocher.
Story: Madame Géquil teaches physics in a vocational high school. She suffers from the pranks of her colleagues and students. But after being struck by lightning, her personality gradually changes...

Ma Femme est une Panthère [*My Wife Is a Panther*] (col., 85 min., 1961]
Dir: Raymond Bailly; *Wri*: Gérard Carlier.
Cast: Jean Richard, Jean Poiret, Michel Serrault, Silvana Blasi, Marcel Lupovici.
Story: A woman's soul has transmigrated into a panther's body and can become human at will.

Le Magnifique [*The Magnificent One*, transl. as *How to Destroy the Reputation of the Greatest Secret Agent*] (col., 90 min., 1973)
Dir: Philippe de Broca; *Wri*: Francis Veber.
Cast: Jean-Paul Belmondo (François/Bob), Jacqueline Bisset (Christine/Tatiana), Vittorio Caprioli, Monique Tarbès, Jean Lefèbvre, Mario David, André Weber, Hubert Deschamps.
Story: François, a writer of spy thrillers, keeps alternating between his reality and the fictional world of his hero, Bob.

La Main [*The Hand*] (col., 90 min., 1969)
Dir: Henri Glaeser; *Wri*: Henri Glaeser, Paul Parisot.
Cast: Nathalie Delon, Michel Duchaussoy, Henri Serre, Pierre Dux, Roger Hanin.
Story: A pair of murderers are forced to cut off their victim's hand when they dispose of his body. But the hand returns to haunt them.

La Main du Diable [*The Devil's Hand*, transl. as *Carnival of Sinners*] (B&W., 82 min., 1942)

Dir: Maurice Tourneur; *Wri*: Jean-Paul Le Chanois, based on a short story by Gérard de Nerval.
Cast: Pierre Fresnay (Roland), Josseline Gaël (Irène), Marcelle Rexlane, Gabrielle Fontan, Pierre Palau, Noël Roquevert, Guillaume de Sax, Pierre Larquey.
Story: Roland, a failed painter, buys a mysterious mummified hand which makes him rich and famous, and enables him to marry Irène, the woman he loves, but by so doing, he has unwittingly sold his soul to the Devil.
Note: Gérard de Nerval is a famous poet and writer of the *fantastique*.

Les Mains d'Orlac [*The Hands of Orlac*] (B&W., 105 min., 1960)
Dir: Edmond Gréville; *Wri*: Edmond Gréville, John Baines, based on the novel by Maurice Renard.
Cast: Mel Ferrer (Orlac), Dany Carrel, Christopher Lee, Lucile Saint-Simon, Balpêtré.
Story: A surgeon (Balpêtré) grafts a killer's hands onto a famous pianist (Ferrer). Before he kills his wife (Carrel), he learns that the killer was in fact innocent.
Note: Maurice Renard is a famous science fiction writer. This is the third film adaptation based on his story, after *Orlacs Hände* in Germany in 1924 (*Dir*: Robert Wiene, starring Conrad Veidt), and *Mad Love* in the U.S. in 1935 (*Dir*: Karl Freund, starring Peter Lorre).

Le Maître du Temps [*The Time Master*] (B&W., 90 min., 1970)
Dir: Jean-Daniel Pollet; *Wri*: Jean-Daniel Pollet, Pierre Kast.
Cast: Jean-Pierre Kalfon, Ruy Guerra.
Story: A man (Kalfon), who may be an alien, owns a ring that allows him to travel through time; he uses it to visit various eras in Brazilian history.

Les Maîtres du Soleil [*The Sun Masters*] (col., 85 min., 1983)
Dir/Wri: Jean-Jacques Aublanc.

Cast: Marcel Amont, Georges Claisse, Maurice Garrel, François Chaumette, Catherine Jarrett, Bernard Marcellin, Jean Davy, Gérard Chaillou.
Story: A retired scientist (Claisse) investigates the disappearance of a colleague (Davy) who had made a breakthrough discovery in light energy. The missing scientist now wants to cleanse the world, but is destroyed by ancient, occult powers.

La Malédiction de Belphegor [*The Curse of Belphegor*] (col., 98 min., 1966)
Dir: Georges Combret; *Wri*: Georges Combret, Michel Dubox.
Cast: Paul Guers, Dominique Boschero, Raymond Souplex, Raymond Bussières, Noëlle Noblecourt, Maurice Chevit, Achille Zavatta, Marcel Charvey, Annette Poivre.
Story: A madman possessed by the pagan god Belphegor, and armed with sophisticated technology, attempts to prevent the staging of what he believes to be a blasphemous play.
Note: No relation to the *Belphegor* television series (see next chapter).

Maléfique [*Malefic*] (col., 90 min., 2002)
Dir: Éric Valette; *Wri*: Alexandre Charlot, Franck Magnier.
Cast: Gérald Laroche, Philippe Laudenbach, Clovis Cornillac, Dimitri Rataud.
Story: Cellmates discover, hidden behind a loose brick, an old journal which belonged to a prisoner from the 1920s who mysteriously disappeared. The book is filled with incantations and symbols of black magic.

Malevil (col., 119 min., 1980)
Dir: Christian de Chalonge; *Wri*: Christian de Chalonge, Pierre Dumayet, based on the novel by Robert Merle.
Cast: Michel Serrault (Emmanuel), Jean-Louis Trintignant (Fulbert), Jacques Dutronc, Jacques Villeret, Robert Dhéry.
Story: After a nuclear war, a few survivors learn to live in peace under Emmanuel's guidance, but they come in conflict with another group led by the fascistic Fulbert.

Note: Robert Merle is a famous writer, author of *The Day of the Dolphin* (1967).

Malpertuis (col., 110 min., 1972)
Dir: Harry Kumel; *Wri*: Jean Ferry, based on the novel by Jean Ray.
Cast: Orson Welles (Cassave), Mathieu Carrière (Yann), Susan Hampshire, Michel Bouquet, Jean-Pierre Cassel.
Story: After Uncle Cassave's death, Yann, a young sailor, inherits his ancient house, Malpertuis, and its weird occupants, who turn out to be the shades of the Olympian Gods once captured by his warlock uncle.
Note: French-language Belgian production. Jean Ray is a major writer of the *fantastique*.

Mama Dracula (col., 90 min., 1980)
Dir: Boris Szulzinger; *Wri*: Boris Szulzinger, Pierre Sterckx, Marc-Henry Wajnberg.
Cast: Louise Fletcher (Mama), Maria Schneider, Marc-Henry & Alexandre Wajnberg.
Story: Another variation of the Countess Bathory/female Dracula tale, used here mostly as a vehicle for two stand-up comedians, the Wajnbergs, two cousins posing as Mama Dracula's twin sons.
Note: French-language Belgian production.

Le Mangeur de Lune [*The Moon Eater*] (col., 103 min., 1994)
Dir: Dai Sijie; *Wri*: Dai Sijie, Nadine Perront.
Cast: Chick Ortega, Rufus, Mohamed Camara, Catherine Hiegel, Geneviève Fontanel, Yann Colette.
Story: Adaptation of a Russian folk tale in which, in order to be freed from a curse, a flying man must be bathed in human blood.

Manika, Une Vie Plus Tard [*Manika, One Life Later*] (col., 100 min., 1988)

Dir: François Villiers; *Wri*: François Villiers, Jean-Pierre Gibrat, Brian Phelan.
Cast: Julian Sands, Ayesha Dharker, Stéphane Audran.
Story: A young Indian girl discovers that she is the reincarnation of another woman.

Le Manoir du Diable [*The House of the Devil*, aka *The Haunted Castle*, *The Devil's Castle*] (B&W., 3+ min., 1896)
Dir/Wri: Georges Méliès.
Story: Brief pantomimed sketch about an encounter with the Devil and various attendant demons.
Note: This feature is intended to evoke amusement and wonder rather than fear. However, because of its themes and characters, it has been considered to be the first horror film ever. The picture also includes a human transforming into a bat, which has led some to label it the first vampire film ever. Its running time was ambitious for its era. A remake was produced a year later under the title *Le Château hanté* [*The Haunted Castle*], which is often confused with this film.

Marguerite de la Nuit [*Marguerite of the Night*] (col., 125 min., 1955)
Dir: Claude Autant-Lara; *Wri*: Ghislaine Autant-Lara, Gabriel Arout, based on the novel by Pierre Mac Orlan.
Cast: Michèle Morgan (Marguerite), Yves Montand (Léon / Mephistophéles), Jean-François Calvé (Faust), Pierre Palau, Massimo Girotti.
Story: Another variation on the classic *Faust* story, in which Marguerite is willing to sacrifice her soul to save Faust, but because Mephistopheles is in love with her, he releases them both.

Marianne de ma Jeunesse [*Marianne of my Youth*] (B&W., 105 min., 1954)
Dir/Wri: Julien Duvivier, based on the novel by Peter von Mendelssohn.

Cast: Marianne Hold, Pierre Vaneck, Isabelle Pia, Gil Vidal, Jean Yonnel.
Story: In the midst of the Bavarian forest, a young man (Vaneck) meets a beautiful, mysterious woman (Hold) who transforms his life.

Marie-Chantal contre Dr. Kha [*Marie-Chantal vs. Dr. Kha*] (col., 114 min., 1965)
Dir: Claude Chabrol; *Wri*: Claude Chabrol, Christian Yve, based on an idea by Jacques Chazot.
Cast: Marie Laforêt (Marie-Chantal), Akim Tamiroff (Dr. Kha), Francisco Rabal, Serge Reggiani, Charles Denner, Roger Hanin, Stéphane Audran.
Story: Marie-Chantal accidentally comes into the possession of the secret of a super-weapon and becomes the target of a variety of spies working for the evil Dr. Kha (Tamiroff) in this light-hearted satire of *James Bond* movies.

Le Martien de Noël [*The Christmas Martian*] (col., 66 min., 1977)
Dir: Bernard Gosselin; *Wri*: Roch Carrier, Louise Forestier.
Cast: Paul Berval, Yvan Canuel, Roland Chenail, François Gosselin, Ernest Guimond.
Story: Children find a friendly Martian in a forest at Christmas time.
Note: French-Canadian production.

Un Martien à Paris [*A Martian in Paris*] (B&W., 90 min., 1960)
Dir: Jean-Daniel Daninos; *Wri*: Jean-Daniel Daninos, Jacques Vilfrid.
Cast: Darry Cowl, Nicole Mirel, Henri Vilbert, Gisèle Grandré, Rolande Ségur, Michèle Verez.
Story: A Martian lands in Paris to study the emotion called love.

Le Masque de la Méduse [*The Mask of Medusa*] (col., 75 min., 2010)
Dir/Wri: Jean Rollin.
Cast: Marie-Simone Rollin (Medusa), Marlène Delcambre (Steno), Sabine Lenoël (Euryale), Delphine Montoban (Cornelius).
Story: A variation on the classic Medusa tale, taking place at the Grand-Guignol theater.
Note: This was Rollin's last film before his death on 15 December 2010.

Matusalem (col., 1993, 107 min.)
Dir/Wri: Roger Cantin.
Cast: Marc Labrèche, Émile Proulx-Cloutier, Steve Gendron, Jessica Barker, Marie-France Monette, Maxime Collin, Jod Léveillé-Bernard.
Story: Every 50 years, on his birthday, a spell forces Philippe to seek the help of a living person to accomplish an important mission. Olivier agrees to help him, which will lead him, and six of his friends, on a whimsical adventure
Note: French-Canadian production

Méandre [*Meander*] (col., 90 min., 2020)
Dir/Wri: Mathieu Turi.
Cast: Gaia Weiss, Peter Franzén.
Story: A young hitchhiker (Weiss) discovers that her driver is a serial killer. She wakes up in a metal tube full of deadly traps. In order not to die, she has to constantly move forward.

La Mémoire Courte [*Short Memory*] (col., 90 min., 1979)
Dir: Eduardo de Gregorio; *Wri*: Edgardo Cozarinsky, Eduardo de Gregorio.
Cast: Philippe Léotard, Nathalie Baye, Bulle Ogier.
Story: A fantastical investigation in a Jose Luis Borges-like setting.
Note: French-Belgian co-production.

La Merveilleuse Visite [*The Marvelous Visit*] (col., 100 min., 1974)
Dir: Marcel Carné; *Wri*: Marcel Carné, Didier Decoin, based on the story by H. G. Wells.
Cast: Gilles Kohler (The Angel), Roland Lesaffre, Deborah Berger, Lucien Barjon, Mary Marquet, Jean-Pierre Castaldi, Yves Barsacq, Jacques Debary.
Story: The inhabitants of a small village in Britanny discover a man who claims to be an angel who fell from the sky.

La Meute [*The Pack*] (col., 85 min., 2010)
Dir/Wri: Franck Richard.
Cast: Yolande Moreau (La Spack), Émilie Dequenne (Charlotte), Benjamin Biolay, Philippe Nahon.
Story: A young female traveler, Charlotte finds herself prisoner of La Spack, a woman who sees her as the next meal for her brood, a pack of ghouls.
Note: Belgian production.

Midi-Minuit [*Noon to Midnight*] (col., 105 min., 1970)
Dir/Wri: Pierre Philippe.
Cast: Sylvie Fennec, Béatrice Arnac, Daniel Emilfork, Jacques Portet, Laurent Vergez, Patrick Jouanne.
Story: A mysterious killer with vampiric tendencies rips his victims apart with iron-clawed gloves.

Les Mille et Une Nuits [*The Thousand and One Nights*] (col., 98 min., 1990)
Dir: Philippe de Broca; *Wri*: Philippe de Broca, Jérôme Tonnerre.
Cast: Thierry Lhermitte (Sultan), Gérard Jugnot (Genie), Vittorio Gassman, Catherine Zeta-Jones (Sheherazade).
Story: Comedic transposition of the classic tale, in which a genie from the 20th century uses modern equipment to save Sheherazade from the Sultan.

Les Mille Merveilles de l'Univers [*The Thousand Wonders of the Universe*] (col., 90 min., 1997)
Dir/Wri: Jean-Michel Roux.
Cast: Tchéky Karyo (Larsen), Julie Delpy (Eva), Chick Ortega (Oscar), Féodor Atkine, Maria de Medeiros, Pascale Bussières, James Hyndman.
Story: NASA receives alien signals from space; on Earth 12,000 people are mysteriously abducted. An astrophysicist investigates.

Le Miracle des Loups [*The Miracle of the Wolves*] (B&W., 3000 M., 1924)
Dir: Raymond Bernard; *Wri*: Jean-José Frappa, Henry Dupuy-Mazuel.
Cast: Charles Dullin (Louis XI), Vanni Marcoux (Charles le Téméraire), Romuald Joubé (Robert), Yvonne Sergyl (Jeanne), Gaston Modot, Philippe Hériat.
Story: Medieval folk tale where two lovers are miraculously saved by wolves.

Le Miracle des Loups [*The Miracle of the Wolves*] (col., 130 min., 1961)
Dir: André Hunebelle; *Wri*: André Hunebelle, Jean Halain.
Cast: Jean-Louis Barrault (Louis XI), Roger Hanin (Charles le Téméraire), Jean Marais (Robert de Neuville), Rosanna Schiaffino (Jeanne de Beauvais).
Story: Same as above.

Le Miraculé [*The Miracle Victim*] (col., 87 min., 1986)
Dir: Jean-Pierre Mocky; *Wri*: Jean-Pierre Mocky, Jean-Claude Romer, Patrick Granier.
Cast: Michel Serrault (Fox-Terrier), Jean Poiret (Papu), Jeanne Moreau.
Story: Papu pretends to be paralyzed to defraud his insurance company. After a trip to Lourdes, he really becomes paralyzed.

Mirages (col., 100 min., 2010)
Dir: Talal Selhami; *Wri*: Christophe Mordellet, Talal Selhami.
Cast: Éric Savin, Karim Saidi, Aïssam Bouali.
Story: Five people from various backgrounds agree to participate in a strange experiment in Morocco. They are placed in a windowless bus that has an accident.
Note: French-Moroccan co-production.

Le Miroir [*The Mirror*] (col., 13 min., 1976)
Dir/Wri: Dominique Maillet, based on a story by Claude Seignolle.
Cast: Anne Jolivet, Albert Pierjac.
Story: A mysterious woman hides a secret behind the bandages which cover her head.

Miss Shumay Jette un Sort [*Miss Shumway Casts a Spell*]
See *Une Blonde Comme Ça*.

Mister Freedom (col., 110 min., 1968)
Dir/Wri: William Klein.
Cast: John Abbey (Mr. Freedom), Donald Pleasance (Dr. Freedom), Jean-Claude Drouot, Philippe Noiret, Delphine Seyrig, Serge Gainsbourg, Yves Montand, Rufus, Sami Frey.
Story: Mr. Freedom fights Moujik Man over the fate of France; a satire on the clash between super-powers, done in a comic-book style.

Mister Frost (col., 105 min., 1989)
Dir: Philippe Setbon; *Wri*: Philippe Setbon, Brad Lynch, Louise Vincent, Deny Hall.
Cast: Jeff Goldblum, Alan Bates, Kathy Baker, Roland Giraud, Jean-Pierre Cassel, François Négret, Daniel Gélin, Maxime Leroux, Vincent Schiavelli.
Story: A murderer (Goldblum) incarcerated in a lunatic asylum tries to convince his doctor (Baker) that he is the Devil.

Le Moine [*The Monk*] (col., 90 min., 1972)

Dir: Ado Kyrou; *Wri*: Luis Buñuel, Jean-Claude Carrière, based on the novel by Matthew Lewis.
Cast: Franco Nero (Ambrosio), Nathalie Delon (Jean), Nicol Williamson, Nadja Tiller.
Story: Adaptation of the celebrated gothic novel about Ambrosio, a monk who is being tempted by the Devil (Delon).
Note: This film was originally written by Carrière for Buñuel to direct.

Le Moine et la Sorcière [*The Monk and the Witch*] (col., 98 min., 1986)
Dir: Suzane Schiffman; *Wri*: Pamela Berger, Suzane Schiffman.
Cast: Tcheky Karyo (Étienne), Christine Boisson (Elda), Jean Carmet, Féodor Atkine.
Story: In the Middle-Ages, Étienne, an inquisitor, accuses Elda, a local woman who is knowledgable about herbs and plants, of being a witch; she is eventually rescued by the local priest (Carmet).

Les Moineaux de Paris [*The Sparrows of Paris*] (B&W., 90 min., 1952)
Dir: Maurice Cloche; *Wri*: Maurice Cloche, André Hornez, Franz Tanzler.
Cast: Jean-Pierre Aumont, Virginia Kelley, Max Elloy, Robert Lombard, Louis Gimberg, Odette Barançay, Louis de Funès, André Dalibert, Philippe Olive, Paul Demange.
Story: The ghost of a Napoleonic soldier (Aumont) searches for a lost medallion and is helped by his young descendent.

Le Monde Tremblera [*The World Will Quake*] (B&W., 108 min, 1939)
Dir: Richard Pottier; *Wri*: Jean Villard, Henri-Georges Clouzot, based on the novel *La Machine à Prédire la Mort* [*The Death-Predicting Machine*] by Charles Robert-Dumas & Roger-Francis Didelot.

Cast: Claude Dauphin (Jean), Roger Duchesne, Madeleine Sologne, Erich Von Stroheim.
Story: Jean, a young inventor, creates a machine that can accurately predict the time of someone's death—including his.

Le Monde Vivant [*The Living World*] (col., 75 min., 2003)
Dir/Wri: Eugène Green.
Cast: Arnold Pasquier (The Ogre), Christelle Prot (His Wife), Alexis Loret, Adrien Michaux.
Story: An ogre keeps two children alive that he intends to eat. Two knights plan to free them. The ogre's wife helps them to get rid of her awful husband.

Monsieur Leguignon, Guérisseur [*Mr. Leguignon, Healer*] (B&W., 90 min, 1953)
Dir: Maurice Labro; *Wri*: Solange Térac, Maurice Labro, based on the radio series by Robert Picq & Pierre Ferrari.
Cast: Yves Deniaud, Jeanne Marken, Nicole Besnard, André Brunot, Michel Roux.
Story: A man discovers that he has the power of healing.

Le Monstre aux Yeux Verts [*The Green-Eyed Monster*] (col., 87 min., 1961)
Dir: Romano Ferrara; *Wri*: Romano Ferrara, Piero Pierotti based on a story by Massimo Rendina.
Cast: Jany Clair, Michel Lemoine, Marco Guglielmi, Maria-Pia Luzi.
Story: An alien humanoid robot causes death by mere contact. He is hunted down and destroyed.
Note: French-Italian co-production.

La Montagne aux Mille Regards [*The Mountain of a Thousand Eyes*] (col., 155 min., 2021)
Dir: Bastien Verney; *Wri*: David Chamberod.
Cast: Aurore Péron, Lilou Collet, Baptiste Ratel, Emmanuel Pétoud, Lisa Excoffon, Daniel Gros, Aimé Traversaz.

Story: In a strange, forgotten land there is a mountain fortress that is the seat of a frightening legend. It is called The Mountain of a Thousand Eyes because one feels watched there... One night, a group of daring young adventurers decides to spend the night there...

Morgane et ses Nymphes [*Morgana and her Nymphs*] (col., 90 min., 1970)
Dir/Wri: Bruno Gantillon.
Cast: Dominique Delpierre, Alfred Baillou, Mireille Saunin, Régine Motte, Ursule Pauly, Michèle Perello, Nathalie Chaîne.
Story: X-rated tale of the wild adventures of two girls in the realm of Faerie.

Mort à l'Écran [*Live from Deathrow*] (col., 35 min., 2008)
Dir/Wri: Alexis & Jonathan Ferrebeuf.
Cast: Lambert Wilson, MC Solaar.
Story: A former boxer, sentenced to death for murder, is offered the chance to be pardoned or not by a court of spectators during a new TV show presented by an unscrupulous host.

La Mort en Direct [*Death on Live TV*, transl. as *Death Watch*] (col., 120 min., 1980)
Dir: Bertrand Tavernier; *Wri*: David Rayfiel, Bertrand Tavernier, based on the novel *The Continuous Katherine Mortenhoe*, aka *The Unsleeping Eye*, by D. G. Compton.
Cast: Romy Schneider (Katherine), Harvey Keitel (Roddy), Harry Dean Stanton (Vincent), Max von Sydow (Gerard), Thérèse Liotard (dubbed by Julie Christie).
Story: Roddy, a television reporter, has a camera implanted in his eye in order to follow and broadcast the journey of Katherine, a woman dying from an incurable disease, as she looks for Gerard, her estranged husband. Eventually, disgusted by his treachery and voyeurism, he allows himself to go blind. We discover that the woman can be cured—It was all part of a plan by Vincent, the head of the TV network, to guarantee a

happy ending and big ratings. But Katherine chooses to die to make a point.
Note: The U.S. release version of this film was badly re-edited by the distributor; in particular, the reasons for Katherione's suicide were totally obfuscated.

Une Mort sans Importance [*A Meaningless Death*] (B&W., 80 min., 1948)
Dir/Wri: Ivan Noé.
Cast: Jean Tissier (Duvernay), Suzy Carrier, Jean-Pierre Kerrien, Marcelle Géniat, Jeanne Fusier-Gir.
Story: Death forces a man (Kerrien) to choose another member of his family to take his place.

La Mort Trouble [*An Unclear Death*] (col., 84 min., 1968)
Dir: Claude d'Anna, Ferid Boughedir; *Wri*: Ferid Boughedir.
Cast: Aly Ben Ayed, Ursule Pauly, Sophie Vaillant, Sylvie Céline.
Story: On a deserted island, a strange butler (Ben Ayed) plays games with three young women.

La Mort de l'Utopie [*The Death of Utopia*] (col., 70 min., 1975)
Dir/Wri: Jorge Amat.
Cast: José-Louis Aguire, Charlotte Trench, Emmanuelle Riva, Juliette Noessi.
Story: After his capture by the police, a mad gunman finds refuge in his imagination.

La Morte-Vivante [*The Living Dead Girl*] (col., 90 min., 1982)
Dir/Wri: Jean Rollin.
Cast: Françoise Blanchard, Marina Pierro, Carina Barone, Mike Marshall, Fanny Magier.
Story: A young girl returns to life.

Mr. Nobody (col., 141 min., 2009)

Dir/Wri: Jaco Van Dormael.
Cast: Jared Leto (Nobody), Sarah Polley, Diane Kruger, Linh-Dan Pham.
Story: The story of Nemo Nobody, an 118-year-old man who is the last mortal on Earth after the human race has achieved quasi-immortality.
Note: Belgian production.

Mutants (col., 85 min., 2099)
Dir: David Morlet. *Wri*: David Morlet, Louis-Paul Desanges
Cast: Hélène de Fougerolles (Sonia), Francis Renaud, (Marco), Dida Diafat.
Story: A virus has transformed the vast majority of humanity into bloodthirsty, zombie creatures. Marco and Sonia are young couple fleeing the "mutants" and trying to fight their way to a military base.

Les Mystères de Paris [*The Mysteries of Paris*] based on the 1843 novel by Eugène Sue.
Story: Hugely popular social-gothic serial pitting the mysterious Prince Rodolphe and the beautiful Fleur-de-Marie (who is eventually revealed to be his illegitimate daughter) against the villainous Maître d'École (Schoolmaster), Chourineur (Stabber) and La Chouette (The Owl) in the darkness-filled mazes and haunts of the Paris underworld.

    Les Mystères de Paris (B&W., 100 min., 1911)
    Dir/Wri: Albert Capellani.
    Cast: Henry Houry, Edmond Duquesne.

    Les Mystères de Paris (B&W. serial, 12 episodes, 1922)
    1: *Le Tapis Franc* (*The French Carpet*); 2: *La Ferme de Bouqueval* (*The Farm at Bouqueval*) ; 3: *Les Justiciers* (*The Avengers*) ; 4: *Le Ménage Pipelet* (*The Pipelet Couple*) ; 5: *Les Suites d'un Bal à l'Ambassade* (*The Sequels of a Ball at the Embassy*); 6: *Misère* (*Misery*); 7: *Le Martyre de Louise Morel* (*The Martyrdom of Louise Morel*) ; 8: *L'Étude de Me. Ferrand* (*The Office of Ferrand,*

Esq.) ; 9: *L'Île du Ravageur* (*The Island of the Destroyer*); 10: *Le Maître d'École et la Chouette* (*The Schoolmaster and the Owl*) ; 11. *Celle qui Venge* (*She who Avenges*) ; 12. *Son Altesse Fleur-de-Marie* (*Her Highness Fleur-de-Marie*)
Dir/Wri: Charles Burguet.
Cast: Georges Lannes (Rodolphe), Huguette Duflos, Camille Bardou, Suzanne Bianchetti, Jeanne Bérangère, Gilbert Dalleu, Régine Dumien, Andrée Lionel, Desdemona Mazza, Gaston Modot, Yvonne Sergyl, Simone Vaudry.

Les Mystères de Paris (B&W., 110 min., 1935)
Dir/Wri: Félix Gandera.
Cast: Henri Rollan (Rodolphe), Madeleine Ozeray (Fleur-de-Marie), Constant Rémy (Maître d'École), Lucien Baroux, Raymond Cordy, Marcelle Géniat, Lucienne Le Marchand, Raoul Marco, Marthe Mussine, Rolla Norman, François Rodon, Nadia Sibirskaïa, Georges Vitray.

Les Mystères de Paris (B&W., 89 min., 1943)
Dir: Jacques de Baroncelli; *Wri*: Maurice Bessy, Pierre Laroche.
Cast: Marcel Herrand (Rodolphe), Caecilia Paroldi (Fleur-de-Marie), Alexandre Rignault (Maître d'École), Lucien Coëdel (Chourineur), Germaine Kerjean (La Chouette), Yolande Laffon, Raphael Patorni, Simone Ribaut, Ginette Roy.

Les Mystères de Paris (B&W., 100 min., 1957)
Dir: Fernando Cerchio; *Wri*: Damiano Damiani.
Cast: Franck Villard, Yvette Lebon, Jacques Castelot.
Note: French-Italian co-production.

Les Mystères de Paris (col., 110 min., 1962)
Dir: André Hunebelle; *Wri*: Jean Halain, Pierre Foucaud, Diego Fabbri.

Cast: Jean Marais (Rodolphe), Dany Robin (Fleur-de-Marie), Jean Le Poulain (Maître d'École), Pierre Mondy (Chourineur), Renée Gardès (La Chouette), Raymond Pellegrin, Georges Chamarat, Noël Roquevert, Madeleine Barbulée, Charles Bouillaud.
Note: French-Italian co-production.

La Naissance de Narcisse [*The Birth of Narcissus*] (col., 88 min., 2018)
Dir/Wri: Hugo Parthonnaud.
Cast: Sergei Philippenko, Olivier Parthonnaud, Laure Massard.
Story: David, a young megalomaniac scientist, decides clone himself…

Narayana (B&W., 60 min., 1920)
Dir/Wri: Léon Poirier, based on *La Peau de Chagrin* (known in English as *The Wild Ass's Skin*) by Honoré de Balzac.
Cast: Laurence Myrga, Marguerite Madys, Edmond Van Daële.
Story: A young man finds a magic piece of shagreen that fulfills his every desire.

Nature Morte Avec Oranges [*Still Life With Oranges*] (col., 125 min., 2016).
Dir/Wri: Dick Turner.
Cast: Frédéric Moulin, Laura d'Assche, Isabelle Ziental.
Story: In a near future where everyone wears invisible chains, a young girl decides to help an alchemist change the order of things.

Le Navire Aveugle [*The Blind Ship*] (B&W., 90 min., 1927)
Dir/Wri: Giuseppe Guarino, based on a novel by Jean Barreyre.
Cast: Colette Darfeuil, Marthe Mellot, Adelqui Migliar.

Story: The passengers and the crew of a ship all go blind, turning the boat into ghost ship.

Ne le Criez pas sur les Toits [*Don't Shout it Over the Rooftops*] (B&W., 99 min., 1943)
Dir: Jacques Daniel-Norman; *Wri*: Jean-Bernard Luc, Alex Joffé.
Cast: Fernandel (Vincent), Meg Lemonnier, Robert Le Vigan, Jacques Varennes, Albert Gercourt, Jacques Berlioz.
Story: After the death of a scientist who was looking for a new superfuel, his assistant, Vincent, becomes that target of villains seeking to steal or suppress the discovery.

Necronomicon (1993)
French-American anthology horror film. It features three distinct segments and a wraparound. Only the segment entitled *The Drowned* is of interest here.
Dir/Wri: Christophe Gans.
Cast: Bruce Payne, Belinda Bauer, Richard Lynch, Maria Ford.
Story: A man usesd the *Necronomicon* to bring his family back to life. However, they are revived as unholy monsters with green glowing eyes and tentacles in their mouths. He chooses to commit suicide.

Ne Jouez Pas Avec Les Martiens [*Don't Play With Martians*] (col., 90 min., 1967)
Dir: Henri Delanoe; *Wri*: Henri Delanoe, Joanne Harwood, based on the novel *Les Sextuplés de Loqmaria* [*The Sextuplets of Loqmaria*] by Michel Labry.
Cast: Jean Rochefort, Macha Méril, André Vallardy, Frédéric de Pasquale, Haydée Politoff, Pierre Dac.
Story: A reporter fakes a Martian landing when sextuplets are born in a Britanny village. Real aliens (not Martians) then arrive to claim the children.

Némo (col., 97 min., 1984)

Dir: Arnaud Sélignac; *Wri*: Arnaud Sélignac, Jean-Pierre Esquenazzi, Telsche Boorman, based on the comic strip by Winsor McCay.
Cast: Seth Kibel (Nemo), Mathilda May (Alice), Katherine Boorman, Michel Blanc, Harvey Keitel, Carole Bouquet, Jason Connery, Charley Boorman, Dominique Pinon.
Story: Little Nemo meets Captain Nemo and Zorro, and saves Alice in Wonderland.

9 doigts [*Nine Fingers*] (col., 98 min., 2018)
Dir/Wri: Frédéric-Jacques Ossang.
Cast: Paul Hamy, Damien Bonnard, Elvire, Gaspard Ulliel.
Story: A man is taken aboard a cargo carrying plutonium.

La Neuvième Porte [*The Ninth Gate*] (col., 133 min., 1999)
Dir: Roman Polanski; *Wri*: John Brownjohn, Enrique Urbizu, Roman Polanski based in the novel *El Club Dumas* by Arturo Pérez-Reverte.
Cast: Johnny Depp (Corso), Lena Olin, Frank Langella, Emmanuelle Seigner.
Story: Corso, a rare book dealer, must authenticate a rare and ancient book that purportedly contains a magical secret for summoning the Devil.
Note: French-Spanish-U.S. co-production

Névrose [*Neurosis*, transl. as *The Revenge of the House of Usher*] (col., 90 min., 1983)
Dir: A.M. Franck (pseudonym of Daniel Lesoeur); *Wri*: Daniel Lesoeur.
Cast: Howard Vernon (Éric Usher), Jean Tolzac, Joan Virly, Françoise Blanchard, Olivier Mathot.
Story: Sequel to Edgar Allan Poe's classic story.
Note: There is a Spanish version with a different cast entitled *El Hundimiento de la Casa Usher*.

New Age (col., 78 min., 2017)
Dir/Wri: Rached M'Dini.

Cast: Jean-Yves Moon, Ines Froissard, Laurent Graziano.
Story: In the year 2030, the evolution of science and of the human condition have reached harmony with Nature.

Ni le Ciel ni la Terre [*Neither Heaven Nor Earth*, transl. as *The Wakhan Front*] (col., 100 min., 2015)
Dir: Clément Cogitore; *Wri*: Clément Cogitore, Thomas Bidegain.
Cast: Jérémie Renier, Kévin Azaïs, Swann Arlaud.
Story: With the withdrawal of troops from Afghanistan approaching, a captain and his section watch over a far-flung valley in Wakhan, bordering Pakistan. A supposedly trouble-free sector, but troops begin mysteriously disappearing.

Night of Vampyrmania (col., 90 min., 1993)
Dir/Wri: Richard J. Thomson.
Cast: Blaise Michel R. ., Luc Cendrier, Richard J. Thomson, Guy Emmanuel, Noé Cendrier
Story: Low-budget horror feature shot on video comprised of three sketches about vampires: *Le Dernier Fils de Dracula* [*Dracula's Last Son*], *Noel Rouge* [*Red XMas*], *Le Taxi de l'Enfer* [*Hell Cab*].

Les Noces Rouges [*Wedding in Blood*] (col., 90 min., 1973)
Dir/Wri: Claude Chabrol.
Cast: Michel Piccoli (Pierre), Stéphane Audran (Lucienne), Claude Piéplu (Paul), Clotilde Joano.
Story: Pierre, an elected official, murders his wife to be with his lover, Lucienne. But her husband Paul blackmails him.

Notre Histoire [*Our Story*] (col., 110 min., 1984)
Dir/Wri: Bertrand Blier.
Cast: Alain Delon (Robert), Nathalie Baye (Donatienne), Michel Galabru, Sabine Haudepin, Jean-François Stévenin, Gérard Darmon, Ginette Garcin.

Story: Robert meets Donatienne, a strange woman with whom he experiences a series of surreal adventures; but he discovers that it was all a dream.

Nuage [*The Cloud*] (col., 81 min., 2007)
Dir/Wri: Sébastien Betbeder.
Cast: Adrien Michaux, Nathalie Boutefeu, Bruno Sermonne, Bruce Myers.
Story: A mysterious cloud descends on a French village and causes havoc in the lives of four people.

Le Nuage Atomique [*The Atomic Cloud*]
See *Le Petit Nuage*.

La Nuée [*The Swarm*] (col., 101 min., 2020)
Dir: Just Philippot; *Wri*: Jérôme Genevray, Franck Victor.
Cast: Suliane Brahim (Virginie).
Story: To save her farm, Virginie decides to breed edible locusts. Gradually, she forges a strange bond with her insects.

La Nuit du Cimetière [*The Night at the Cemetery*]
See *La Rose De Fer*.

La Nuit a dévoré le Monde [*The Night Eats the World*] (col., 94 min., 2018)
Dir: Dominique Rocher; *Wri*: Jérémie Guez, Guillaume Lemans, Dominique Rocher, based on a novel by Pit Agarman.
Cast: Anders Danielsen Lie (Sam), Golshifteh Farahani, Denis Lavant.
Story: Sam (Danielsen Lie) is caught in the midst of a zombie apocalypse that suddenly overtakes Paris.
Note: This Dominique Rocher is a male director born in 1983, not to be confused with Dominique Rocher, a female author of popular horror novels (1929-2016).

La Nuit Fantastique [*The Fantastic Night*] (B&W., 103 min., 1941)

Dir: Marcel L'Herbier; *Wri*: Louis Chavance.
Cast: Fernand Gravey (Denis), Saturnin Fabre (Thalès), Micheline Presle (Irène), Jean Parédès, Charles Granval, Bernard Blier, Marcel Levesque.
Story: Denis, a student, helps Irène, a magician's daughter, escape from an unwanted marriage.

La Nuit des Horloges [*The Night of Clocks*] (col., 92 min., 2007)
Dir/Wri: Jean Rollin.
Cast: Ovidie (Isabelle), Sabine Lenoël, Natalie Perrey, Jean-Loup Philippe.
Story: Isabelle inherits the country house of her cousin, a famous writer. The places is haunted by his characters and fantasies.

La Nuit de la Mort [*The Night of Death*] (Col., 90 min., 1980)
Dir: Raphaël Delpard; *Wri*: Raphaël Delpard, Richard Joffo.
Cast: Isabelle Goguey (Martine), Charlotte de Turckheim (Nicole), Betty Beckers, Michel Flavius, Ernest Menzer.
Story: Young nurses unwittingly provide fresh flesh and blood to the pensioners of an old folks' home who refuse to age.

La Nuit des Pétrifiés [*The Night of the Petrified*]
See *La Plus Longue Nuit Du Diable*.

La Nuit s'achève [*The Night is Over*] (B&W., 103 min., 1949)
Dir: Pierre Méré; *Wri*: J. A. Faux, Pierre Malfille, Philippe Brunet.
Cast: Victor Francen (Dr. Coudray), Ludmilla Tcherina, Georges Rollin, Gérard Landry.
Story: Melodramatic love story in which Dr. Coudray is able to transplant the eyes of his son onto another man's head.

La Nuit Tous Les Chats Sont Gris [*At Night All Cats Are Grey*] (col., 90 min., 1977)
Dir: Gérard Zingg; *Wri*: Gérard Zingg, Philippe Dumarçay.
Cast: Gérard Depardieu, Laura Betti, Robert Stephens, Charlotte Crow.
Story: A British writer invents the character of a French bandit to entertain his young niece. The fictional character comes to life and eventually the author must kill him.

La Nuit des Traquées [*The Night of the Hunted*] (aka *Filles Traquées* [*Hunted Girls*]) (col., 90 min., 1980)
Dir/Wri: Jean Rollin.
Cast: Brigitte Lahaie, Vincent Gardner, Dominique Journet.
Story: A relentless psychotic killer pursues a young couple.
Note: Not to be confused with the eponymous 1959 thriller by Bernard Roland.

Nuits Rouges [*Red Nights*, transl. as *Shadowman*] (col., 105 min., 1973)
Dir: Georges Franju; *Wri*: Jacques Champreux.
Note: Feature-length film version shot simultaneously with, and edited down from the television series *L'Homme Sans Visage* (see next section).

Obsession (B&W., 60 min., 1934)
Dir: Maurice Tourneur; *Wri*: Paul Bringuier, based on the play *L'Homme Mystérieux* [*The Mysterious Man*] by André de Lorde and Alfred Binet.
Cast: Louise Lagrange, Charles Vanel, Paul Amiot, Georges Paulais, Jean Yonnel, Louise Marquet.
Note: Based on a popular *Grand-Guignol* play. This film bears no relation to Julien Duvivier's 1954 anthology film *Obsessions* (a.k.a. *Flesh and Fantasy*), Jean Delannoy's 1954 *Obsession* (based on a Wiliam Irish novel), and Brian de Palma's 1976 *Obession*.

L'Oeil du Malin [*The Evil Eye*, transl. as *The Third Lover*] (B&W., 80 min., 1961)
Dir/Wri: Claude Chabrol.
Cast: Jacques Charrier (Albin), Stéphane Audran (Hélène), Walter Reyer.
Story: Chilling tale of obsessional evil, in which a journalist, Albin, tries to destroy a couple.

L'Oeil Qui Ment [*The Lying Eye*, transl. as *Dark at Noon*] (col., 100 min., 1992)
Dir: Raoul Ruiz; *Wri*: Raoul Ruiz, Paul Fontaine-Salas.
Cast: John Hurt, Didier Bourdon, Lorraine Evanoff, David Warner, Daniel Prévost.
Story: After World War I, a surgeon travels to a Portuguese village which is filled with miracles and supernatural occurrences; he eventually learns to accept these events.
Note: French-Portuguese co-production.

Ogre (col., 103 min., 2021)
Dir: Arnaud Malherbe; *Wri*: Arnaud Malherbe , Sebastian Sepulveda.
Cast: Ana Girardot (Chloé), Giovanni Pucci, Samuel Jouy.
Story: Chloé starts a new life as a teacher with her 8-year-old son in a desolated part of France. She soon falls under the spell the local charismatic, mysterious doctor. Then a child disappears and a monster prowls.

L'Oiseau de Paradis [*The Bird of Paradise*] (col., 89 min., 2020)
Dir: Paul Manate; *Wri*: Cécile Ducrocq, Paul Manate.
Cast: Sebastian Urzendowsky (Teivi), Blanche-Neige Huri (Yasmina), Patrick Descamps.
Story: Teivi, a young amoral parliamentary assistant involved in a case of real estate corruption, meets Yasmina, a distant Maori cousin with mystical powers, who makes a strange prediction. Convinced that she can help him, he sets out to find her in Tahiti.

On A Volé Charlie Spencer ! [*They Stole Charlie Spencer!*] (col., 96 min., 1986)
Dir/Wri: Francis Huster.
Cast: Béatrice Dalle, Francis Huster, Isabelle Nanty, Jacques Spiesser.
Story: A mild-mannered bank clerk has heroic dreams of being a real he-man.

Ophelia (B&W., 102 min., 1962)
Dir: Claude Chabrol; *Wri*: Paul Gégauff.
Cast: Alida Valli (Claudia), Claude Serval (Adrien), Juliette Mayniel.
Story: Surreal, Kafkaesque tale which recasts *Hamlet* as a contemporary murder mystery.

Oppressions (col., 85 min., 1987)
Dir: Jean Cauchy; *Wri*: Jean Cauchy, Agnès Bromberg.
Cast: Louise Bertaux (Constance), Philippe Lemaire, Hugues Proffy, Didier Cauchy, Philippe Hérisson, Vincent de Bouard.
Story: In a future where the melting polar ice has created a water world, Constance escapes from her father (Lemaire), and goes looking for her two childhood loves.

L'Or [*Gold*] (B&W., 120 min., 1934)
Dir: Serge de Poligny, Karl Hartl; *Wri*: Rolf E. Vanloo.
Cast: Brigitte Helm (Florence), Pierre Blanchar (François), Jacques Dumesnil, Rosine Deréan, Line Noro.
Story: François, a scientist, discovers how to turn lead into gold, but eventually chooses to destroy his research.
Note: This is the French version of a French-German co-production with UFA. The German version stars Brigitte Helm, Hans Albers, and Friedrich Kayssler. Some of its special effects were later reused in *Magnetic Monster* (1953).

L'Ordinateur des Pompes Funèbres [*The Mortuary Computer*] (col., 85 min., 1975)

Dir: Gérard Pirès; *Wri*: Jean-Patrick Manchette, Gérard Pirès, based on the novel by Walter Kemply.
Cast: Jean-Louis Trintignant (Fred), Mireille Darc (Charlotte), Bernadette Lafont, Bernard Fresson, Lea Massari, Claude Piéplu.
Story: Fred, a computer scientist, uses his programming skills to get rid of his wife and all his enemies.
Note: Jean-Patrick Manchette is a popular thriller writer.

L'Or et le Plomb [*Gold and Lead*] (col., 85 min., 1966)
Dir/Wri: Alain Cuniot, based on *Le Monde Comme Il Va* [*The World as it Goes*] by Voltaire.
Cast: Alain Cuniot, Emmanuelle Riva, Max-Paul Fouchet, Michel Legrand, Jean Massin.
Story: A man from another planet interviews people to decide if Earth is worth saving.

Les Orgies du Comte Porno [*The Orgies of Count Porno*] (col., 60 min., 1984)
Dir/Wri: Joanna Morgan.
Cast: Alain L'Yle.
Story: An evil, leather-masked Master (the Devil?) orders his disciples to torture helpless women.
Note: A fairly sick and weird combination of X-rated and gore film.

Orphée [*Orpheus*] (B&W., 112 min., 1949)
Wri/Dir: Jean Cocteau.
Cast: Jean Marais (Orpheus), Marie Déa (Eurydice), François Périer (Heurtebise), Maria Casarès, Juliette Gréco, Jacques Varennes, Pierre Bertin, Édouard Dermit, Roger Blin.
Story: Modern transposition of the classic Orpheus myth.

OSS 117

A series of films based on the popular *James Bond*-like French espionage book series created in 1949 by Jean Bruce (Jean Brochet) and continued after his death in 1963 by his wife,

Josette Bruce. OSS 117 is the codename of Hubert Bonnisseur de la Bath, an American agent born in Louisiana in a family with French ancestry, who worked first for the OSS, then the CIA, then the NSC.

OSS 117 n'est pas mort [*OSS 117 Is Not Dead*] (B&W., 80 min., 1956)
Dir: Jean Sacha; *Wri*: Jacques Berland, Jean Levitte.
Cast: Ivan Desny (OSS 117), Magali Noël, Danik Patisson, Georges Lannes, Marie Déa.
Story: OSS 117 investigates the leak of strategic documents.

Le Bal des espions [*Dance of the Spies*, transl. as *Danger in the Middle East*] (B&W., 92 min., 1960)
Dir: Michel Clément, Umberto Scarpelli; *Wri*: Daniel Boulanger.
Cast: Michel Piccoli (Cannon), Françoise Arnoul, Rosanna Schiaffino.
Story: A spy tricks rival gangs in the Middle East into fighting each other.
Note: For legal reasons, OSS 117 is renamed Brian Cannon.

OSS 117 Se Déchaîne [*OSS 117 Strikes Back*] (B&W., 110 min., 1963)
Dir/Wri: André Hunebelle; *Wri*: Pierre Foucaud, Richard Caron, Patrice Rondard.
Cast: Kerwin Mathews (OSS 117), Irina Demick, Daniel Emilfork, Yvan Chiffre.
Story: OSS 117 thwarts an enemy spy ring in Corsica.

Banco à Bangkok pour OSS 117 [*Panic in Bangkok for Agent OSS 117*, transl. as *Shadow of Evil*] (col., 92 min., 1964)
Dir: André Hunebelle; *Wri*: Pierre Foucaud, Raymond Borel, Michel Lebrun, Richard Caron, Patrice Rondard.

Cast: Kerwin Mathews, Robert Hossein, Pier Angeli, Dominique Wilms, Henri Virlojeux.
Story: An Indian sect plans to use infected rats to create a worldwide epidemic.

Furia à Bahia pour OSS 117 [*Fury in Bahia for OSS 117*, transl. as *Mission for a Killer*] (col., 84 min., 1965)
Dir: André Hunebelle; *Wri*: Jean Halain, Pierre Foucaud.
Cast: Frederick Stafford (OSS 117), Mylène Demongeot, Raymond Pellegrin, Perrette Pradier, Annie Andersson, François Maistre, Jacques Riberolles.
Story: OSS 117 goes up against a gang which uses a drug that turns its victims into zombies.

Atout Coeur à Tokyo pour OSS 117 [*Trump of Hearts in Tokyo for OSS 117*, transl. as *Terror in Tokyo*] (col., 90 min., 1966)
Dir: Michel Boisrond; *Wri*: Pierre Foucaud, Marcel Mithois, Terence Young.
Cast: Frederick Stafford (OSS 117), Marina Vlady, Henri Serre, Colin Drake, Tetsuko Yoshimura.
Story: OSS 117 thwarts Japanese blackmailers who have built a super-weapon.

Cinq Gars pour Singapour [*Five Boys for Singapore*] (col., 95 min., 1967)
Dir: Bernard Toublanc-Michel; *Wri*: Sergio Amidei, Pierre Kalfon.
Cast: Sean Flynn (Art Smith), Marika Green, Terry Downes.
Story: Art Smith investigates the disappearances of several US Marines in Singapore.
Note: For legal reasons, OSS 117 is renamed Art Smith.

Le Vicomte Règle ses Comptes [*The Viscount Settles His Account*] (col., 90 min., 1967)
Dir: Maurice Cloche; Wri: Georges Farrel, Luis Marquina.

Cast: Kerwin Mathews (Vicomte Clint de la Roche), Sylvia Sorrente, Jean Yanne, Fernando Rey.
Story: The Viscount investigates a case of bank fraud.
Note: For legal reasons, OSS 117 is renamed Vicomte Clint de la Roche.

Pas de Roses pour OSS 117 [*No Roses for OSS 117*, transl. as *Murder for Sale* or *Double Agent*] (col., 105 min., 1968)
<u>Dir</u>: Jean-Pierre Desagnat, André Hunebelle; *Wri*: Jean-Pierre Desagnat, Michel Lévine, Renzo Cerrato, Pierre Foucaud.
Cast: John Gavin (OSS 117), Robert Hossein, Margaret Lee, Curd Jurgens, Luciana Paluzzi, George Eastman.
Story: OSS 117 goes after a ring of hitmen who murder politicians.

OSS 117 prend des Vacances [*OSS 117 Takes a Vacation*] (col., 92 min., 1969)
Dir: Pierre Kalfon; *Wri*: Pierre Kalfon, Pierre Philippe.
Cast: Luc Merenda (OSS 117), Elsa Martinelli, Edwige Feuillère, Geneviève Grad, Norma Bengell.
Story: In Cuba, OSS 117 thwarts a band of fascist terrorists.

OSS 117 tue le taon [*OSS 117 Kills the Yellowjacket*] (col., 75 min., 1971)
Dir: André Leroux; *Wri*: Josette Bruce, André Leroux.
Cast: Alan Scott (OSS 117), Aude Loring, Vania Vilers, Reinhard Kolldehoff.
Story: OSS 117 investigates the disappearance of an American scientist in Europe.
Note: Made-for-TV movie.

Le Caire, Nid d'Espions [*Cairo, Nest of Spies*] (col., 99 min., 2006)
Dir: Michel Hazanavicius; *Wri*: Jean-François Halin.

Cast: Jean Dujardin (OSS 117), Bérénice Bejo, Aure Atika, Philippe Lefebvre.
Story: 1955. OSS 117 (who now works for the French spy service SDECE) is sent on a mission to Cairo to investigate the disappearance of his best friend and fellow spy Jack Jefferson, only to stumble into a web of international intrigue.
Note: Parody of the earlier films depicting OSS 117 as an idiotic Frenchman with narrow-minded views on race, religion, and gender roles.

Rio Ne Répond Plus [*Lost in Rio*] (col., 100 min., 2009)
Dir: Michel Hazanavicius; *Wri*: Jean-François Halin.
Cast: Jean Dujardin (OSS 117), Louise Monot, Rüdiger Vogler, Alex Lutz.
Story: OSS 117 sent to Brazil in order to retrieve a microfilm list of French Nazi sympathizers, only to once again unknowingly set foot into a bigger international intrigue.
Note: Same as above.

Alerte Rouge en Afrique Noire [*From Africa with Love*] (col., 116 min., 2021)
Dir: Nicolas Bedos; *Wri*: Jean-François Halin.
Cast: Jean Dujardin (OSS 117), Pierre Niney, Natacha Lindinger.
Story: Set in 1981, 14 years after *Lost in Rio*, OSS 117 is sent on a mission in Black Africa (unknown country) where he teams up with a young agent, OSS 1001.
Note: Same as above.

Out Un: Spectre (col., 260 min., 1971-74)
Dir/Wri: Jacques Rivette, based on a story by Honoré de Balzac.
Cast: Michael Lonsdale, Bulle Ogier, Jean-Pierre Léaud, Bernadette Lafont, Françoise Fabian.
Story: In contemporary Paris, a young man tries to locate thirteen people implicated in a mysterious conspiracy.

Note: This film was originally conceived as a 12 hour 40 min. production, but was released in a 4 hour 20 min. version.

Oxygène [*Oxygen*] (col., 100 min., 2021)
Dir: Alexandre Aja; *Wri*: Christie LeBlanc.
Cast: Mélanie Laurent (Elizabeth), Mathieu Amalric, Malik Zidi.
Story: In the near future, Elizabeth Hansen wakes up in a cryogenic capsule. Alone and amnesic, she doesn't know how she got there. The situation becomes more complicated when her oxygen starts running out.
Note: Co-produced by Netflix.

Le Pacte des Loups [*The Brotherhood of the Wolves*] (col., 142 min., 2001)
Dir: Christophe Gans; *Wri*: Stéphane Cabel, Christophe Gans.
Cast: Samuel Le Bihan (Fronsac), Vincent Cassel, Monica Bellucci, Jérémie Renier, Mark Dacascos (Mani).
Story: In 18th-century France, Chevalier de Fronsac and Mani of the Iroquois tribe are sent to investigate the mysterious slaughter of hundreds by an unknown creature in the province of Gévaudan.
Note: The plot is loosely based on a real-life series of killings and the famous legend of the beast of Gévaudan.

Le Pain Quotidien [*The Daily Bread*] (B&W., 20 min., 1970)
Dir/Wri: Philippe Bordier.
Cast: Jean Callas, Martine Broustra.
Story: Science fiction.

Panique [*Panic*] (col., 90 min., 1977)
Dir: Jean-Claude Lord; *Wri*: Jean-Claude Lord, Jean Salvy.
Cast: Paule Bailargeon, Jan Coutu, Lise Thouin.
Story: A journalist investigates an industrial threat to Canadian ecology.
Note: French-Canadian production.

La Papesse (col., 95 min., 1974)
Dir: Mario Mercier; *Wri*: Robert Paillardon.
Cast: Lisa Lavanne, Érika Maaz, Jean-François Delatour.
Story: A young couple joins a sect of devil worshippers. During their abominable initiation rituals, he is killed and she goes mad.

Papy fait de la Résistance [*Papy Joins the Resistance*] (col., 100 min., 1983)
Dir: Jean-Marie Poiré; *Wri*: Christian Clavier, Martin Lamotte, Jean-Marie Poiré.
Cast: Christian Clavier, Michel Galabru (Papy), Gérard Jugnot, Martin Lamotte (Bourdelle, a.k.a. Super-Résistant), Dominique Lavanant, Jacques Villeret, Josiane Balasko, Jean-Claude Brialy, Michel Blanc, Jean Carmet.
Story: Comedy about the French Resistance.
Note: The only genre element is the inclusion of a French super-hero, "Super-Resistant," with the traditional secret identity of a meek person.

Paradis pour Tous [*Paradise for All*] (col., 110 min., 1982)
Dir: Alain Jessua; *Wri*: Alain Jessua, André Ruellan.
Cast: Patrick Dewaere (Alain), Jacques Dutronc (Dr. Valois), Fanny Cottençon (Jeanne), Stéphane Audran (Edith), Philippe Léotard, Jeanne Goupil, Patrice Kerbrat.
Story: Alain, a chronically depressed man, becomes the first subject of Dr. Valois, a scientist who has discovered a brain operation which turns people into happy, yet soulless, beings. The experiment is a success—a frightening success.

Paradisio (B&W., 90 min., 1961)
Dir: Jacques Henrici; *Wri*: Laurence Zeitlin, Henri Halle.
Cast: Arthur Howard.
Story: A man owns a pair of X-ray glasses which make clothes invisible.
Note: French/German/British "nudie" film featuring 3-D sequences.

Parano (col., 82 min., 1994)
Anthology film comprised of six stories, linked together.
Dir: Yann Piquer; *Wri*: Yann Piquer, Alain Robak, Manuel Flèche, Anita Assal, John Hudson.
Cast: Jean-Marie Madeddu, Gustave Parking, Smaïn, Alain Chabat, Patrick Bouchitey, Jean-François Gallotte.

1. *Parano* (linking story)
Story: A beautiful paranoid girl tells stories to a shy young man who ends up strangling her to shut her up.

2. *Nuit d'Essence* [*Gasoline Night*]
Story: A pyromaniac is traumatized by the death of his family.

3. *Panic FM*
Story: A pizza delivery man hears a horrible news story on the radio.

4. *Déroute* [*Retreat*]
Story: After a car crash, a couple is doomed to relive their recent fight.

5. *Sado et Maso Vont en Bateau* [*Sado & Maso Go Boating*]
Story: A man falls in love with a masochistic woman.

6. *Joyeux Anniversaire* [*Happy Birthday*]
Story: A woman plots her husband's death by getting him into a diving suit and then arranging for him to be carried away in a water-dropping plane.

Paris n'existe pas [*Paris Does Not Exist*] (B&W., 95 min., 1968)
Dir/Wri: Robert Benayoun.
Cast: Danièle Gaubert, Richard Leduc, Serge Gainsbourg, Monique Lejeune.

Story: A young artist discovers that he can mentally travel back through time.

Paris Qui Dort [*Paris Sleeps*, transl. as *The Crazy Ray*] (B&W., 61 min./1480 M., 1923)
Dir/Wri: René Clair.
Cast: Henri Rollan, Albert Préjean, Marcel Vallée, Madeleine Rodrigue.
Story: A scientist's ray plunges Paris into a cataleptic state, except for the Eiffel Tower watchman and the passengers of an airplane.

Parking (col., 95 min., 1985)
Dir/Wri: Jacques Demy.
Cast: Francis Huster (Orphée), Keito Ito (Eurydice), Jean Marais (Hadès), Marie-France Pisier, Laurent Malet, Gérard Klein, Hugues Quester.
Story: Another modern transposition of the Orpheus myth; this time, Orpheus is a modern pop star.

La Particule Humaine [*The Human Particle* aka *Grain*] (col. 127 min., 2018)
Dir: Semih Kaplanoglu; *Wri*: Semih Kaplanoglu, Leyla Ipekci.
Cast: Jean-Marc Barr (Erin), Ermin Bravo (Akman), Lubna Azabal.
Story: In the near future, a sudden climate change is driving life on Earth to extinction. In this new world with redrawn borders, populations are parked in camps while waiting to be able to integrate the cities closed behind magnetic shields. The path of Professor Erin, a genetic engineer specializing in seeds, will cross, in the Dead Lands region, that of the scientist Cemil Akman, a strange man who has chosen to turn his back on modern life.
Note: French-Turkish co-production.

Les Particules [*Particles*] (col., 98 min., 2019)
Dir: Blaise Harrison; *Wri*: Mariette Désert, Blaise Harrison.

Cast: Thomas Daloz, Néa Lüders, Salvatore Ferro, Léo Couilfort, Nicolas Marcant, Emma Josserand.
Story: A group of friends starts to observe strange phenomena around them when a powerful particle accelerator in the world beneath their feet tries to recreate the conditions of the Big Bang.
Note: Swiss production.

Pas De Linceul Pour Billy Brakko [*No Shroud for Billy Brakko*] (col., 5 min., 1983)
Dir: Jean-Pierre Jeunet, based on a story by Marc Caro.
Cast: Marc Caro, Zorin, Phil Casoar, Jean Bouise (Narrator).
Story: A futuristic private eye investigates a murder.

Pas Question le Samedi [*Never on Saturdays*] (B&W., 105 min., 1964)
Dir: Alex Joffé; Wri: Jean Ferry, Alex Joffé.
Cast: Robert Hirsch (Chaim and his entire family), Misha Scheroff.
Story: With the help of his father's and grandfather's ghosts, the son of Chaim tries to locate the rest of his family.
Note: Franco-Israeli co-production.

Le Passage [*The Passage*] (col., 84 min., 1986)
Dir/Wri: René Manzor.
Cast: Alain Delon (Jean), Christine Boisson (Catherine), Alain Musy (David), Jean-Luc Moreau, Alberto Lomeo.
Story: Death itself tries to prevent Jean, an animation director, from making a film about world peace. With the help of his young son, the director outwits Death.

Le Passe-Muraille [*The Walker Through the Walls*]
See *Garou-Garou, Le Passe-Muraille*.

Le Pays sans Étoiles [*The Starless Country*] (B&W., 100 min., 1945)

Dir/Wri: Georges Lacombe, based on the novel by Pierre Véry.
Cast: Gérard Philipe (Simon/Frédéric), Piere Brasseur, Jany Holt.
Story: A young lawyer experiences visions of a murder he may (or may not) have committed. Are they visions of the past, or of the future?
Note: Pierre Véry is a noted mystery and fantasy writer. His works include two well-known thrillers, *L'Assassinat du Père Noël* [*The Murder of Santa Claus*] and *Les Disparus de Saint-Agil* [*Disappearances at Saint-Agil*], both made into films.

Peau d'Âne [*Donkey Skin*] (col., 89 min., 1970)
Dir/Wri: Jacques Demy, based on the fairy tale by Charles Perrault.
Cast: Catherine Deneuve (Donkey Skin), Jean Marais (Blue King), Jacques Perrin (Prince Charming), Delphine Seyrig, Micheline Presle, Fernand Ledoux, Sacha Pitoëff, Henri Crémieux.
Story: Gorgeous adaptation of the classic fairy tale in which a Princess (Deneuve) who wants to avoid an unwanted marriage flees into the forest and lives disguised by a donkey skin.

La Pension [*The Retirement Home*] (col., 35 min., 1987)
Dir: Marc Cadieux; *Wri*: Marc Cadieux, Lionel Kopp.
Cast: Christian Charmetant, Isabelle Petit-Jacques, François Nègre, Jimmy-Léonar Aeton, Hervé Briaux, Emmanuelle Devos, Jérôme Keen.
Story: A mysterious "home" inhabited by eccentrics is revealed to be the antechamber of death.

Perceval le Gallois (col., 138 min., 1978)
Dir/Wri: Éric Rohmer, based on the stories by Chrétien de Troyes.
Cast: Fabrice Luchini (Perceval), André Dussolier (Gauvain), Marc Eyraud (King Arthur), Marie-Christine Barrault (Guine-

vere), Gérard Falconetti, Arielle Dombasle, Michel Etcheverry.
Story: The legendary tale of pure-hearted Perceval, who leaves his mother's castle to join King Arthur and his Knights of the Round Table, and eventually searches for the Holy Grail.

Perdues dans New York [*Lost in New York*] (col., 52 min., 1991)
Dir/Wri: Jean Rollin.
Cast: Natalie Perrey, Catherine Herengt, Adeline Abitbol (all Michelle at various ages), Marie-Laurence, Catherine Lesret, Funny Abitbol (ditto Marie), Sophie Maret, Catherine Rival.
Story: Marie and Michelle find a magic amulet which allows them to travel through time and space. They land in New York.

Le Péril Rampant [*The Crawling Menace*] (col., 25 min., 1981)
Dir/Wri: Alberto Yaccelini.
Cast: Pierre Julien, Bernard Born, Maurice Vallier, Jeanne Biras, Gérard Heffmann, Jean-Claude Dreyfus, Michèle Loubet, Jean-Pierre Elga, Gilbert K. Jakubzcyk.
Story: An homage to serials, presented as the sixth chapter of a fictional serial, *Les Aventures du Serpent* [*The Adventures of the Serpent*].

Personal Shopper (col., 105 min., 2016)
Dir/Wri: Olivier Assayas.
Cast: Kristen Stewart (Maureen), Anders Danielsen Lie, Lars Eidinger.
Story: Maureen, a young American in Paris, earns her living as a personal shopper for a celebrity. Like her missing twin brother, she possesses the ability to communicate with spirits.

Perversions Sexuelles [*Sexual Perversions*] (aka *Le Gout du Sang* [*The Taste of Blood*], *Le Sang des Autres* [*The Blood of Others*], *Les Chemins de la Violence* [*The Paths of Violence*],

La Volupté de l'Horreur [*Voluptuous Horror*], *Le Secret de la Momie* [*The Mummy's Secret*]) (col., 90 min., 1972).
Dir: Ken Ruder (pseudonym of Pierre Chevalier); *Wri*: Alexandro Marti Gelabert.
Cast: Catherine Frank, Michael Flynn, Sandra Reeves, Patricia Lee, Julie Prescott, Georges Rigaud.
Story: A resurrected mummy drains the blood from young women to survive.
Note: Not to be confused with Claude Chabrol's 1983 adaptation of Simone de Beauvoir's novel, *Le Sang des Autres*. The final title is explained by the fact that this film was eventually released on the X-rated circuit. There is a Spanish version (*El Secreto de la Momia Egipcia*) directed by Alexandro Marti Gelabert, starring Teresa Gimpera, Frank Brana, Martin Trévières.

Le Petit Nuage [*The Little Cloud*] (aka *La Chasse au Nuage* [*The Hunt for the Cloud*] and *Le Nuage Atomique* [*The Atomic Cloud*]) (B&W., 82 mins., 1954)
Dir: Antoine Allard, Armand Bachelier, Charles Dekeukeleire; *Wri*: Antoine Allard, Armand Bachelier, Joseph Bertrand.
Cast: Marcel Berteau, Marcel Cornelis, Hubert Daix, Paul Frankeur, Guy-Lou, Robert Lussac, Pierre Trabaud.
Story: Fantasy
Note: Belgian production.

Le Petit Poucet [*Tom Thumb*] (col., 80 min., 1972)
Dir: Michel Boisrond; *Wri*: Michel Boisrond, Marcel Jullian, based on the fairy tale by Charles Perrault.
Cast: Titoyo (Tom Thumb), Jean-Pierre Marielle (Ogre), Marie Laforêt, Jean-Luc Bideau, Michel Robin, Marianne Ridoret.
Story: Adaptation on the classic fairy tale about a boy abandoned in the forest who encounters an Ogre with Seven-League Boots.

Le Petit Poucet [*Tom Thumb*] (col., 90 min., 2001)
Dir/Wri: Olivier Dahan, based on the fairy tale by Charles Perrault..
Cast: Nils Hugon, Catherine Deneuve, Romane Bohringer, Pierre Berriau, Hanna Berthaut.
Story: Same as above.

Le Petit Poucet [*Tom Thumb*] (col., 81 min., 2011)
Dir: Marina de Van; *Wri*: Bertrand Santini, Marina de Van, based on the fairy tale by Charles Perrault.
Cast: Denis Lavant, Adrien de Van, Rachel Arditi.
Story: Same as above.

La Petite Bande [*The Little Gang*] (col., 91 min., 1982)
Dir: Michel Deville; *Wri*: Gilles Perrault.
Cast: François Marthouret (Stranger), Roland Amstutz, Nathalie Bécue, Françoise Lugagne.
Story: Six runaway English boys experience a series of adventures in France, until they are captured by a secret sect which steals little boys' youth; but they are rescued by a mysterious guardian angel-like hero (Marthouret).
Note: Gilles Perrault is a famous espionage thriller writer.

Petite Maman (col., 72 min., 2021)
Dir/Wri: Céline Sciamma
Cast: Joséphine Sanz (Nelly), Gabrielle Sanz (Marion), Nina Meurisse (Mother), Margot Abascal, Stéphane Varupenne.
Story: Nelly, an 8-year-old girl, has just lost her beloved grandmother and is helping her parents clean out her mother's childhood home. One day, her mom abruptly leaves, and Nelly meets Marion, a girl her age as she''s building a tree house in the woods.

La Petite Marchande d'Allumettes [*The Little Match Girl*] (B&W., 29 min., 1928)
Dir/Wri: Jean Renoir, based on a story by Hans Christian Andersen.

Cast: Catherine Hessling, Jean Storm, Manuel Raabi.
Story: Short feature adaptation of the classic story about the poor little match girl who freezes to death. She dreams of toys and a handsome officer who comes flying through the air to rescue her.

Les Petites Jouisseuses [*Small Pleasures*] (col., 85 min., 1979)
Dir/Wri: Homère Bongo.
Cast: Lise Badia, Brigitte Blanche.
Note: X-rated film about a female vampire.

Les Petites Saintes y touchent [*The Little Saintly Girls Touch It*, transl. as *Seven Women for Satan*] (col., 90 min., 1974)
Dir/Wri: Michel Lemoine.
Cast: Martine Azencot, Aurore Benn, Jacques Bernard, Jerry Brouer, Joelle Coeur, Catherine Flaubert, Robert Icart, Michel Lemoine, Stéphane Lorry, Maria Mancini, Patricia Mionnet, Catherine Mouton, Manu Pluton, Marie-Hélène Règne, Howard Vernon, Nathalie Zeiger.
Story: Erotic horror.

Peut-être [*Maybe*] (col., 109 min., 1999)
Dir/Wri: Cédric Klapisch.
Cast: Romain Duris (Arthur), Jean-Paul Belmondo (Ako), Géraldine Pailhas (Lucie), Julie Depardieu, Emmanuelle Devos, Liliane Rovère, Bass Dhem, Léa Drucker, Hélène Fillières, Dominique Frot.
Story: On New Year's Eve 2000, Lucie asks Arthur to give her a child, but he doesn't feel ready to be a father. Then Arthur finds himself transported seventy years later into the future, to a Paris half-buried under sand. He then meets Ako, an old man who claims to be his son.

La Plus Longue Nuit du Diable [*The Devil's Longest Night*, transl. as *The Devil's Nightmare*] (col., 95 min., 1971)

(aka *Au Service du Diable* [*In the Devil's Service*], *Le Château du Vice* [*The Castle of Vice*], *La Nuit des Pétrifiés* [*The Night of the Petrified*]).
Dir: Jean Brismée; *Wri*: Patrice Rhomm, Charles Lecocq, André Hunebelle, Jean Brismée.
Cast: Erika Blanc, Jean Servais, Daniel Emilfork (Satan), Jacques Monseu, Ivana Novak, Shirley Corrigan.
Story: A long night of terror grips the passengers of a coach when it becomes lost in the Black Forest. They find refuge in a castle and become involved in a battle between good and evil. The eldest daughter of a family becomes the agent of the Devil because of an ancient curse.

Le Plus Vieux Métier du Monde [*The Oldest profession in the World*] (col., 120 min., 1967)
Six sketches about prostitution. Only the sixth one belongs to the genre:
Anticipation - L'An 2000 [*Science Fiction - The Year 2000*]
Dir/Wri: Jean-Luc Godard.
Cast: Jacques Charrier, Anna Karina, Marilu Tolo, Jean-Pierre Léaud.
Story: In the year 2000, a prostitute working for the state and a spaceman rediscover the notion of kissing.

Le Pont du Nord [*The North Bridge*] (col., 129 min., 1981)
Dir: Jacques Rivette; *Wri*: Jacques Rivette, Jérôme Prieur.
Cast: Bulle Ogier (Marie), Pascale Ogier (Baptiste), Pierre Clémenti, Jean-François Stévenin (Max).
Story: Marie, a bank robber just out of prison, meets Baptiste who claims to come from "somewhere else." Together, they investigate a surreal mystery that includes a briefcase stuffed with secret documents, a mechanical, fire-breathing dragon and a mysterious police force whose members are all named Max.

Les Portes de la Nuit [*The Gates of Night*] (B&W., 120 min, 1946)

Dir: Marcel Carné; *Wri*: Jacques Prévert, Joseph Kosma.
Cast: Jean Vilar (Destiny), Yves Montand, Nathalie Nattier, Pierre Brasseur, Serge Reggiani, Saturnin Fabre, Julien Carette, Mady Berry, Dany Robin, Raymond Bussières, Sylvia Bataille, Christian Simon.
Story: In post-war Paris, Destiny incarnates as a vagrant whose predictions fail to help a young couple.

Le Portrait de Dorian Gray [*The Picture of Dorian Gray*] (col., 90 min., 1977)
Dir/Wri: Pierre Bouteron, based on the story by Oscar Wilde.
Cast: Raymond Gérôme (Lord Henry), Marie-Hélène Breillat, Patrice Alexandre, Denis Manuel.
Story: Film adaptation of a play written by Bouteron based on Wilde's famous story about an ageless man.

Les Possédés du Diable [*Possessed by the Devil*] (aka Lorna l'Exorciste [*Lorna the Exorcist*]) (col., 85 min., 1974)
Dir: Clifford Brown (pseudonym of Jess Franco); *Wri*: Jesus Franco Manera, Robert de Nesle.
Cast: Pamela Stanford, Lina Romay, Guy Delorme, Jacqueline Parent.
Story: A rich industrialist once made a pact to deliver his 18-year old daughter to the mysterious Lorna.
Note: French-Spanish co-production.

Possession (col., 127 min., 1981)
Dir/Wri: Andrzej Zulawski.
Cast: Isabelle Adjani (Anna), Sam Neill (Marc), Heinz Bennent, Margit Carstensen.
Story: Anna cheats on her husband, Marc, with a creature of unknown origins, which takes on her husband's form the more she has sex with it. After their deaths, their doppelgangers fall in love.
Note: French-German co-production.

La Possibilité d'une Île [*The Possibility of an Island*] (col., 85 min., 2008)
Dir/Wri: Michel Houellebecq, based on his novel.
Cast: Benoît Magimel, Ramata Koite.
Story: The only survivor of the devastation of the human species, Daniel 25 sees his life change completely when, following messages he receives on his computer, he discovers that there is a survivor, like him.

La Poupée [*The Doll*] (col., 90 min., 1961)
Dir: Jacques Baratier; *Wri*: Jacques Audiberti.
Cast: Sonne Teal (Android), Zbigniew Cybulski, Claudio Gora, Daniel Emilfork, Catherine Milinaire, Jacques Dufilho, Sacha Pitoëff.
Story: In a South American country, a rebel scientist invents a duplicating machine and uses it to create an android double of the dictator's mistress.

La Poupée Rouge [*The Red Doll*] (col., 80 min., 1969)
Dir/Wri: Francis Leroi.
Cast: Aude Olivier, Gaétane Lorre, André Oumansky, François Guilloteau.
Story: Political fiction about a revolution in an imaginary country.

Les Prédateurs de la Nuit [*The Night Predators*, transl. as *Faceless*] (col., 93 min., 1988)
Dir: Jess Franco; *Wri*: Fred Castle (pseudonym of René Château).
Cast: Helmut Berger (Dr. Flamand), Chris Mitchum (Sam), Telly Savalas (Terry), Howard Vernon (Orloff), Caroline Munro, Brigitte Lahaie, Stéphane Audran.
Story: In this transposition of Franju's *Les Yeux Sans Visage*, Dr. Flamand (Berger) kidnaps a young model (Munro) to graft her face onto his disfigured sister's (Lahaie). Howard Vernon guest-stars as Dr. Orloff.

Le Prix du Danger [*The Prize of Peril*] (col., 99 min., 1982)
Dir: Yves Boisset; *Wri*: Jean Curtelin, Yves Boisset, based on a short story by Robert Sheckley.
Cast: Gérard Lanvin (François), Michel Piccoli (Frédéric Mallaire), Marie-France Pisier, Bruno Cremer, Andréa Ferréol, Gabrielle Lazure, Catherine Lachens.
Story: The *Prize of Peril* is a TV game show where contestants must escape killers in order to collect their prizes. François, a contestant who has discovered that the game is fixed, is committed.
Note: Robert Sheckley is a famous American science fiction writer. He wrote the short story which became the basis for the film *The Tenth Victim* (1965). The original story, published in 1958 inspired Stephen King's *The Running Man* (1982). A French court later ruled that the film adaptation of The Running Man was plagiarized from *The Prize of Peril*. The same story had also been adapted into a 1970 German telefilm *Das Millionenspiel* directed by Tom Toelle, with Jörg Pleva and Dieter Thomas Heck.

Le Professeur Raspoutine (col., 85 min., 1981)
Dir/Wri: Gérard Gregory, Andrei Fehrer, André White.
Cast: Christine Lodes, Magali Pell, Marina Delestrade.
Story: Professor Rasputin and his wife runs a clinic for people with sexual problems.
Note: Swedish-French X-rated film with genre elements.

Providence (col., 100 min., 1976)
Dir: Alain Resnais; *Wri*: David Mercer.
Cast: John Gielgud (Clive), Dirk Bogarde (Claud), Ellen Burstyn (Sonia), David Warner, Elaine Stritch, Peter Arne, Anna Wing, Tania Lopert, Dennis Lanson.
Story: A dying writer's nightmares take on fearsome shapes in the city of Providence, RI.

Proxima (col., 107 min., 2019)

Dir: Alice Winocour; *Wri*: Alice Winocour, Jean-Stéphane Bron.
Cast: Eva Green (Sarah), Matt Dillon, Lars Eidinger, Zélie Boulant-Lemesle (Stella), Sandra Hüller.
Story: Sarah is an astronaut who trains hard at the Cologne Space Center. She lives alone with her 8-year-old daughter, Stella. When Sarah is chosen to go aboard a one-year space mission, called Proxima, her life and that of Stella are turned upside down.

Quartier Lointain [*A Distant Neighborhood*] (col., 98 min., 2010)
Dir: Sam Garbarski; *Wri*: Philippe Blasband, Sam Garbarski, Jérôme Tonnerre, based on the manga by Jirō Taniguchi.
Cast: Pascal Greggory (Thomas (adult)), Jonathan Zaccaï (Bruno), Léo Legrand (Thomas (young)), Alexandra Maria Lara (Anna).
Story: Thomas, a middle-aged family man visits his mother's grave and is transported back in time, being a teenager again, but with all of his adult memories.

4 h 44 Dernier jour sur Terre [*4:44 Last Day on Earth*] (col., 90 min., 2011)
Dir/Wri: Abel Ferrara.
Cast: Willem Dafoe, Natasha Lyonne, Shanyn Leigh.
Story: The relationship between two people as they await the end of all life on Earth.
Note: French-Chilean-U.S. co-production.

Queen Lear (col., 90 min., 1980)
Dir/Wri: Mokhtar Chorfi.
Cast: Joe Dallesandro, Laura Garcia Lorca, Fabrice Josso, Jean Gosselin.
Story: Ghostly variation on *King Lear*.
Note: French-Swiss co-production.

Les Raisins de la Mort [*The Grapes of Death*, transl. as *Pesticide*] (col., 89 min., 1978)
Dir/Wri: Jean Rollin.
Cast: Marie-Georges Pascal, Serge Marquand, Félix Marten, Brigitte Lahaie.
Story: Polluted grapes turn grape growers into a bloodthirsty mob.

Rapa-Nui (B&W., 6 episodes, 1800 meters, 1928)
Dir/Wri: Mario Bonnard, based on the novel by André Armandy.
Cast: André Roanne (Jean), Ijane Haid (Oédidée / Claire), Hugo Werner-Kahle, Jean Albers, Robert Leffler, Van Riel, Claude Mérelle.
Story: Explorers seek the treasures of Atlantis on the island of Rapa-Nui.

Le Rat Noir d'Amérique [*The American Black Rat*] (col., 21 min., 1982)
Dir/Wri: Jérôme Enrico.
Cast: André Julien, Philippe du Janerand, Philippe Goyard, Louis Julien, Pierre Arditi, Pia Courcelles.
Story: A writer meets the characters he has just created.

Rayés des Vivants [*Banned from the Living*] (B&W., 90 min., 1952)
Dir: Maurice Cloche; *Wri*: Henri Danjou.
Cast: Daniel Ivernel (Pierre Baupré), Marthe Mercadier, Christiane Lénier, François Chaumette.
Story: The life of Pierre Baupré, a hardened criminal, is eventually transformed by a surgical, personality-altering procedure.

Realive (col., 107 min., 2018)
Dir/Wri: Mateo Gil.
Cast: Tom Hughes (Marc), Charlotte Le Bon, Oona Chaplin (Naomi).

Story: Marc has just learned that he is seriously ill and that he only has one year left to live. Unable to accept his own death, he decides to have his body frozen. Sixty years later, in 2084, he becomes the first man to be resurrected. It is then that he discovers that the love of his life, Naomi, has been with him all along in ways he could never have foreseen.
Note: French-Spanish co-production.

Le Récit de Rebecca [*Rebecca's Story*] (col., 20 min. 1964)
Dir/Wri: Paul Vecchiali, based on *The Ms. Found in Zaragoza* by Jean Potocki.
Cast: Jean-Pierre Bonnefous, Jean-Paul Cisife, Marika Green (Rebecca).
Story: Adaptation of the classic story.

Régime Sans Pain [*Regime Without Bread*] (col., 75 min., 1985)
Dir/Wri: Raoul Ruiz.
Cast: Anne Alvaro, Olivier Angèle, Gérard Maimone, Gilles Arbona.
Story: Surrealistic story about Jason III, king of the rock music-based principality of Vercors, in his search for a new personality.

Rei-Dom, ou La Légende des Kreuls [*Rei-Dom, or The Legend of the Kreuls*] (col., 100 min., 1989)
Dir/Wri: Jean-Claude Gallotta.
Cast: Pascal Gravat, Christophe Delachaux, Éric Alfieri, Muriel Boulay, Mathilde Altaraz, Robert Seyfried, Deborah Salmirs, Viviane Serry.
Story: The survivor of a car crash imagines himself in a fantasy universe where he is a warrior, the last defender of the peaceful people of Kreul.

La Reine de Nacre [*The Mother-of-Peaerl Queen*] (col., 15 min., 2001)
Dir/Wri: Bernard Werber, Sébastien Drouin,

Cast: Jean-Christophe Barc, Julia Masini, Sylvain Rougerie.
Story: A series of crimes is patterned after a game of chess.
Note: Bernard Werber is a renowned genre author.

La Reine des Vampires [*The Queen of Vampires*]
See *Le Viol du Vampire*.

Rencontre avec le Dragon [*Meeting a Dragon*] (col., 109 min., 2003)
Dir: Hélène Angel; *Wri*: Hélène Angel, Jean-Claude Janer, Agnès de Sacy.
Cast: Daniel Auteuil (Guillaume), Sergi López (Raoul), Emmanuelle Devos.
Story: Guillaume travels with his friend Raoul de Vautadour who has a sinister secret: Every night he turns into a beast.

Rendez-Moi Ma Peau [*Give Me Back My Skin*] (col., 90 min., 1980)
Dir/Wri: Patrick Schulmann.
Cast: Erik Colin, Bee Michelin.
Story: In this satirical comedy, a clumsy witch causes two young people to switch bodies (but each retains his own voice).

Rendez-Vous à Bray [*Rendezvous at Bray*] (col., 90 min., 1971)
Dir/Wri: André Delvaux, based on a story by Julien Gracq.
Cast: Anna Karina, Bulle Ogier, Mathieu Carrière.
Story: In 1917, a young man spends a strange weekend in a mysterious castle.

Le Rendez-Vous en Forêt [*Rendezvous in the Forest*] (col., 80 min., 1972)
Dir/Wri: Alain Fleischer.
Cast: Catherine Jourdan, Laurence Trimble, Maria Meriko, Heinz Bennent, Renée Gardes.

Story: Modern version of *Beauty and the Beast* with witchcraft elements.

Rendez-Vous Hier [*Rendezvous Yesterday*] (col., 26 min., 1981)
Dir: Gérard Marx; *Wri*: Gérard Marx, Dominique Lancelot.
Cast: Richard Bohringer, Michel Derville, Peter Berlig, Catherine Jarrett.
Story: A man travels back in time through his ancestral memory.

Requiem pour un Vampire [*Requiem for a Vampire*]
See *Vierges et Vampires*.

Réseau Particulier [*Singular Network*] (col., 85 min., 1982)
Dir: Joe de Palmer; *Wri*: Joe de Lara.
Cast: Jean-Pierre Armand, Carmelo Petix, Isabelle Tara.
Story: Secret Agent James Love 069 (!) battles the inventor of a secret virus in this soft-core erotic parody.

La Revanche des Mortes Vivantes [*The Revenge of the Living Dead Girls*] (col., 85 min., 1985)
Dir/Wri: Peter B. Harsone.
Cast: Kathryn Charly, Veronik Cantazaro.
Story: Poisoned milk creates a plague of female zombies.
Note: X-rated horror film, including a scene where a young woman is vaginally impaled.

Les Revenants [*The Revenants*, transl as *They Came Back*] (col., 105 min., 2004)
Dir: Robin Campillo; *Wri*: Robin Campillo, Brigitte Tijou.
Cast: Géraldine Pailhas, Jonathan Zaccaï, Frédéric Pierrot, Victor Garrivier, Catherine Samie.
Story: The recently deceased of an anonymous French town suddenly return to life, calmly streaming forth from a cemetery in a silent procession. Unlike typical zombies, the Re-

turned seek only to reintegrate themselves into society--or so it seems
Note: This film generated two TV spin-offs: *Les Revenants*, a French TV series (see next section), and *The Returned*, a U.S. TV remake.

Ricky (col., 90 min., 2009)
Dir: François Ozon; *Wri*: François Ozon, Emmanuèle Bernheim, based on *Moth* by Rose Tremain.
Cast: Alexandra Lamy, Sergi López, Mélusine Mayance.
Story: A human baby develops a set of functional wings, and his parents try to cope with the child's abnormality.

Roboflash Warrior (col., 90 min., 1995)
Dir/Wri: Richard J. Thomson.
Cast: Laurent Dallias, Hafida Bachir, Franck Morelli, Mickaël Pabst, Patrick Aldebert.
Story: In 2020, a Terminator-like android pursues a band of survivors from a nuclear holocaust.
Note: Low-budget horror feature shot on video

Rocambole
Based on the famous character created in 1857 by popular writer Pierre-Alexis Ponson du Terrail. Rocambole is a daring adventurer who fights for good but is often on the wrong side of the law; he is the first modern literary super-hero.

Rocambole (B&W. serial, 3 hr 20 min., 1914)
Dir/Wri: Georges Denola.
Cast: Gaston Silvestre (Rocambole), Jean Aymé, Louis Blanche, Georges Dorival, Cécile Guyon, Madeleine Céliat, Émile Mylo, Delphine Renot, Paul Escoffier, Jean Hervé, Andrée Pascal.
Story: Serial comprised of three episodes: *La Jeunesse de Rocambole* [*Rocambole's Youth*], *Les Exploits de Rocambole* [*Rocambole's Adventures*] and *Rocambole et l'Héritage du Marquis de Morfontaine* [*Rocambole & The Marquess de Morfontaine's Inheritance*].

Les Amours de Rocambole [*Rocambole's Loves*] (B&W. serial, ?? min., 1924)
Dir/Wri: Charles Maudru.
Cast: Maurice Thorèze (Rocambole), Claude Mérelle (Baccarat), Albert Decoeur (Sir William), Noëlle Roland, Pierre Fresnay, Janie Péra, Jean Peyrière, Émilien Richard.
Story: Sir William and Rocambole, the leaders of the Club of the Jacks of Hearts, help an Indian woman in love with her cousin to win his heart. Serial comprised of two episodes entitled *Les Premières Armes de Rocambole* [*Rocambole's First Adventures*] and *Les Amours de Rocambole* [*Rocambole's Loves*].

Rocambole (B&W., 91 min., 1933)
Dir: Gabriel Rosca; *Wri*: Yvan Noé, Gérard Soubise.
Cast: Rolla Norman (Rocambole), Gil Clary, Ginette Gaubert, Leda Ginelly, Jim Gérald, Max Maxudian, Philippe Hersent, Georges Melchior.

Rocambole (B&W., 105 min., 1947)
Dir: Jacques de Baroncelli; *Wri*: Léon Roth, André-Paul Antoine.
Cast: Pierre Brasseur (Rocambole), Sophie Desmarets (Baccarat), Lucien Nat (Sir William), Robert Arnoux, Loredana, Roland Armontel.
Story: Film in two parts entitled *Rocambole* and *La Revanche de Baccarat* [*Baccarat's Revenge*]. The story is loosely based on the first serial, in which Rocambole and Baccarat start as adversaries and end up joining forces to defeat the evil Sir William/Andréa.

Rocambole (col., 95 min., 1963)
Dir: Bernard Borderie; *Wri*: Ugo Liberatore. Fulvio Gicca Palli.

Cast: Channing Pollock (Rocambole), Nadia Gray (Baccarat), Guy Delorme, Edy Vessel, Alberto Lupo, Rik Battaglia.
Story: In 1903 London, Rocambole unmasks German spies.
Note: French-Italian co-production.

Rogopag (1963)
Sketch film; only the second sketch is of interest:
Le Nouveau Monde [*The New World*] (B&W., 20 min.)
Dir/Wri: Jean-Luc Godard.
Cast: Jean-Marc Bory, Alexandra Stewart.
Story: A nuclear explosion modifies the behavior of the Parisians.
Note: French-Italian co-production. The movie title is an abbreviation of the authors' last names: **Ro**ssellini, **Go**dard, **Pa**solini, **G**regoretti.

The Room (col., 1090 min., 2019)
Dir: Christian Volckman; *Wri*: Éric Forestier, Christian Volckman.
Cast: Olga Kurylenko, Kevin Janssens.
Story: A young couple who discover a way to fulfill all of their material desires, but then go too far by using it to create a child.
Note: French-Belgian-Luxembourg co-production.

Le Rose et le Blanc [*Pink and White*] (col. 100 min., 1982)
Dir: Robert Pansard-Besson; *Wri*: Robert Pansard-Besson, Jean Echenoz.
Cast: Raymond Pellegrin, Bulle Ogier, Michael Lonsdale, Yves Afonso, Valérie Lagrange.
Story: In a Parisian building, strange events cause the entanglement of the fantasies of a novelist with the dreams of the other tenants.

La Rose Écorchée [*The Flayed Rose*, transl. as *The Blood Rose*] (col., 92 min., 1970)
Dir: Claude Mulot; *Wri*: Claude Mulot, Edgar Oppenheimer, Jean Larriaga.
Cast: Philippe Lemaire (Frédéric), Annie Duperey (Anne), Howard Vernon (Professor Romer), Elisabeth Tessier (Moira), Michèle Perello, Olivia Robin.
Story: Moira, Frédéric's mistress, pushes his wife, Anne, into a fire. She is disfigured. Frédéric then decides to find a plastic surgeon (Prof. Ro mer) to redo her face.
Note: Uncredited remake of *Les Yeux Sans Visage*.

La Rose de Fer [*The Iron Rose* transl. as *The Crystal Rose*] (aka *La Nuit du Cimetière* [*Night at the Cemetery*]) (col., 81 min., 1973)
Dir/Wri: Jean Rollin.
Cast: Françoise Pascal, Pierre Dupont, Mireille Dargent.
Story: Two lovers spend the night in a cemetery.

Le Rouge de Chine [*China Red*] (B&W./col., 80 min., 1979)
Dir/Wri: Jacques Richard
Cast: Agathe Vannier, Jacques Richard, Bojena Horackova, Bernard Dubois, Jacques Robiolles.
Story: Five characters share their lives in a vast castle. Each in his own way is in search of the absolute: J. wanders about, B. polishes weapons, C. seeks amorous adventures, A. and J. pursue an idyll which takes them on an initiation journey.
Note: Avant-garde non-narrative film shot in a mixture of ultra-high contrast black and white and muted grainy colour images. The film incorporates images of Louis Feuillade's *The Vampires*.

Rouletabille
Based on the famous character of the journalist-detective created in 1907 by popular writer Gaston Leroux, author of the classic *Phantom of the Opera*. Genre elements are few and far between, but Leroux being the French equivalent of Sir Arthur

Conan Doyle, the inclusion of *Rouletabille* in this filmography seems warranted.

Le Mystère de la Chambre Jaune [*The Mystery of the Yellow Room*] (B&W., 905 M., 1913)
Dir/Wri: Maurice Tourneur.
Cast: Marcel Simon (Rouletabille), Paul Escoffier (Larsan), Laurence Duluc (Mathilde).
Story: Rouletabille solves a murder in a locked room.

Le Parfum de la Dame en Noir [*The Scent of the Woman in Black*] (B&W., 1220 M., 1914)
Dir/Wri: Émile Chautard.
Cast: Marcel Simon (Rouletabille), Jean Garat, Maurice de Féraudy, Fernande Van Doren.
Story: Rouletabille solves another seemingly impossible murder.
Note: A 1919 American version of this serial was also produced, directed by Chautard, starring Lorin Baker, Ethel Grey Terry and George Cowl.

Rouletabille chez les Bohémiens [*Rouletabille and the Gypsies*] (Serial, B&W., 10 Eps., 8000 M., 1922)
1. *Le Livre des Ancêtres* [*The Book of the Ancestors*]; 2. *L'Arrestation* [*The Arrest*]; 3. *L'Instruction* [*The Investigation*]; 4. *La Poursuite* [*The Pursuit*]; 5. *La Page Déchirée* [*The Torn-Up Page*]; 6. *L'Enlèvement* [*The Kidnapping*]; 7. *A Severe Turn*; 8. *Le Signe* [*The Sign*]; 9. *Les Noces* [*The Wedding*]; 10. *Le Châtiment* [*The Punishment*].
Dir: Henri Fescourt; *Wri*: Gaston Leroux.
Cast: Gabriel de Gravone (Rouletabille), Joe Hamman, Romuald Joubé, Edith Jehanne, Jean Dehelly, Suzanne Talba.
Story: Rouletabille recovers a sacred book stolen from the gypsies.
Note: Simultaneously novelized by Leroux.

Le Mystère de la Chambre Jaune [*The Mystery of the Yellow Room*] (B&W., 108 min., 1930)
Dir/Wri: Marcel L'Herbier.
Cast: Roland Toutain (Rouletabille), Marcel Vilbert (Larsan), Huguette Duflos (Mathilde), Edmond Van Daële (Darzac), Maxime Desjardins.

Le Parfum de la Dame en Noir [*The Scent of the Woman In Black*] (B&W., 109 min., 1931)
Dir/Wri: Marcel L'Herbier.
Cast: Roland Toutain (Rouletabille), Marcel Vilbert (Larsan), Huguette Duflos (Mathilde), Edmond Van Daële (Darzac), Léon Belières, Wera Engels.

Rouletabille Aviateur [*Rouletabille Aviator*] (B&W., 100 min., 1932)
Dir: Étienne Szekely; *Wri*: Pierre Veber.
Cast: Roland Toutain (Rouletabille), Léon Belières, Lisette Lanvin, Germaine Aussey, Maurice Maillot.
Story: Rouletabille solves a murder at an airfield.

Rouletabille Joue et Gagne [*Rouletabille Plays and Wins*] (B&W., 95 min., 1947)
Dir: Christian Chamborant; *Wri*: Pierre Lestringuez.
Cast: Jean Piat (Rouletabille), Marie Déa, Suzanne Dehelly, Michel Vitold, Lucas Gridoux.
Story: Rouletabille solves a murder in the South of France.

Rouletabille contre la Dame de Pique [*Rouletabille vs. The Queen of Spades*] (B&W., 88 min., 1948)
Dir: Christian Chamborant; *Wri*: Pierre Lestringuez.
Cast: Jean Piat (Rouletabille), Marie Déa, Suzanne Dehelly, Lucas Gridoux, Fernand Gilbert, Jérôme Goulven.
Story: Rouletabille's fiancée confesses she may have killed a spy.

Le Mystère de la Chambre Jaune [*The Mystery of the Yellow Room*] (B&W., 90 min., 1949)
Dir: Henri Aisner; *Wri*: Wladimir Pozner.
Cast: Serge Reggiani (Rouletabille), Marcel Herrand (Larsan), Hélène Perdrière (Mathilde),
Lucien Nat (Darzac).

Le Parfum de la Dame en Noir [*The Scent of the Woman in Black*] (B&W., 100 min., 1949)
Dir: Louis Daquin; *Wri*: Wladimir Pozner.
Cast: Serge Reggiani (Rouletabille), Marcel Herrand (Larsan), Hélène Perdrière (Mathilde),
Lucien Nat (Darzac).

Le Mystère de la Chambre Jaune [*The Mystery of the Yellow Room*] (B&W., 90 min., 1965)
Dir: Jean Kerchbron; *Wri*: Jean Gruault.
Cast: Claude Brasseur, Marika Green, Catherine Rouvel.
Note: Made for TV movie.

Le Mystère de la Chambre Jaune [*The Mystery of the Yellow Room*] (col., 118 min., 2003)
Dir: Bruno Podalydès.
Cast: Denis Podalydès (Rouletabille), Jean-Noël Brouté (Sainclair), Sabine Azéma (Mathilde), Olivier Gourmet (Darzac), Pierre Arditi (Larsan), Michael Lonsdale, Claude Rich.

Le Parfum de la Dame en Noir [*The Scent of the Woman in Black*] (col., 115 min., 2005)
Dir: Bruno Podalydès.
Cast: Denis Podalydès (Rouletabille), Jean-Noël Brouté (Sainclair), Sabine Azéma (Mathilde), Olivier Gourmet (Darzac), Pierre Arditi (Larsan), Zabou Breitman.

Rubber (col., 82 min., 2010)

Dir: Quentin Dupieux; *Wri*: Quentin Dupieux, Jake Householder.
Cast: Stephen Spinella, Roxane Mesquida, Jack Plotnick, Haley Ramm, Wings Hauser, Ethan Cohn.
Story: Somewhere in the American desert, a tire named Robert suddenly comes to life. After standing upright, he discovers he has psychokinesis powers.

Le Sadique aux Dents Rouges [*The Sadist with Red Teeth*] (col., 100 min., 1970)
Dir/Wri: Jean-Louis Van Belle.
Cast: Jane Clayton, Albert Simono, Daniel Mossman.
Story: A young artist is obsessed by the thought of becoming a vampire.

Saint Ange (col., 98 min., 2004)
Dir/Wri: Pascal Laugier.
Cast: Virginie Ledoyen (Anna), Lou Doillon, Catriona McCall.
Story: In 1958, Anna accepts a job as a housekeeper of Saint Ange, an abandoned orphanage in the French Alps. The place is haunted.

Les Saisons du Plaisir [*The Seasons of Pleasure*] (col., 88 min., 1988)
Dir/Wri: Jean-Pierre Mocky.
Cast: Charles Vanel (Van Bert), Denise Grey, Jacqueline Maillan, Bernadette Lafont, Jean Poiret, Eva Darlan, Stéphane Audran, Richard Bohringer, Darry Cowl, Fanny Cottençon.
Story: Van Bert, a wealthy centenarian, gathers his family and friends to decide who will inherit his fortune. Meanwhile the world is approaching nuclear war.

Salammbo (B&W., 3500 Meters, 1924)
Dir/Wri: Pierre Marodon, based on the novel by Gustave Flaubert.

Cast: Jeanne de Balzac (Salammbo), Rolla Norman (Matho), Victor Vina (Hamilcar).
Story: The doomed love story of Salammbo, the daughter of Carthagenian general Hamilcar, with Matho, leader of the rebel mercenaries.
Note: Gustave Flaubert is a famous novelist.

San Antonio ne pense qu'à ça [*San Antonio Only Thinks About That*] (col., 90 min., 1981)
Dir/Wri: Joël Seria, based on the character created by Frédéric Dard.
Cast: Philippe Gasté, Pierre Doris, Hubert Deschamps.
Story: Police Commissioner San Antonio fights Miss Tenebra and KGB spies to reclaim a pair of X-ray glasses.
Note: Loosely based on a popular series of humorous detective novels.

Le Sang des Autres [*The Blood of Others*]
See *Perversions Sexuelles*.

Le Sang d'un Poète [*The Blood of a Poet*] (B&W., 49 min., 1930)
Dir/Wri: Jean Cocteau.
Cast: Enrique Rivero (The Poet), Lee Miller, Feral Benga, Pauline Carton.
Story: A series of surreal scenes orchestratred by the poetic genius of Jean Cocteau.

Scheherazade (B&W., 90 min., 1962)
Dir: Pierre Gaspard-Huit; *Wri*: Marc-Gilbert Sauvajon, Pierre Gaspard-Huit.
Cast: Anna Karina (Scheherazade), Gérard Barray, Antonio Vilar, Giulano Gemma, Marilu Tolo, Fernando Rey, Fausto Tozzi, Gil Vidal.
Story: Another adaptation of the *Thousand and One Nights*.

Le Secret de la Momie [*The Mummy's Secret*]

See *Perversions Sexuelles*.

Le Secret de Sarah Tombelaine [*The Secret of Sarah Tombelaine*] (col., 90 min., 1990)
Dir: Daniel Lacambre; *Wri*: Claude Gilbert, Daniel Lacambre.
Cast: Irène Jacob (Sarah) Marc de Jonge, Harry Cleven, François Caron, Rémy Roubakha, Jean-Paul Roussillon, Jenny Alpha, Gabriel Cattand, Jean Markalé, Hélène Simonnet.
Story: Sarah, a young woman, is about to be sacrificed to a dragon living under Mount Saint-Michael; she is rescued by an engineer (Cleven).

Les Secrets Professionnels du Docteur Apfelgluck [*The Professional Secrets of Dr. Apfelgluck*] (col., 86 min., 1990)
Dir: Hervé Palud, Allessandro Capone, Mathias Ledoux, Stéphane Clavier, Thierry Lhermitte; *Wri*: Philippe Bruneau, Thierry Lhermitte.
Cast: Thierry Lhermitte, Gérard Jugnot, Jacques Villeret, Michel Blanc, Zabou, Christian Clavier, Josiane Balasko.
Story: Several sketches in this comedy revolve around fantasy elements: an unbeatable game show contestant, true X-ray glasses, a journey through the afterlife, murderous innkeepers.

Les Seigneurs d'Outre Monde [*The Lords of Beyond*] (col., 140 min., 2016)
Dir: Rémi Hoffmann; *Wri*: Rémi Hoffmann, Fenriss.
Cast: Jonathan Durieux (Jarwin), Djamel Bride (Rashalden), Soizic Fonjallaz, Olivier Grignard, Bernard Belin, Claudine Jacquemard.
Story: For 1000 years, Rashalden, the banished Lord of Beyond, seeks to return to destroy the human race. Jarwin de Kalmeril, a carefree prince, is unaware of the threat, yet, the future of the world of Eravys depends on him.

La Sentinelle [*The Sentinel*] (col., 144 min., 1992)
Dir: Arnaud Desplechin; *Wri*: Arnaud Desplechin, Pascale Ferran, Noémie Lvovsky, Emmanuel Salinger.

Cast: Emmanuel Salinger (Mathias), Jean-Louis Richard (Bleicher), Bruno Todeschini (William), Marianne Denicourt (Marie), Valérie Dréville, Emmanuelle Devos, Jean-Luc Boutté.
Story: Mathias, the son of a French diplomat, returns to France and discovers a mysterious shrunken head in his luggage. This morbid discovery takes him on a surreal journey in the twilight world of espionnage.

Les Sept Péchés Capitaux [*The Seven Deadly Sins*] (1961)
Sketch film; only the seventh sketch is of interest:
La Colere (*Anger*) (B&W., 15 min.)
Dir: Sylvain Dhomme, Max Douy, Eugène Ionesco; *Wri*: Eugène Ionesco.
Cast: Dominique Paturel, Marie-José Nat.
Story: A man finds a fly in his soup, which triggers a chain of events that results in the atomic destriction of the planet.
Note: French-Italian co-production. Eugène Ionesco is a famous playwright.

La Septième Dimension [*The Seventh Dimension*] (col., 90 min., 1987)
Anthology film comprised of six stories, linked together.
Wri: Laurent Dussaux, Elvire Murail, Nicolas Cuche.
Cast: Francis Frappat (Henri), Marie-Armelle Deguy (Hélène), Jean-Michel Dupuis (Louis).

Le Savant Fou [The Mad Scientist]
Dir: Stéphan Holmes.

Le Mariage [The Wedding]
Dir: Peter Winfield.

Le Chasseur de Rêves [The Dream Hunter]
Dir: Olivier Bourbeillon.

Le Duel
Dir: Laurent Dussaux.

La Fille qui Boit [The Drinking Girl]
Dir: Manuel Boursinhac.

Henri en Egypte [Henri in Egypt]
Dir: Benoît Ferreux.
Story: Henri, a pharmacist, is secretly in love with Hélène, a 50s movie star. One night, Louis, an old partner of the actress, knocks on his door. The two men enter the seventh dimension, the fantastic world of Hélène's movies. Henri searches for Hélène through it, while fighting Louis. The stories take the characters:
1. to Doctor Jekyll's lab; 2. To the Middle Ages; 3: to the time of King Arthur; 4: to a sorcerous duel; 5: to a medieval castle during the Inquisition; and finally, 6: to Ancient Egypt.

La Septième Porte [*The Seventh Door*] (B&W., 88 min., 1946)
Dir: André Zwobada; *Wri*: Jean Aurenche, Pierre Bost.
Cast: Georges Marchal (Ali), Maria Casarès, Jean Servais.
Story: A *Thousand and One Nights* story in which Ali disobeys his master's command never to open the Seventh Door. His punishment is to see his entire future revealed to him.

Sérail [*Seraglio*] (col., 90 min., 1976)
Dir/Wri: Eduardo de Gregorio.
Cast: Leslie Caron, Bulle Ogier, Marie-France Pisier, Colin Redgrave.
Story: A novelist (Redgrave) meets three strange women in a house he wants to purchase. He is eventually imprisoned in the house.

Le Seuil du Vide [*The Threshold of the Void*] (B&W., 90 min., 1971)

Dir: Jean-François Davy; *Wri*: Jean-François Davy, André Ruellan, based on his novel (written under the pseudonym of Kurt Steiner).
Cast: Dominique Erlanger, Pierre Vaneck, Jean Servais, Odette Duc, Catherine Rich, Michel Lemoine.
Story: A young girl (Erlanger) becomes the prey of a cult of immortals who steal her youth.
Note: André Ruellan is a noted science fiction and horror writer.

Seuls [*Alone*] (col., 98 mins., 2017)
Dir: David Moreau; *Wri*: David Moreau, Guillaume Moulin, based on the comic book by Bruno Gazzotti & Fabien Vehlmann.
Cast: Stéphane Bak (Dodji), Sofia Lesaffre (Leïla), Kim Lockhart (Camille), Jean-Stan DuPac (Terry), Paul Scarfoglio (Yvan), Thomas Doret.
Story: Sixteen-year-old Leïla wakes up in a world where all the adults have disappeared. She meets four other young people: Dodji, Yvan, Camille and Terry. Together, they will try to understand what happened and learn to survive—but are they really alone?

Le Sexe Qui Parle [*Talking Sex*, transl. as *Pussy Talk*] (col. 90 min., 1975)
Dir/Wri: Frédéric Lansac (pseudonym of Claude Mulot).
Cast: Pénélope Lamour, Béatrice Harnois, Nils Hotz, Ellen Earl-Coupey, Sylvia Bourdon, Vicky Messica.
Story: Award-winning X-rated film in which a man discovers his penis can talk. *Note*: A sequel, *Triples Introductions (Le Sexe Qui Parle II)*, also written and directed by Lansac, starring France Lomay, Richard Lemieuvre, and Gwenda Farnel, was released in 1978.

Sexorcismes [*Sexorcism*] (aka *Exorcisme* [*Exorcism*], *Exorcisme et Messes Noires* [*Exorcism and Black Masses*], *Expé-

riences Sexuelles au Château des Jouisseuses [*Sexual Experiences at the Castle of Pleasure*]) (col., 93 min., 1975)
Dir: Jess Franco); *Wri*: David Khunne (aka Jess Franco), James C. Gardner (aka Jean-Claude Garnier), Henri Bral de Boitselieu.
Cast: Lina Romay, Jess Franck (Jess Franco), Monica Swinn, Lynn Monteil, Catherine Laferrière, Caroline Rivière.
Story: A religious fanatic tortures people whom he thinks are possessed by the Devil.
Note: French-Belgian co-production.

Signé Furax [*Signed: Furax*] (col., 90 min., 1980)
Dir/Wri: Marc Simenon, based on a story by Pierre Dac & Francis Blanche.
Cast: Bernard Haller (Furax), Mylène Demongeot (Malvina), Jean Le Poulain, Michel Galabru, Jean-Pierre Darras, Alfred Pasquali.
Story: The evil Babus steal Paris' monuments by dehydrating them, then pin the blame on retired master criminal Edmond Furax.
Note: Based on a popular radio serial.

Si J'Avais Mille Ans [*If I Was a Thousand-Years-Old*] (col., 86 min., 1983)
Dir/Wri: Monique Enckell.
Cast: Daniel Olbrychski, Jean Bouise, Marie Dubois, Dominique Pinon.
Story: Every year at Halloween, the ghosts of medieval knights invade a small island in Britanny A thousand years earlier, the villagers refused to turn over to them a girl they had condemned to die.

Si J'Étais Toi [*If I Were You*, transl, as *The Secret*] (col., 93 min., 2007)
Dir: Vincent Pérez; *Wri*: Ann Cherkis.
Cast: David Duchovny, Olivia Thirlby, Lili Taylor.

Story: A wife and mother passes away, and spirit returns in her daughter's body.
Note: Remake of *Himitsu*, a 1999 Japanese film directed by Yojiro Takita, written by Hiroshi Saitô.

Si Jeunesse Savait [*If Youth Only Knew*] (B&W., 95 min., 1947)
Dir: André Cerf; *Wri*: André Cerf, Marc-Gilbert Sauvajon.
Cast: Jules Berry (Vigne), Jean Tissier, Saturnin Fabre, Suzet Maïs.
Story: Banker Vigne asks a genie to make him thirteen-year-old again, but eventually chooses to revert to adulthood to preserve his business.

Si le Soleil Ne Revenait Pas [*If The Sun Never Came Back*] (col., 120 min., 1987)
Dir/Wri: Claude Goretta, based on a story by Charles-Ferdinand Ramuz.
Cast: Catherine Mouchet (Isabelle), Charles Vanel (Anzevui), Philippe Léotard, Raoul Billerey, Claude Évrard.
Story: In the winter of 1937, an old wizard, Anzevui, scares a Swiss village buried under the snow when he annonces that the sun will not come back. But a young girl, Isabelle, helps the villagers regain hope.
Note: Swiss production.

Silver Slime (col., 15 min., 1981)
Dir/Wri: Christophe Gans.
Cast: Isabelle Wendling, Aïssa Djabri.
Story: Homage to Mario Bava.

Siméon (col., 115 min, 1992)
Dir: Euzhan Palcy; *Wri*: Euzhan Palcy, Jean-Pierre Rumeau.
Cast: Jean-Claude Duverger (Siméon), Jacob Desvarieux (Isidore), Jocelyne Beroard (Roselyne), Lucinda Messager (Orélie).

Story: Elderly music teacher Siméon dies and to keep his memory alive his granddaughter Orélie cuts off her braid, thus condemning him to become a *Soucouyant*. Siméon takes the opportunity to convince his son Isidore to continue his musical work.
Note: Musical.

Simon les Nuages [*Simon of the Clouds*] (col. 81 min., 1990)
Dir/Wri: Roger Cantin.
Cast: Hugolin Chevrette-Landesque (Simon), Jessica Barker, Bernard Carez, Edgar Fruitier, Charles-André Gill-Therrien, Anaïs Goulet-Robitaille, Naad Joseph, Isabelle Lapointe.
Story: A young boy, Simon, leads other children on a secret expedition to a dream-like land inhabited by all kinds of vanished species.
Note: Canadian production.

Simple Mortel [*Mere Mortal*] (col., 85 min., 1991)
Dir/Wri: Pierre Jolivet.
Cast: Philippe Volter, Christophe Bourseiller, Nathalie Roussel, Roland Giraud, Marcel Maréchal, Arlette Thomas.
Story: A linguist (Volter) receives messages in ancient Gaelic from a mysterious, seemingly all-powerful entity who orders him to accomplish a series of actions (including murdering one of his friends) in order to save the world.

Une Sirène à Paris [*A Mermaid in Paris*] (col., 102 min., 2020)
Dir: Mathias Malzieu; *Wri*: Stéphane Landowski, Mathias Malzieu, based on his novel.
Cast: Nicolas Duvauchelle (Gaspard), Marilyn Lima (Lula the Mermaid), Romane Bohringer, Rossy de Palma, Tchéky Karyo , Alexis Michalik.
Story: Gaspard rescues a mermaid in Paris and slowly falls in love with her.

Un Soir, Par Hasard [*One Night, By Chance*] (B&W., 90 min., 1964)
Dir: Ivan Govar; *Wri*: Ivan Govar, André Allard, Pierre Sabatier, based on the novel by René Collard.
Cast: Pierre Brasseur, Anita Stroyberg, Jean Servais.
Story: A couple is offered a method of immortality.

Un Soir, Un Train [*One Night, A Train*] (col., 91 min., 1968)
Dir/Wri: André Delvaux, based on a story by Johan Daisne.
Cast: Yves Montand (Mathias), Anouk Aimée (Anne), Adriana Bogdan, François Beukelaers.
Story: Mathias loses his girlfriend Anne on a train. When the train stops, he finds himself in a strange town. He eventually awakens and discovers that the train had an accident and Anne is dead.

Les Soleils de l'Île de Pâques [*The Suns of Easter Island*] (col., 94 min., 1971)
Dir/Wri: Pierre Kast.
Cast: Norma Bengell, Françoise Brion, Alexandra Stewart, Jacques Charrier, Maurice Garrel, Marcello Romo, Zozimo Bulbul.
Story: Aliens summon six men and women to Easter Island to evaluate mankind's progress. Disgusted by the violence they discover, they leave.

La Sorcière [*The Witch*] (B&W., 97 min., 1955)
Dir: André Michel; *Wri*: Jacques Companez.
Cast: Marina Vlady (Aino), Maurice Ronet (Laurent), Nicole Courcel, Michel Etcheverry.
Story: In a Swedish village, a newly arrived man falls in love with a girl who may be a witch.

Soudain le Vide [*Enter the Void*] (col., 161 min., 2009)
Dir: Gaspar Noé; *Wri*: Gaspar Noé, Lucile Hadzihalilovic.
Cast: Nathaniel Brown (Oscar), Paz de la Huerta, Olly Alexander.

Story: Oscar is shot dead by the police in a Tokyo bar. As his soul detaches from his body, he remembers his promise to his sister never to abandon her. Then begins a long wandering of the mind through Tokyo.

La Soupe aux Choux [*The Cabbage Soup*] (col., 98 min., 1981)
Dir: Jean Girault; *Wri*: Louis de Funès, Jean Halain, based on the novel by René Fallet.
Cast: Louis de Funès (Claude), Jean Carmet (Le Bombé), Jacques Villeret (La Denrée), Christine Dejoux, Claude Gensac, Henri Genès.
Story: An alien who loves cabbage soup resurrects an old farmer's wife. Eventually, made aware that the world has passed him by, the farmer and his friend leave Earth.

Sous le Soleil de Satan [*Under the Sun of Satan*] (col., 113 min., 1987)
Dir: Maurice Pialat; *Wri*: Sylvie Danton, based on the novel by Georges Bernanos.
Cast: Gérard Depardieu (Abbé Donissan), Sandrine Bonnaire, Maurice Pialat.
Story: In 1926, Abbot Donissan experiences a crisis of faith and performs a miracle.

Spermula (col., 110 min., 1976)
Dir/Wri: Charles Matton.
Cast: Dayle Haddon (Spermula), Udo Kier, Ginette Leclerc, Georges Géret, François Dunoyer, Jocelyne Boisseau.
Story: A sect of telepathic women led by the beautiful Spermula tries to take over the world, but fails. Spermula sacrifices her immortality for a night of true passion.

Star Suburb: La Banlieue des Étoiles (col., 26 min., 1982)
Dir/Wri: Stéphane Drouot.
Cast: Caroline Appere, Marcelle Turlure.

Story: In her futuristic apartment, a girl who can't sleep listens to a galactic radio station presenting a new game show.

Stress (col., 90 min., 1984)
Dir: Jean-Louis Bertucelli; *Wri*: André Grall.
Cast: Guy Marchand (Alex), Carole Laure (Nathalie), Patrice Kerbrat (Gérard), André Dussolier, Germaine Monero.
Story: Gérard's heart has been transplanted in Alex and seeks revenge against Nathalie, his former girlfriend who drove him to commit suicide.

Subtil Concept [*Subtle Concept*] (B&W., 21min., 1980)
Dir/Wri: Gérard Krawczyk, based on the short story *Mr. Big* by Woody Allen.
Cast: Alan Wenger, Rebecca Pauly, Nicholas Bang, Daniel Croheim, Ed Marcus.
Story: A hardboiled private eye is hired to find out who killed God.

Le Suicide de Frank Einstein [*Frank Einstein's Suicide*] (col., 45 min., 1984)
Dir/Wri: René Manzor.
Cast: Alan Wenger.
Story: Another variation on the Frankenstein theme.

Suivez Mon Regard [*Follow My Glance*] (col., 85 min., 1986)
Dir/Wri: Jean Curtelin.
Cast: Pierre Arditi, Stéphane Audran, Jean-Claude Brialy, Claude Chabrol, Gérard Darmon, Andréa Ferréol, Brigitte Lahaie, Léo Malet, Macha Méril, Zabou.
Story: Surreal series of short sketches, often parodic or nonsensical. Genre elements include the return of Christ, what happens after death, mysterious disappearances of people and their dogs, etc.

Superlove (col., 88 min., 1997)

Dir: Jean-Claude Janer; *Wri*: Hélène Angel, Jean-Claude Janer, Agnès de Sacy.
Cast: Grégoire Colin (Mario), Isabelle Carré (Mary), Carmen Maura.
Story: A woman claiming to be the Virgin Mary appears to Mario, a provincial hairdresser who dreams of becoming a successful singer. He presents her to her parents who adopt her immediately and install her in their pavilion.

Supernova (Expérience #1) [*Supernova : Experiment #1*] (col., 89 min., 2003)
Dir: Pierre Vinour; *Wri*: Pierre Vinour, Pascal Mieszala.
Cast: Philippe Nahon (Simon), Catherine Wilkening, Clément Sibony.
Story: Simon, a minister, is about to commit suicide, but changes his mind. Then a rain of meteors begins to fall...

La Surface Perdue [*The Lost Surface*] (B&W., 19 min., 1966)
Dir: Dolorès Grassian; *Wri*: Dolorès Grassian, Paul Pellas.
Cast: Bernard Fresson, Philippe Moreau, Jean Champion.
Story: Three surveyors lost a surface. The topography center tells them that it cannot exist, that their calculations are wrong. Disappointed, the three surveyors remain perplexed by this very real surface under their eyes.

Sur La Terre Comme Au Ciel [*On Earth As In Heaven*] (col., 80 min., 1991)
Dir: Marion Hänsel; Wri: Marion Hänsel, Paul Le, Jaco Van Dormael, Laurette Vankeerberghen.
Cast: Carmen Maura (Maria), Didier Bezace, Samuel Mussen, Jean-Pierre Cassel, Johan Leysen, Serge-Henri Valcke, Pascale Tison.
Story: A fetus mysteriously tells his mother that he and the other fetuses have decided not to be born until the world becomes a better place. She eventually convinces him otherwise.
Note: Belgian-French-Spanish co-production.

Sursis pour un Vivant [*Reprieve for a Living Man*] (B&W., 88 min., 1958)
Dir: Victor Merenda; *Wri*: Frédéric Dard, based on the short story *Thanatos Palace Hôtel* by André Maurois.
Cast: Henri Vidal (Jean Monnier), Dawn Addams (Nadia), Lino Ventura.
Story: A writer (Vidal) wishing to die but afraid to commit suicide goes to a mountain hotel where he will be killed painlessly. But after he falls in love, he no longer wants to die...
Note: French-Italian co-production. André Maurois is a famous writer and essayist. Frédéric Dard is a noted thriller writer.

Sybille (col., 15 min., 1979)
Dir/Wri: Robert Cappa.
Cast: Manuel Bonnet, Jean Montagne, Brigitte Roudier, Gilles Kohler.
Story: A man buys a film reel showing a mysterious woman. Every time he projects the film, new scenes appear until the woman reaches into his reality, killing him.

Sylvie et le Fantôme [*Sylvie and the Ghost*] (B&W., 102 min., 1945)
Dir: Claude Autant-Lara; *Wri*: Jean Aurenche, based on a play by Alfred Adam.
Cast: Odette Joyeux (Sylvie), Pierre Larquey (Baron Édouard), Jacques Tati (The Ghost), François Périer, Jean Desailly, Gabrielle Fontant, Julien Carette, Louis Salou, Claude Marcy.
Story: Sylvie is in love with a gallant ghost. During a party for her sixteenth birthday, she discovers what real love is.

Le Syndrome de l'Espion [*The Spy Syndrome*] (col., 70 min., 1989)
Dir: Daniel Petitcuenot; *Wri*: Daniel Petitcuenot, Kristine Joray.

Cast: Christian Pageault, Philippe Schmid, Bob Watson Barr, Robert Ground, Liliane David.
Story: While filming a movie, a filmmaker becomes involved in a three-way battle between American, Russian, and Jupiterian spies, all vying for the same, mysterious mineral.

Le Temps de Mourir [*A Time to Die*] (col., 90 min., 1969)
Dir: André Farwagi; *Wri*: Alain Morineau, André Farwagi.
Cast: Bruno Cremer (Max), Anna Karina, Jean Rochefort, Catherine Rich, Daniel Moosmann, Billy Kearns.
Story: A mysterious girl (Karina) shows Max a film portraying his own murder. By trying to prevent it, Max actually causes the murder to take place.

Tendre Dracula [*Tender Dracula*]
See *La Grande Trouille*.

La Tendre Ennemie [*The Tender Enemy*] (B&W., 69 min., 1936)
Dir: Max Ophuls; *Wri*: Curt Alexander, Max Ophuls, based on a play by André-Paul Antoine.
Cast: Jacqueline Daix (Line), Simone Berriau (Annette), Georges Vitray, Marc Valbel, Catherine Fonteney.
Story: The ghost of Line's father and her mother's lover join forces to save her from an unwanted marriage.

La Tentation de Barbizon [*The Temptation of Barbizon*] (B&W., 100 min., 1945)
Dir: Jean Stelli; *Wri*: André-Paul Antoine.
Cast: François Périer (The Devil), Simone Renant (The Angel), André Bervil, Juliette Faber, Pierre Larquey, Daniel Gélin.
Story: The Devil (posing as a film producer) tries to break up a young couple, while an Angel (posing as a film star) attempts to bring them back together.

Terminus [transl. as *End of the Line*] (col., 110 min., 1986)

Dir: Pierre-William Glenn; *Wri*: Pierre-William Glenn, Patrice Duvic, based on a story by Alain Gillot.
Cast: Johnny Hallyday, Karen Allen, Jürgen Prochnow, Julie Glenn, Gabriel Damon, Dominique Valera, Dieter Shidor.
Story: In a post-apocalyptic future, the driver of a giant battle-truck (Hallyday) and a girl (Allen) try to escape from a totalitarian regime.
Note: French-German co-production.

Terreur [*Terrror*, transl. as *The Perils of Paris*] (B&W., 90 min., 1924)
Dir/Wri: Édouard José.
Cast: Pearl White, Robert Lee, Henry Bandin, Arlette Marchal.
Story: Criminals are after the Power Ray invented by the heroine's father.
Note: This is second serial in the *Perils of Pauline* series which started in 1914, and later became a Universal serial (starring Evalyn Knapp) in 1933.

Le Testament du Dr. Cordelier [*The Testament of Dr. Cordelier*, transl. As *The Doctor's Horrible Experiment*, *Experiment in Evil*] (B&W., 100 min., 1959/1961)
Dir/Wri: Jean Renoir, based on the novel by Robert-Louis Stevenson.
Cast: Jean-Louis Barrault (Dr. Cordelier/Opale), Teddy Bills, Michel Vitold, Jean Topart, Micheline Gary, Gaston Modot.
Story: French transposition of *Dr. Jekyll and Mr. Hyde*.
Note: This film was originally made in 1959 and screened that year at the Venice Film Festival. However, its release was delayed because of a conflict between film and television distributors; it was ultimately released on French TV in November 1961.

Le Testament d'Orphée [*The Testament of Orpheus*] (B&W., 77 min., 1959)
Wri/Dir: Jean Cocteau.

Cast: Jean Cocteau (Orpheus), Jean Marais (Oedipus), François Périer (Heurtebise), Maria Casarès, Édouard Dermit.
Story: Cocteau plays himself as a dying poet revisiting his life and works in this new transposition of the Orpheus myth. Cameo appearances by Pablo Picasso, Charles Aznavour, Jean-Pierre Léaud and Yul Brynner.

Tête à Tête [*Head to Head*] (col., 75 min., 1994)
Dir: Jean-Hugues Lime, Yves Benoît; *Wri*: Jean-Hugues Lime.
Cast: Régis Laspalès (Prosper), Jean-Hugues Lime (Paul), Christian Pernot (Henri), Laurence Semonin, Didier Bénureau, Philippe Chevallier.
Story: Paul and Henri are friends until the latter dies in a plane crash. A goofy undertaker, Prosper, gives Paul Henri's head, which he kept and which has mysteriously remained alive. But Paul finds living with a talking head unbearable.

Thank You, Satan (col., 85 min., 1988)
Dir: André Farwagi; *Wri*: André Farwagi, Christian Carini, Nelly Allard, Jean Cosmos.
Cast: Carole Laure, Patrick Chesnais, Marie Fugain, Muriel Brenner, Sandrine Caron, Annie Legrand (Satan), Bernard Le Coq, Éric Blanc.
Story: A fourteen-year-old girl (Fugain) signs a pact with Satan to solve her family's romantic problems.
Note: French-Canadian production.

Themroc (col., 105 min., 1972)
Dir/Wri: Claude Faraldo.
Cast: Michel Piccoli (Themroc), Béatrice Romand, Marilu Tolo, Francesca Coluzzi, Jeanne Herviale, Patrick Dewaere, Miou-Miou, Romain Bouteille, Coluche.
Story: Themroc is a lonely man who leads a savage revolt against society.

Time Demon (col., 90 min., 1996)

Dir/Wri: Richard J. Thomson.
Cast: Laurent Dallias, Elodie Chérie, Elisabeth Henriques, Dominick Breuil, Jean-François Gallotte.
Story: Hitler travels back in time.
Note: Low-budget horror feature shot on video

Tintin
Based on the popular series of graphic novels created in 1929 by Hergé.

Tintin et le Mystère de la Toison d'Or [*Tintin and the Mystery of the Golden Fleece*] (col., 94 min., 1961)
Dir: Jean-Jacques Vierne; *Wri*: André Barret, Rémo Forlani.
Cast: Jean-Pierre Talbot (Tintin), Georges Wilson (Haddock), Georges Loriot (Calculus), Charles Vanel (Father Alexander), Dario Moreno (Midas Papas), Marcel Bozzuffi (Angorapoulos), Dimitrios Starenios (Scoubidovitch).
Story: Haddock inherits an old steamer which contains the key to a hidden treasure. Professor Calculus discovers a pill which, when dropped in the fuel tank, makes the boat go at incredible speeds.

Tintin et les Oranges Bleues [*Tintin and the Blue Oranges*] (col., 110 min., 1964)
Dir: Philippe Coudroyer; *Wri*: André Barret.
Cast: Jean-Pierre Talbot (Tintin), Jean Bouise (Haddock), Félix Fernandez (Prof. Calculus), Francky François, André Marie (Thomson & Thompson), Jenny Orléans, Max Eloy.
Story: Tintin outwits an Arab Sheik who has kidnaped a scientist who has created a new type of orange that can grow in the desert.

Titane (col., 108 min., 2021)
Dir/Wri: Julia Ducournau.
Cast: Vincent Lindon (Vincent), Agathe Rousselle (Alexia), Garance Marillier.

Story: Alexia, seriously injured in a road accident as a child, is saved by the placement of a titanium implant in her skull. Around the age of 30, she is seized with murderous impulses. At the same time, Vincent, a firefighter, believes he has found his son Adrien, who has been missing for ten years. In reality, it is Alexia, who has taken on the appearance of a young man to escape the police.

Tom et Lola (col., 97 min., 1989)
Dir: Bertrand Arthuys; *Wri*: Bertrand Arthuys, Christian de Chalonge, Muriel Teodori, Luc Goldenberg.
Cast: Neil Stubbs (Tom), Mélodie Collin (Lola), Cécile Magnet, Marc Berman, Catherine Frot, Célian Varini, Janine Souchon, Sophie Arthuys, Olivier Belmont, Nadia Chapuis.
Story: The surreal adventures of two children with immune deficiencies who escape their hospital "bubble."

Torticola contre Frankensberg [*Torticola vs. Frankensberg*] (B&W., 34 min., 1952)
Dir: Paul Paviot; *Wri*: Albert Vidalie, Louis Sapin.
Cast: Vera Norman (Lorelei), François Patrice (Éric), Roger Blin (Frankensberg), Michel Piccoli (Torticola), Helena Manson, Marc Boussac.
Story: In this surreal parody of gothic horror films, Dr. Frankensberg's monster, Torticola, revolts and frees the beautiful captive Lorelei and Eric the wolf-man.

Le Toubib [*The Doc*] (col., 95 min., 1979)
Dir: Pierre Granier-Deferre; *Wri*: Pierre Granier-Deferre, Pascal Jardin, based on the novel by Jean Freustié.
Cast: Alain Delon (Desprès), Véronique Jannot (Harmonie), Bernard Giraudeau (François), Francine Bergé, Michel Auclair, Catherine Lachens, Bernard Le Coq.
Story: During a third world war, Desprès, a cynical, *M.A.S.H.*-type doctor, falls in love with Harmonie, a beautiful, idealistic nurse, but she is eventually killed by a mine.

Note: The original novel took place in the present, not the future.

Le Tour d'Écrou [*The Turn of the Screw*] (col., 92 min., 1992)
Dir/Wri: Rusty Lemorande, based on the novel by Henry James.
Cast: Patsy Kensit (Jenny), Stéphane Audran (Mrs Grose), Julian Sands, Marianne Faithfull.
Story: Faithful adaptation of the classic story about two children haunted by the ghosts of the previous caretakers.
Note: French-British co-production obviously inspired by Jack Clayton's 1961 *The Innocents*.

Tous les Dieux du Ciel [*All the Gods in the Sky*] (col., 98 min., 2019)
Dir/Wri: Quarxx.
Cast: Jean-Luc Couchard (Simon), Melanie Gaydos (Estelle), Thierry Frémont.
Story: Simon lives in an isolated farm with his sister Estelle, bedridden in a vegetative state…

Toute Une Vie [*A Whole Life*, transl. as *And Now My Love*] (col., 150 min., 1974)
Dir: Claude Lelouch; *Wri*: Claude Lelouch, Pierre Uytterhoeven.
Cast: Marthe Keller, André Dussolier, Charles Denner, Carla Gravina, Charles Gérard.
Story: This multi-generational family saga begins in 1918 and ends in the year 2000 when an expectant couple (Keller, Dussolier) must hide in order to escape compulsory abortion.

Traitement de Choc [*Shock Treatment*, transl. as *Doctor in the Nude*] (col., 91 min., 1972)
Dir/Wri: Alain Jessua.
Cast: Alain Delon (Dr. Devillers), Annie Girardot (Hélène), Michel Duchaussoy, Robert Hirsch, Jean-François Calvé.

Story: Dr. Devillers secretly uses organs harvested from his Portuguese workers to keep his rich clientele young. A patient, Hélène, discovers the truth and kills him.
Note: Alain Jessua also wrote the novelization of the film.

36-15 Code Père Noël [*SantaClaus.com*] (col., 90 min., 1989)
Dir/Wri: René Manzor.
Cast: Brigitte Fossey, Louis Ducreux, Alain Musy, Patrick Floersheim (Santa Claus), François-Eric Gendron.
Story: In a deserted house, a nine-year-old child fights a serial killer disguised as Santa Claus. The boy's grandfather eventually comes to his rescue.

Le Trésor des Îles Chiennes [*The Treasure of Dog Island*] (col., 115 min., 1989)
Dir/Wri: Frédéric-Jacques Ossang.
Cast: Stéphane Ferrara, Diogo Dória, Michel Albertini, Mapi Galán.
Story: An expedition is sent to the Dog Islands to find an engineer who has discovered a new form of energy.

Le Triangle de Mimizan [*The Mimizan Triangle*] (B&W., 16 min., 1981)
Dir/Wri: Florence Barnett, Jean-Louis Philippon.
Cast: The inhabitants of the town of Mimizan.
Story: Based on the real-life shipwreck of a tanker off the western coast of France, the filmmakers build a pseudo-documentary, where local inhabitants convincingly spin a yarn about an ancient curse.

Le Trio Infernal [*The Infernal Threesome*] (col., 110 min., 1974)
Dir: Francis Girod; *Wri*: Francis Girod, Jacques Rouffio, based on a novel by Solange Fasquelle.
Cast: Michel Piccoli (Georges), Romy Schneider (Philomène), Mascha Gomska (Catherine), Andréa Ferréol.

Story: In 1919, Georges, a lawyer, his mistress, Philomène, and her sister Catherine commit numerous murders to collect life insurance premiums.

Triples Introductions
See *Le Sexe Qui Parle*.

Les Trois Couronnes du Matelot [*The Three Crowns of the Sailor*] (B&W/Col., 117 min., 1982)
Dir: Raoul Ruiz; *Wri*: Raoul Ruiz, Emilio de Solar, François Ede.
Cast: Jean-Bernard Guillard, Philippe Deplanche, Jean Badin, Claude Derepp, Lisa Lyon, Frank Oger, Paule Brunet.
Story: For the price of three crowns, a sailor agrees to tell a student three horror tales.

Trois Vies et Une Seule Mort [*Three Lives and Only One Death*] (col., 123 min., 1996)
Dir: Raoul Ruiz; *Wri*: Raoul Ruiz, Pascal Bonitzer.
Cast: Marcello Mastroianni (Mateo Strano), Anna Galiena (Tania), Marisa Paredes (Maria), Melvil Poupaud, Chiara Mastroianni, Féodor Atkine, Arielle Dombasle, Jean-Yves Gautier, Jacques Pieiller, Pierre Bellemare, Roland Topor.
Story: Mateo lives in a bizarre apartment, speaks with fairies who stole his real life and has lived four different lives.

Le Troisième Cri [*The Third Scream*] (col., 90 min., 1973)
Dir/Wri: Igaal Niddam.
Cast: Jacques Denis, Myriam Mézières, Christine Fersen, Leyla Aubert.
Story: A dozen persons become trapped inside an anti-nuclear bunker.
Note: French-language Swiss production.

Trompe l'Oeil (col., 105 min., 1974)
Dir: Claude d'Anna; *Wri*: Claude d'Anna, Marie-France Bonin.

Cast: Max von Sydow, Laure Deschanel, Micheline Presle.
Story: A pregnant woman returns after having disappeared and without any memories of what happened to her. She and her husband are then stalked by a mysterious stranger. At the end, the woman flies away with a bird-man.

Le Tronc [*The Torso*] (col., 80 min., 1992)
Dir: Karl Zéro, Bernard Faroux; *Wri*: Karl Zéro.
Cast: Rose Thierry, Jean-Pol Dubois, Alexis Nitzer, Yvon Back, Stéphane Bignon.
Story: Allegorical comedy in which a man who has been made limbless by his lover (Thierry) undergoes a series of adventures before returning to his love.

Trop, C'est Trop [*Too Much Is Too Much*] (col., 90 min., 1974)
Dir/Wri: Didier Kaminka.
Cast: Didier Kaminka, Philippe Ogouz, Georges Beller, Claudia Wells, José-Luis de Villalonga.
Story: Three men born on the same day fall in love with a girl also born that day. After her death, they commit suicide and find themselves in Hell. There, Lucifer arranges for the girl to bear three boys and one girl identical to the protagonists.

Trouble Every Day (col., 105 min., 2001)
Dir: Claire Denis; *Wri*: Claire Denis, Jean-Pol Fargeau.
Cast: Vincent Gallo (Dr. Brown), Tricia Vessey (June Brown), Béatrice Dalle (Coré), Alex Descas (Dr. Sémeneau), Florence Loiret, Nicolas Duvauchelle, Raphaël Neal, José Garcia.
Story: An American couple, Dr. Brown and his wife June, go to Paris, to find neuroscientist Dr. Léo Sémeneau and his wife, Coré, a murderous maniac.

Le Tunnel [*The Tunnel*] (B&W., 80 min., 1933)
Dir: Kurt Bernhardt; *Wri*: Kurt Bernhardt, Reinhart Steinbicker, Alexandre Arnoux, based on the novel by Bernhardt Kellermann.

Cast: Jean Gabin (MacAllan), Madeleine Renaud (Mary), Edmond Van Daële, Robert Le Vigan.
Story: The engineer in charge of the construction of a transatlantic tunnel succeeds in his task, despite his wife's death at the hands of saboteurs.
Note: This is the French version of a multinational coproduction. Two other versions were shot simultaneously with different casts: a German version, *Der Tunnel*, also directed by Bernhardt, with Paul Hartmann, Olly von Flint, and Gustav Gründgens; and an English version, *Transatlantic Tunnel*, directed by Maurice Elvey, with Richard Dix, Leslie Banks, and Madge Evans (1935). Alexandre Arnoux (1884-1973) is a science fiction writer.

Tykho Moon (col., 107 min., 1997)
Dir: Enki Bilal; *Wri*: Enki Bilal, Dan Franck.
Cast: Julie Delpy, Michel Piccoli, Marie Laforêt, Richard Bohringer, Jean-Louis Trintignant, Johan Leysen.
Story: The leaders of a lunar colony which looks like Paris are the victims of a spreading cancer which turns their skins blue. The president (Piccoli) searches for the only man with the cure.

Ubac (col., 80 min., 1986)
Dir: Jean-Pierre Grasset; *Wri*: Pierre Chaussat, Michel Cyprien, Richard Bohringer, Jean-Pierre Grasset.
Cast: Richard Bohringer, Suzanna Borges, Pierre Malet, Larry Lamb, Rufus.
Story: At fifty-year intervals, a hunter (Lamb) and a pulp writer (Bohringer) are drawn to a mysterious lost valley inside the Amazon.

L'Unique [*The Only One*] (col., 90 min., 1985)
Dir: Jérôme Diamant-Berger; *Wri*: Jérôme Diamant-Berger, Olivier Assayas, Jean-Claude Carrière.
Cast: Julla Migenes-Johnson, Tchéky Karyo, Sami Frey, Charles Denner, Jezabel Carpi, Fabienne Babe, Thierry Rode.

Story: A music superstar (Migenes-Johnson) is replaced by a hologram designed by a mad scientist (Frey).

Valérian et la Cité des Mille Planètes [*Valerian and the City of a Thousand Planets*] (col., 137 mins., 2017)
Dir: Luc Besson; *Wri*: Luc Besson based on the comic book by Pierre Christin & Jean-Claude Mézières.
Cast: Dane DeHaan (Valérian), Cara Delevingne (Laureline), Clive Owen, Rihanna, Ethan Hawke, Herbie Hancock, Kris Wu, Rutger Hauer.
Story: Valerian and Laureline, two special operatives for the space station of Alpha, have to protect the city from an evil force that threatens not only its existence, but the future of the universe.

La Vampire Nue [*The Nude Vampire*] (col., 90 min., 1969)
Dir/Wri: Jean Rollin.
Cast: Olivier Martin, Caroline Cartier, Ly Letrong, Michel Delahaye, Maurice Lemaître, Bernard Musson, Jean Aron.
Story: A scientist (Martin) tries to discover the secret of the vampires' existence and eventually learns that they are mutants.

Le Vampire de Dusseldorf [*The Dusseldorf Vampire*] (B&W., 86 min., 1964)
Dir: Robert Hossein; *Wri*: Robert Hossein, Charles Dessailly.
Cast: Robert Hossein (Kurten), Marie-France Pisier.
Story: The story of a notorious German serial killer of the 1930s.

Les Vampires [*The Vampires*] (Serial, B&W., 10 eps., 1915)
1: *La Tête Coupée* [*The Cut-Off Head*]; 2: *La Bague qui Tue* [*The Killing Ring*]; 3: *Le Cryptogramme Rouge* [*The Red Cryptogram*]; 4: *Le Spectre*; 5: *L'Évasion du Mort* [*The Deadman's Escape*]; 6: *Les Yeux qui Fascinent* [*The Mesmerizing Eyes*]; 7: *Satanas*; 8: *Le Maître de la Foudre* [*The Light-*

ning Master]; 9: *L'Homme des Poisons* [*A Man of Poisons*]; 10: *Les Noces Sanglantes* [*The Bloody Wedding*].
Dir/Wri: Louis Feuillade.
Cast: Édouard Mathé (Philippe Guérande), Marcel Levesque (Oscar), Jean Aymé (Great Vampire), Musidora (Irma Vep), Fernand Herrmann (Moreno), Stacia Napierkowska (Marfa), Louis Leubas (Satanas), Frederik Moriss (Venenos).
Story: Philippe Guérance, a heroic journalist (Mathé), and hisd pal Oscar Mazamette, fight the sinister machinations of the Vampires gang, led by a series of evil masterminds: the Great Vampire, Moreno, Satanas, and Venenos, and their female accomplice, Irma Vep.

Un Vampire au Paradis [*A Vampire in Paradise*] (col., 100 min., 1990)
Dir/Wri: Abdelkrim Bahloul.
Cast: Farid Chopel (Nosfer), Bruno Crémer, Brigitte Fossey, Laure Marsac, Hélène Surgère, Abdel Kechiche, Jean-Claude Dreyfus, Saïd Amadis, Michel Peyrelon, Benoît Giros, Mathieu Poirier, Françoise Rigal.
Story: A young girl from a bourgeois family (Marsac) is bitten by Nosfer, a Muslim vampire, and begins to speak Arabic. After having located the vampire, who is accidentally shot, she and her family travel to North Africa where she meets a young Arab who suffers from the reverse curse.

Vera (B&W., 21 min, 1966)
Dir: Francis Morane; *Wri*: Francis Morane, Guy Breton, based on the story by Auguste de Villiers de L'Isle-Adam.
Cast: Madeleine Constant (Vera), Jean Signe (Roger).
Story: A disconcerted husband who has just lost his wife is going to find her again, in his dreams or in another reality.

La Vérité sur l'Imaginaire Passion d'un Inconnu [*The Truth About the Imaginary Passion of an Unknown Man*] (col., 85 min., 1973)
Dir/Wri: Marcel Hanoun.

Cast: Michel Morat, Anne Wiazemsky, Isabelle Weingarten, Michael Lonsdale.
Story: In the near future, a retarded girl finds an unknown man crucified like Christ. No one can discover the man's identity.

Vibroboy (col., 28 min., 1993)
Dir: Jan Kounen; *Wri*: Jan Kounen, Carlo de Boutiny.
Cast: Dominique Bettenfeld, Valérie Druguet, Michel Vuillermoz, Fabien Béhar.
Story: Semi-pornographic parody of super-hero films. A man is possessed by an Aztec warrior's spirit.

Vidocq (col., 98 min., 2001)
Dir: Pitof; *Wri*: Pitof, Jean-Christophe Grangé.
Cast: Gérard Depardieu (Vidocq), Guillaume Canet (Étienne), Moussa Maaskri, Inès Sastre, André Dussollier, Edith Scob.
Story: Paris, 1830. Just as he was about to apprehend an individual calling himself the Alchemist, detective Eugène-François Vidocq disappeared into the flaming shaft of a glass blower. A young provincial journalist, Étienne Boisset, takes over Vidocq's investigations. He then discovers that the latter was investigating a mysterious serial killer.

La Vie Amoureuse de l'Homme Invisible [*The Invisible Man's Love Life,* transl. as *Dr. Orloff and the Invisible Man*] (col., 86 min., 1971)
Dir/Wri: Pierre Chevalier.
Cast: Howard Vernon.
Story: X-rated film in which Prof. Orloff creates an amorous invisible monster. (It turns out to be an ape.)

Ma Vie Est Un Enfer [*My Life Is Hell*] (col., 106 min., 1991)
Dir: Josiane Balasko; *Wri*: Joël Houssin, Josiane Balasko.
Cast: Josiane Balasko (Leah), Daniel Auteuil (Abargadon), Richard Berry, Michael Lonsdale (Gabriel), Catherine Samie, Jean Benguigui, Luis Rego, Catherine Hiegel, Jessica Forde,

Max Vialle, Ticky Holgado, Bertrand Blier, Joël Houssin, Daniel Riche.
Story: Leah sells her soul to the demon Abargadon, but the archangel Gabriel turns Abargadon back into a mortal, who now neads Leah's help to escape eternal damnation.
Note: Joël Houssin is a science fiction writer.

La Vie Est Un Roman [*Life Is a Novel*, transl. as *Life Is a Bed of Roses*] (col., 111 min., 1983)
Dir: Alain Resnais; *Wri*: Jean Gruault.
Cast: Vittorio Gassman (Walter), Ruggero Raimondi (Forbek), Geraldine Chaplin, Fanny Ardant, Pierre Arditi, Sabine Azéma, André Dussollier, Robert Manuel, Martine Kelly.
Story: In the same castle, three stories interconnect: In 1919, Utopian Count Forbek attempts a psychic experiment; in 1982, a conference on imagination proves to be a failure; finally, children project themselves in a fairy tale land of adventure.
Note: This film features sets designed by Enki Bilal.

Une Vierge chez les Morts Vivants [*A Virgin Among the Living Dead*] (aka *Christina, Princesse de l'Erotisme* [*Christina, Princess of Erotism*]) (col., 90 min., 1971)
Dir/Wri: Jess Franco & Jean Rollin.
Cast: Christina von Blanc, Britt Nichols, Paul Muller, Anne Libert, Howard Vernon.
Story: Christina discovers that her aunt and uncle are zombies.

Vierges et Vampires [*Virgins and Vampires*, transl. as *Caged Virgins, Crazed Virgins, Dungeon of Horror*] (aka *Requiem pour un Vampire* [*Requiem for a Vampire*]) (col., 81 min., 1971)
Dir/Wri: Jean Rollin.
Cast: Marie-Pierre Castel, Mireille d'Argent, Philippe Gasté, Louise Dhour.
Story: A mildly erotic variation on the theme of vampire women.

Vif-Argent [*Quicksilver*] (col., 104 min., 2019)
Dir: Stéphane Batut; *Wri*: Stéphane Batut, Christine Dory, Frédéric Videau.
Cast: Thimotée Robart (Juste), Judith Chemla (Agathe).
Story: Juste has just died and a soul ferryman allows him to stay a little longer in order to collect his last memories. He meets Agathe who seems to recognize him.

Le Village des Ombres [*The Village of Shadows*] (col., 103 min., 2010)
Dir: Fouad Benhammou; *Wri*: Fouad Benhammou, Pascal Jaubert, Lionel Olenga.
Cast: Christa Theret, Barbara Goenaga, Cyrille Thouvenin.
Story: A group of friends spend a weekend in the village of Ruiflec. Once there, some mysteriously disappear. The others, while looking for their companions, try to stay alive and escape the grip of the Village of Shadows.

Vincent n'a pas d'écailles [*Vincent has no scales*] (col., 78 min., 2014)
Dir/Wri: Thomas Salvador.
Cast: Thomas Salvador (Vincent), Vimala Pons (Lucie), Youssef Hajdi.
Story: Vincent, a discreet young man, settles in a region of lakes and rivers. He meets Lucie, with whom he falls in love. Soon, he reveals his secret to her: an extraordinary power when he comes in contact with water.

Vingt Mille Lieues sous les Mers [*Twenty Thousand Leagues Under the Seas*] (B&W., 14 min.,1907).
Dir/Wri: Georges Méliès inspired by the novel from Jules Verne.
Story: The film is a comedic version of Verne's classic following a fisherman who dreams of traveling by submarine to the bottom of the ocean, where he encounters both realistic and fanciful sea creatures, including a chorus of naiads.

Vinyan (col., 96 mion., 2008)
Dir: Fabrice Du Welz; *Wri*: Fabrice Du Welz, David Greig, Oliver Blackburn.
Cast: Emmanuelle Béart, Rufus Sewell, Julie Dreyfus.
Story: In Phuket in 2005, Jeanne and Paul lost their son during the 2004 tsunami. Unable to accept his death, they remained to live there. One day, Jeanne thinks she sees the silhouette of her child on an amateur video. Paul is skeptical, but agrees to follow her deep into the jungle. Their journey leads them into a supernatural world populated by hostile children.

Le Viol du Vampire [*The Vampire's Rape*], followed by **La Reine des Vampires** [*The Queen of Vampires*] (B&W., 90 min., 1968)
Dir/Wri: Jean Rollin.
Cast: Solange Pradel, Ursule Pauly, Nicole Romain, Bernard Letrou, Catherine Deville, Marquis Polho, Jacqueline Sieger (Vampire Queen), Ariane Sapriel.
Story: A young man frees four women vampires and pays the price. After defeating a vampire cult, the young man and his wife, now turned into vampires, sacrifice their lives.
Note: First vampire movie directed by Rollin, in black-and-white with amateur actors.

Virtual Revolution (col., 92 min., 2016)
Dir/Wri: Guy-Roger Duvert.
Cast: Mike Dopud, Jane Badler, Jochen Hägele
Story: In 2047, almost the entire population of Paris has their minds permanently immersed in virtual worlds. A killer is employed to kill the rebels...

Le Visionarium – Un Voyage à travers le Temps [*A Journey Through Time*] (col., 18 min., 1992)
Dir/Conception: Jeff Blyth.
Cast: Michel Leep (voice of the Timekeeper), Myriam Boyer (voice of 9-Eyes), Michel Piccoli (Jules Verne), Jeremy Irons

(H G Wells), Gérard Depardieu, Franco Nero (Leonardo), Jean Rochefort (Louis XV), Nathalie Baye (Mme de Pompadour), Patrick Bauchau (Interpreter).

Story: Nine-Eye is sent through time by the Timekeeper, so that she can send back surrounding images as she records them in whichever era she finds herself.

Note: A Circle-Vision 360° film that was presented at three Disney parks around the world. It was the first Circle-Vision show that was arranged and filmed with an actual plot and not just visions of landscapes, and the first to utilize Audio-Animatronics. *Le Visionarium* marked the first time that the Circle-Vision film process was used to deliver a narrative story line.

Le Visiteur du Futur [*The Visitor from the Future*] (col., 102 min., 2022)
Dir/Wri: François Descraques
Cast: Florent Dorin (the Visitor), Arnaud Ducret (Gilbert), Enya Baroux (Alice), Raphaël Descraques, Slimane-Baptiste Berhoun, Mathieu Poggi, Audrey Pirault, Lénie Chérino, Simon Astier.
Story: Alice opposes the construction of a nuclear power plant initiated by her father, Gilbert. It is then that a strange Visitor takes them to 2555, a future devastated by the explosion of the power plant.

Les Visiteurs [*The Visitors*] (col., 102 min., 1994)
Dir: Jean-Marie Poiré; *Wri*: Jean-Marie Poiré, Christian Clavier.
Cast: Jean Reno (Godefroy), Christian Clavier, Valérie Lemercier, Marie-Anne Chazel, Isabelle Nanty, Christian Bujeau, Gérard Séty, Michel Peyrelon, Didier Pain.
Story: Godefroy, a medieval knight, and his squire (Clavier) are magically transported to the 20th century, where they meet Godefroy's descendant (Lemercier). Eventually, he returns to his own time, but the squire chooses to remain in the present.

Note: This comedic fantasy film was an enormous success at the French box office. A version was dubbed in English by Mel Brooks for release in the American market but not used.

Les Visiteurs 2 : Les Couloirs du Temps [*The Visitors 2: The Time Corridors*] (col., 118 min., 1997)
Dir: Jean-Marie Poiré; *Wri*: Jean-Marie Poiré, Christian Clavier.
Cast: Jean Reno (Godefroy), Christian Clavier, Marie-Anne Chazel, Muriel Robin.
Story: In order to get married, Gorefroy must return to the 20th century. Sequel to *Les Visiteurs*.

Les Visiteurs du Soir [*The Visitors at Dusk*, transl. as *The Devil's Envoys*] (B&W., 123 min., 1942)
Dir: Marcel Carné; *Wri*: Jacques Prévert, Pierre Laroche.
Cast: Jules Berry (The Devil), Arletty (Dominique), Alain Cuny (Gilles), Marie Déa, Marcel Herrand, Fernand Ledoux, Simone Signoret.
Story: The Devil sends Gilles and Dominique, two minstrels, to spread despair among mankind. However, Gilles falls in love with a local baron's daughter (Déa). Buy nothing the Devil does can break that love.

Les Visiteuses [*The Female Visitors*] (col., 90 min., 2014)
Dir/Wri: Alain Payet.
Cast: Roberto Malone, Alain L'Yle, Élodie Chérie, Christophe Clark, Tabatha Cash.
Story: X-rated pastiche of *Les Visiteurs*.

Viva la Vie [*Hurray for Life*] (col., 110 min., 1984)
Dir/Wri: Claude Lelouch.
Cast: Michel Piccoli, Charlotte Rampling, Jean-Louis Trintignant, Évelyne Bouix, Raymond Pellegrin, Charles Gérard, Laurent Malet.

Story: Two UFO abductees (Piccoli, Bouix) return with a message of peace for mankind. In reality, it seems to have been an elaborate hoax, or possibly a dream.

La Voie Lactée [*The Milky Way*] (col., 92 Min, 1969)
Dir: Luis Buñuel; *Wri*: Luis Buñuel, Jean-Claude Carrière.
Cast: Paul Frankeur, Laurent Terzieff, Alain Cuny, Édith Scob (Marie), Bernard Verley (Jesus), Michel Piccoli (Marquis de Sade), Julien Bertheau, Georges Marchal, Jean Piat, Delphine Seyrig.
Story: On their way to Compostelle, two modern-day pilgrims have visions and meet historical figures (Jesus, the Marquis de Sade, etc.).

La Volupté de l'Horreur [*Voluptuous Horror*]
See **Perversions Sexuelles**.

La Vouivre (col., 102 min., 1988)
Dir/Wri: George Wilson, based on the story by Marcel Aymé.
Cast: Lambert Wilson (Arsène), Laurence Treil (La Vouivre), Jean Carmet, Suzanne Flon (Louise), Jacques Dufilho, Macha Méril, Kathie Kriegel, Jean-Jacques Moreau, Paola Lanzi.
Story: A young soldier back from World War I falls under the deadly spell of a mysterious spirit woman who lives in the swamps of his homeland.

Le Voyage Imaginaire [*The Imaginary Journey*] (B&W., 20 min., 1925)
Dir/Wri: René Clair.
Cast: Jean Borlin, Albert Préjean, Jim Gérald, Paul Ollivier, Dolly Davis.
Story: A bank employee falls asleep and has adventures in the land of dreams.

Le Voyage à travers l'Impossible [*The Impossible Journey*] (B&W., 24 min., 1904)
Dir/Wri: Georges Méliès.

Cast: Georges Méliès, Manuel Delpierre, Fernande Albany, Victor André.
Story: The members of the Incoherent Geographic Society travel toward the Sun aboard an interplanetary train.

Le Voyage dans la Lune [*A Trip to the Moon*] (B&W., 14 min., 1902)
Dir/Wri: Georges Méliès, inspired by the novel by Jules Verne.
Cast: Georges Méliès, Bleuette Bernon, Victor André, Henri Delannoy.
Story: The Astronauts' Club sends a rocket to the Moon, where its passengers are imprisoned by the Selenites before escaping and returning to Earth.

Week-End (col., 95 min., 1967)
Dir/Wri: Jean-Luc Godard.
Cast: Jean Yanne, Mireille Darc, Jean-Pierre Kalfon, Jean-Pierre Léaud, Yves Beneyton, Paul Gégauff, Yves Alfonso.
Story: A Parisian couple go to the country for the weekend; they pass dozens of dead bodies in car wrecks; they meet Emily Brontë and Cagliostro. Later, they are captured by anarchists, whom the wife joins. They kill and eat her husband.

What A Flash (col., 95 min., 1971)
Dir/Wri: Jean-Michel Barjol.
Cast: Maria Vincent, Bernadette Lafont, Vanina Michel, Catherine Lachens, Jean-Pierre Lombard, Jean-Claude Dauphin, Serge Marquand, Pierre Vassiliu.
Story: A dozen people are trapped aboard a spaceship.

Les Yeux sans Visage [*Eyes Without a Face*, transl. as *The Horror Chamber of Dr. Faustus*] (B&W., 88 min., 1959)
Dir: Georges Franju; *Wri*: Pierre Boileau & Thomas Narcejac, Jean Redon, Claude Sauter, based on the novel by Jean Redon.

Cast: Pierre Brasseur (Dr. Genessier), Edith Scob (Christiane), Alida Valli (Louise), Juliette Mayniel, Béatrice Altariba, Claude Brasseur, François Guérin, Alexandre Rignault.

Story: Dr. Genessier, a corrupt surgeon, responsible for the accident which disfigured his daughter Christiane, attempts to graft other girls' faces onto hers, but fails. She revolts, goes insane and kills her father.

Note: Jean Redon is a thriller writer. His novel was published in 1959 by Fleuve Noir's *Angoisse* imprint. The same story was the uncredited basis for Jess Franco's *L'Horrible Dr. Orloff*, *Les Prédateurs de la Nuit* and *La Rose Écorchée*.

Zéro Un (2003)
Anthology film of ten short features produced by Luc Besson.

1. *Au suivant!* [*Next !*]
Dir/Wri: Jeanne Biras.
Cast: Juliette Duval, Patrick Ligardes, Isabelle Nanty.

2. *Silver Moumoute*
Dir: Christophe Campos; *Wri*: Gildas Keraly.
Cast: Jean Dell, Zinedine Soualem.

3. *Offside*
Dir/Wri: Leanna Creel.
Cast: Sam McConkey.

4. *Arrêt d'Urgence* [*Emergency Stop*]
Dir: Jean-Jacques Dumonceau; *Wri*: Thierry Ardiller.
Cast: Caroline Beaune, Bruno Solo.

5. *Pourkoi... passkeu* [*Why... Because*]
Dir: Gilles Lellouche; *Wri*: Tristan Aurouet.
Cast: Léa Drucker, Gilles Lellouche.

6. *Carcan* [*Cast*]
Dir/Wri: Stéphane Levallois.
Cast: Delphine Delambre, Tatiana Korsakova.

7. *Chickendales*
Dir/Wri: Niko Meulemans, Adriaan Van den Hoof.
Cast: Agnès Guignard.

8. *The Same*
Dir/Wri: Mark Palansky
Cast: Jason Wee Man Acuña, Josh Hartnett, Jacqui Maxwell.

9. *The Freak*
Dir/Wri: Aristomenis Tsirbas.

10. *Aujourd'hui madame* [*Today, Madame*]
Dir/Wri: César Vayssié.
Cast: Patrick Fontana, Zoé Félix, Fabyenne Llorens.

Zombi Child (col., 103 min., 2019)
Dir/Wri: Bertrand Bonello.
Cast: Wislanda Louimat (Melissa), Louise Labèque (Fanny), Mackenson Bijou (Clairvius), Nehémy Pierre-Dahomey (Baron Samedi), Katiana Milfort).
Story: In 1962, Clairvius, a Haitian man, is buried alive by white colonists, only to be brought back as an undead zombi slave. 55 years later, a teenage girl Fanny makes friends with Mélissa, who moved from Haiti to France after the 2010 earthquake. After it is revealed that Mélissa's family is associated with voodoo, Fanny convinces Mélissa's aunt, a mambo, to perform a ritual in order to cure Fanny's heartbreak over a recent breakup. The ritual goes awry, however, leaving Fanny possessed by Baron Samedi himself.
Note: The film is inspired by the life of Clairvius Narcisse, a drug-addicted Haitian who supposedly wandered as a zombie and a slave after being declared dead in 1962. This case was already treated in Wes Craven's *The Serpent and the Rainbow.*

Zoo Zéro (col., 95 min., 1978)

Dir/Wri: Alain Fleischer.
Cast: Catherine Jourdan (Eva), Klaus Kinski (Yavé), Alida Valli (Yvonne), Pierre Clémenti, Rufus, Christine Chappey, Lisette Malidor.
Story: In a devastated city, Eva, a singer, reaches a zoo owned by her father Yavé, and frees the animals which take over from Man.

List of Films

We have indicated in **bold** the titles that are of special importance.

2019 Après la Chute de New York
À la Conquête du Pôle
À ton image
L'Abîme des Morts-Vivants
Ada dans la Jungle
ADN, l'Âme de la Terre
Adrénaline - Le Film
L'Affaire des Divisions Morituri
After Blue (Paradis sale)
L'Age d'Or
Aimez-Vous les Femmes ?
Aladin ou la Lampe merveilleuse
Alerte au Sud
Ali Baba et les Quarante Voleurs
Alice, ou La Dernière Fugue
Alice chez les Satyres
Alien Crystal Palace
L'Alliance
Alone
Alphaville
Les Amazones du Temple d'Or
L'Amour à Mort
Un Amour de Poche
Un Amour de Sorcière
L'Ampélopède
L'An 01
L'Âne Qui A Bu La Lune
L'Ange
L'Ange et la Femme
Angel-A
Les Anges Gardiens
L'Angle Mort
Animal
Anna Oz
L'Année Dernière à Marienbad
Les Années Lumière
À Nous la Liberté !
À Pied, à Cheval et en Spoutnik
Aquariens
L'Araignée d'Eau
L'Arbre Sous La Mer
Arako
Les Arcanes du Jeu
L'Arche de Noé
Les Ardentes
Arès
Armaguedon
Arsène Lupin
Atarrabi et Mikelats
L'Atlantide

Atomik Circus
Attack of Serial Killers from Outer Space
Au Coeur de la Vie
Au-delà du sang
Au Rendez-Vous de la Mort Joyeuse
Au Service du Diable
L'Autre Sang
L'Autre Vie de Richard Kemp
L'Avant-Dernier
Les Aventures d'Eddie Turley
Les Aventures Extraordinaires d'Adèle Blanc-Sec
L'Avion
Babel
Baby Blood
Babylon A.D.
Balaoo, ou Des Pas Au Plafond
Le Bal des Folles
Ballade de la Féconductrice
Le Ballon Sorcier
Banlieue 13
Banlieue 13 : Ultimatum
Barbarella
Barbe-Bleue
Barbe-Bleue
Le Baron Fantôme
Baxter
La Beauté du Diable
Belle
La Belle et la Bête
La Belle et la Bête

La Belle Captive
La Belle Histoire
La Belle Image
Les Belles de Nuit
Belphegor
Belphégor, le Fantôme du Louvre
La Bête
Bien Profond dans ton Âme
Big Bug
Black Moon
Une Blonde Comme Ça
Blondie Maxwell Ne Perd Jamais
Blondine
Blood Machines
Blueberry, L'Expérience Secrète
Le Boucher
Boulevard de l'Étrange
Buffet Froid
Le Bunker de la Dernière Rafale
Bunker Palace Hotel
La Cage
Calmos
Camille redouble
Cartes sur Table
Cauchemar Blanc
La Cavalcade des Heures
Le Cerf-Volant du Bout du Monde
C'est Arrivé Près De Chez Vous
La Chambre Ardente
La Chambre Verte

Les Charlots contre Dracula
Le Charme Discret de la Bourgeoisie
La Charrette Fantôme
La Chasse au Nuage
Le Château de la Dernière Chance
Le Château des Messes Noires
Le Château de la Mort Lente
Le Château du Passé
Le Château du Vice
Le Chemin d'Azatoth
Les Chemins de la Violence
Cherchez l'Erreur
Chéri-Bibi
Le Chevalier de la Nuit
Les Chevaliers de la Table Ronde
La Chevelure
Les Chiens
Les Chinois à Paris
Christina, Princesse de l'Erotisme
Chrysalis
La Chute de la Maison Usher
Le Ciel sur la Tête
Le Cinquième Élément
La Cité des Enfants Perdus
La Cité Foudroyée
La Cité de l'Indicible Peur
La Cité de la Peur
Clash
Clérambard
Club Extinction
Coeur de Coq
Coincidences
Coma
Le Coma des Mortels
Combat contre l'amour en songe
Comédie de l'Innocence
La Comète
Comment je suis devenu super-héros
La Comtesse Noire
La Concentration
Le Concile de Pierre
Confessions d'un Barjo
Coplan FX-18
    Action Immédiate
    Coplan, Agent Secret FX-18
    Coplan prend des risques
    Coplan FX-18 Casse Tout
    Coplan Ouvre le Feu à Mexico
    Coplan Sauve Sa Peau
Cosmodrama
Les Couleurs du Diable
Coup de Jeune
Le Couple Idéal
Les Créatures
Le Cri du Hibou
Du Crime Considéré Comme Un Des Beaux Arts

Le Crime du Dr. Chardin
Croisières Sidérales
Crying Freeman
La Dame de Pique
Le Danger vient de l'Espace
Dans la Brume
Dans les Griffes du Maniaque
Dans le Ventre du Dragon
Dante 01
Dead Shadows
Le Déclic
Delicatessen
Demain la Veille
Demain les Mômes
Le Démon dans l'Île
Les Démoniaques
Les Démons
Le Dernier Chaperon Rouge
Le Dernier Combat
Le Dernier Homme
Le Dernier Voyage
La Dernière Vie de Simon
Les Derniers Jours
Les Derniers Jours du Monde
Les Deux Mondes
Les Deux Orphelines Vampires
Deux Vierges pour Satan
Devil Story
Le Diable et les Dix Commandements
Les Diablesses
Les Diaboliques

Didier
Diesel
Dinosaurs from the Deep
Dites-le avec des Fleurs
Djinns
Docteur Jekyll et les Femmes
Docteur M
Docteur Petiot
Documents Interdits
Documents Secrets
Le Don d'Adèle
Don't Grow Up
Dora, ou La Lanterne Magique
Dracula Père et Fils
Duelle
Dying God
L'Éclaireur
Eclipse sur un Ancien Chemin vers Compostelle
Écoute Voir
L'Écume des Jours
L'Éden et Après
Eden Log
Elle Voit Des Nains Partout
En êtes-vous bien sûr ?
Les Enfants
L'Ennemi sans Visage
Entr'acte
Un Escargot dans la Tête
L'Eternel Retour
...Et Mourir de Plaisir
L'Étrange Fiancée
L'Étrangleur

L'Éveillé du Pont de l'Alma [
L'Évènement Le Plus Important Depuis Que l'Homme A Marché Sur La Lune
Évolution
Exit
Exorcisme
Exorcisme et Messes Noires
Les Expériences Érotiques de Frankenstein
Expériences Sexuelles au Château des Jouisseuses
Extinction
Extraneus
L'Extraterrestre
Faeryland
Fahrenheit 451
Fantômas
    Fantômas
    Juve Contre Fantômas
    Le Mort Qui Tue
    Fantômas contre Fantômas
    Le Faux Magistrat Fantômas
    Mr. Fantômas
    Fantômas
    Fantômas contre Fantômas
    Fantômas
    Fantômas Se Déchaîne
    Fantômas contre Scotland Yard
Le Fantôme de la Liberté
Le Fantôme de Longstaff
Le Fantôme du Moulin-Rouge
Fascination
Le Faucheur
La Femme aux Bottes Rouges
La Femme Objet
La Fiancée de Dracula
La Fiancée des Ténèbres
Fifi la Plume
Figures de cire
Filles Traquées
La Fin du Monde
La Folie du Dr. Tube
La Forêt Désenchantée
Le Fou du Labo 4
France, Société Anonyme
François 1er
Frankenstein 90
Frankenstein: La Véritable Histoire
Les Frenchmen, les Premiers Super-Héros français
Les Frères Pétard
Le Frisson des Vampires
Futur Antérieur
Le Futur aux Trousses
Galaxie
Les Garçons Sauvages
Garou-Garou, Le Passe-Muraille
Les Gaspards
Gawin
Le Gendarme et les Extra-Terrestres

Généalogies d'un Crime
Giorgino
Glissements Progressifs du Plaisir
Goal of the Dead
Le Golem
Golem, L'Esprit de l'Exil
Goto, L'Île d'Amour
La Goulve
Les Gourmandes du Sexe
Le Gout du Sang
Grand Guignol
Le Grand Tout
La Grande Frousse
La Grande Trouille
Grave
Le Grimoire d'Arkandias
La Guerre du Feu
Les Gueux au Paradis
Gwendoline
Hélas Pour Moi
Hémophilia
Hibernatus
High Life
Histoire de Chanter
Histoires Abominables
Histoires Extraordinaires
Holy Motors
Home Sweet Home
Homicide By Night
L'Homme au Cerveau Greffé
L'Homme à l'Oreille Cassée
L'Homme qui Revient de Loin
L'Homme qui Revient de Loin
L'Homme Qui Vendit Son Âme au Diable
L'Homme Qui Vendit Son Âme
Les Hommes Veulent Vivre !
La Horde
L'Horrible Dr. Orloff
Horsehead
Hostile
House of Time
House of VHS [
Huis Clos
Hu-Man
L'Ibis Rouge
I.F.1 Ne Répond Plus
Il Etait Une Fois Le Diable
L'Île d'Épouvante
L'Île de la Mort
L'Île Mystérieuse
Ils
Ils Sont Fous, Ces Sorciers
Ils Sont Grands, Ces Petits
L'Imprécateur
L'Inconnu de Shandigor
L'Invité de la 11ème Heure
It Was on Earth That I Knew Joy
IXE-13
J'accuse
J'ai Rencontré le Père Noël

James Bande 00 Sexe
Le Jardinier
Je Ne Sais Pas
Jessica Forever
Je t'aime, Je t'aime
La Jetée
Des Jeunes Gens Modernes
Les Jeux de la Comtesse Dolingen de Gratz
Les Jeux Sont Faits
Je Vous Salue Marie
J'irai comme un cheval fou
Jos Carbone
Le Joueur d'Échecs
Le Joueur de Flûte
Le Joueur de Quilles
Le Jour de la Comète
Judex
Juliette, ou La Clé des Songes
Kaamelott - Premier Volet
Kamikaze
Kandisha
Le Lac des Morts-Vivants
Lady Blood
Landru
Léonor
Lèvres de Sang
Les Lèvres Rouges
Libra
Les Liens de Sang
Liliom
Le Lit de la Vierge
Litan
Livide

Le Locataire
Lorna l'Exorciste
Le Loup-Garou
Le Loup des Malveneur
Lucy
La Lune dans le Caniveau
La Machine
La Machine à Découdre
Madame Hyde
Ma Femme est une Panthère
Le Magnifique
La Main
La Main du Diable
Les Mains d'Orlac
Le Maître du Temps
Les Maîtres du Soleil
La Malédiction de Belphegor
Maléfique
Malevil
Malpertuis
Mama Dracula
Le Mangeur de Lune
Manika, Une Vie Plus Tard
Le Manoir du Diable
Marguerite de la Nuit
Marianne de ma Jeunesse
Marie-Chantal contre Dr. Kha
Le Martien de Noël
Un Martien à Paris
Le Masque de la Méduse
Matusalem
Méandre
La Mémoire Courte

La Merveilleuse Visite
La Meute
Midi-Minuit
Les Mille et Une Nuits
Les Mille Merveilles de l'Univers
Le Miracle des Loups
Le Miraculé
Mirages
Le Miroir
Miss Shumay Jette un Sort
Mister Freedom
Mister Frost
Le Moine
Le Moine et la Sorcière
Les Moineaux de Paris
Le Monde Tremblera
Le Monde Vivant
Monsieur Leguignon, Guérisseur
Le Monstre aux Yeux Verts
La Montagne aux Mille Regards
Morgane et ses Nymphes
Mort à l'Écran
La Mort en Direct
Une Mort sans Importance
La Mort Trouble
La Mort de l'Utopie
La Morte-Vivante
Mr. Nobody
Mutants
Les Mystères de Paris
La Naissance de Narcisse
Narayana
Nature Morte avec des Oranges
Le Navire Aveugle
Ne le Criez pas sur les Toits
Necronomicon
Ne Jouez Pas Avec Les Martiens
Némo
9 doigts
La Neuvième Porte
Névrose
New Age
Ni le Ciel ni la Terre
Night of Vampyrmania
Les Noces Rouges
Notre Histoire
Nuage
Le Nuage Atomique
La Nuée
La Nuit du Cimetière
La Nuit a dévoré le Monde
La Nuit Fantastique
La Nuit des Horloges
La Nuit de la Mort
La Nuit des Pétrifiés
La Nuit s'achève
La Nuit Tous Les Chats Sont Gris
La Nuit des Traquées
Nuits Rouges
Obsession
L'Oeil du Malin
L'Oeil Qui Ment
Ogre
L'Oiseau de Paradis

On A Volé Charlie Spencer !
Ophelia
Oppressions
L'Or
L'Ordinateur des Pompes Funèbres
L'Or et le Plomb
Les Orgies du Comte Porno
Orphée
OSS 117
   OSS 117 n'est pas mort
   Le Bal des espions
   OSS 117 Se Déchaîne
   Banco à Bangkok pour OSS 117
   Furia à Bahia pour OSS 117
   Atout Coeur à Tokyo pour OSS 117
   Cinq Gars pour Singapour
   Le Vicomte Règle ses Comptes
   Pas de Roses pour OSS 117
   OSS 117 prend des Vacances
   OSS 117 tue le taon
   Le Caire, Nid d'Espions
   Rio Ne Répond Plus
   Alerte Rouge en Afrique Noire
Out Un: Spectre

Oxygène
Le Pacte des Loups
Le Pain Quotidien
Panique
La Papesse
Papy fait de la Résistance
Paradis pour Tous
Paradisio
Parano
Paris n'existe pas
Paris Qui Dort
Parking
La Particule Humaine
Les Particules
Pas De Linceul Pour Billy Brakko
Pas Question le Samedi
Le Passage
Le Passe-Muraille
Le Pays sans Étoiles
Peau d'Âne
La Pension
Perceval le Gallois
Perdues dans New York
Le Péril Rampant
Personal Shopper
Perversions Sexuelles
Le Petit Nuage
Le Petit Poucet
La Petite Bande
Petite Maman
La Petite Marchande d'Allumettes
Les Petites Jouisseuses
Les Petites Saintes y touchent
Peut-être

La Plus Longue Nuit du Diable
Le Plus Vieux Métier du Monde
Le Pont du Nord
Les Portes de la Nuit
Le Portrait de Dorian Gray
Les Possédés du Diable
Possession
La Possibilité d'une Île
La Poupée
La Poupée Rouge
Les Prédateurs de la Nuit
Le Prix du Danger
Le Professeur Raspoutine
Providence
Proxima
Quartier Lointain
4 h 44 Dernier jour sur Terre
Queen Lear
Les Raisins de la Mort
Rapa-Nui
Le Rat Noir d'Amérique
Rayés des Vivants
Realive
Le Récit de Rebecca
Régime Sans Pain
Rei-Dom, ou La Légende des Kreuls
La Reine de Nacre
La Reine des Vampires
Rencontre avec le Dragon
Rendez-Moi Ma Peau
Rendez-Vous à Bray
Le Rendez-Vous en Forêt
Rendez-Vous Hier
Requiem pour un Vampire
Réseau Particulier
La Revanche des Mortes Vivantes
Les Revenants
Ricky
Roboflash Warrior
Rocambole
Rogopag
The Room
Le Rose et le Blanc
La Rose Écorchée
La Rose de Fer
Le Rouge de Chine
Rouletabille
    Le Mystère de la Chambre Jaune
    Le Parfum de la Dame en Noir
    Rouletabille chez les Bohémiens
    Le Mystère de la Chambre Jaune
    Le Parfum de la Dame en Noir
    Rouletabille Aviateur
    Rouletabille Joue et Gagne
    Rouletabille contre la Dame de Pique
    Le Mystère de la Chambre Jaune
    Le Parfum de la Dame en Noir
    Le Mystère de la Chambre Jaune

Le Mystère de la Chambre Jaune
Le Parfum de la Dame en Noir
Rubber
Le Sadique aux Dents Rouges
Saint Ange
Les Saisons du Plaisir
Salammbo
San Antonio ne pense qu'à ça
Le Sang des Autres
Le Sang d'un Poète
Scheherazade
Le Secret de la Momie
Le Secret de Sarah Tombelaine
Les Secrets Professionnels du Docteur Apfelgluck
Les Seigneurs d'Outre Monde
La Sentinelle
Les Sept Péchés Capitaux
La Septième Dimension
La Septième Porte
Sérail
Le Seuil du Vide
Seuls
Le Sexe Qui Parle
Sexorcismes
Signé Furax
Si J'Avais Mille Ans
Si J'Étais Toi
Si Jeunesse Savait
Si le Soleil Ne Revenait Pas
Silver Slime
Siméon
Simon les Nuages
Simple Mortel
Une Sirène à Paris
Un Soir, Par Hasard
Un Soir, Un Train
Les Soleils de l'Île de Pâques
La Sorcière
Soudain le Vide
La Soupe aux Choux
Sous le Soleil de Satan
Spermula
Star Suburb: La Banlieue des Étoiles
Stress
Subtil Concept
Le Suicide de Frank Einstein
Suivez Mon Regard
Superlove
Supernova (Expérience #1)
La Surface Perdue
Sur La Terre Comme Au Ciel
Sursis pour un Vivant
Sybille
Sylvie et le Fantôme
Le Syndrome de l'Espion
Le Temps de Mourir
Tendre Dracula
La Tendre Ennemie
La Tentation de Barbizon
Terminus
Terreur

Le Testament du Dr. Cordelier
Le Testament d'Orphée
Tête à Tête
Thank You, Satan
Themroc
Time Demon
Tintin
    Tintin et le Mystère de la Toison d'Or
    Tintin et les Oranges Bleues
Titane
Tom et Lola
Torticola contre Frankensberg
Le Toubib
Le Tour d'Écrou
Toute Une Vie
Tous les Dieux du Ciel
Traitement de Choc
36-15 Code Père Noël
Le Trésor des Îles Chiennes
Le Triangle de Mimizan
Le Trio Infernal
Triples Introductions
Les Trois Couronnes du Matelot
Trois Vies et Une Seule Mort
Le Troisième Cri
Trompe l'Oeil
Le Tronc
Trop, C'est Trop
Trouble Every Day
Le Tunnel

Tykho Moon
Ubac
L'Unique
Valérian et la Cité des Mille Planètes
La Vampire Nue
Le Vampire de Dusseldorf
Les Vampires
Un Vampire au Paradis
Vera
La Vérité sur l'Imaginaire Passion d'un Inconnu
Vibroboy
Vidocq
La Vie Amoureuse de l'Homme Invisible
Ma Vie Est Un Enfer
La Vie Est Un Roman
Une Vierge chez les Morts Vivants
Vierges et Vampires
Vif-Argent
Le Village des Ombres
Vincent n'a pas d'écailles
Vingt Mille Lieues sous les Mers
Vinyan
Le Viol du Vampire
Virtual Revolution
Le Visionarium
Le Visiteur du Futur
Les Visiteurs
Les Visiteurs 2 : Les Couloirs du Temps
Les Visiteurs du Soir
Les Visiteuses
Viva la Vie

La Voie Lactée
La Volupté de l'Horreur
La Vouivre
Le Voyage Imaginaire
Le Voyage à travers l'Impossible
Le Voyage dans la Lune

Week-End
What A Flash
Les Yeux sans Visage
Zéro Un
Zombi Child
Zoo Zéro

Index

Abascal, Margot, 180
Abbey, John, 151
Abelanski, Lionel, 92
Abitbol, Adeline, 178
Abitbol, Funny, 178
Abossolo M'Bo, Émile, 68
About, Edmond, 122
Abril, Victoria, 36, 141
Achard, Marcel, 99
Acosta, Juana, 53
Acuña, Jason Wee Man, 233
Adam, Alfred, 211
Addams, Dawn, 211
Adelin, Louis, 52
Adjani, Isabelle, 92, 139, 183
Adrien, Gilles, 66, 76
Adrien, Yves, 132
Aeton, Jimmy-Léonar, 177
Afkir, Walid, 136
Afonso, Yves, 193
Agarman, Pit, 162
Aguire, José-Louis, 155
Aguttes, Florence, 65
Aimée, Anouk, 207
Aisner, Henri, 197
Aithnard, Alain, 37
Aja, Alexandre, 172
Alane, Bernard, 118

Albany, Fernande, 231
Albers, Hans, 126, 166
Albers, Jean, 187
Albertazzi, Giorgio, 45
Alberti, Guido, 39
Albertini, Michel, 218
Albin, Valentine, 103
Alcée, Gisèle, 78
Aldebert, Patrick, 191
Alerme, André, 48, 117
Alessandrin, Patrick, 57
Alexander, Curt, 212
Alexander, David, 91
Alexander, Olly, 207
Alexandre, Patrice, 183
Alexandrov, Constantin, 60
Alfa, Michèle, 123
Alfieri, Éric, 188
Alfonso, Yves, 110, 231
Allain, Marcel, 14, 104
Allan, Richard, 107
Allard, André, 207
Allard, Antoine, 179
Allard, Nelly, 214
Allégret, Marc, 100
Allen, Karen, 213
Allen, Woody, 209
Alone, René, 41
Alpha, Jenny, 200
Alric, Catherine, 77
Altan, Francesco, 36

Altaraz, Mathilde, 188
Altariba, Béatrice, 232
Alvarez, Germinal, 54
Alvaro, Anne, 188
Alvina, Anicée, 114, 120
Amadis, Saïd, 223
Amalric, Mathieu, 54, 90, 172
Amat, Jorge, 155
Amédée, 42
Ameline, Maud, 67
Amidei, Sergio, 169
Amidou, Souad, 104
Amiot, Paul, 164
Amont, Marcel, 144
Amstutz, Roland, 180
Anconina, Richard, 78
Andersen, Hans Christian, 180
Andersson, Annie, 169
André, Marcel, 59
André, Victor, 231
Andréa, Pat, 84
Andreu, Gaby, 117
Andriot, Josette, 72
Andriot, Lucien, 27
Anémone, 60, 83, 117
Angel, Hélène, 189, 210
Angèle, Olivier, 188
Angeli, Pier, 169
Angelo, Jean, 51
Anger, Cédric, 80
Anglade, Jean-Hugues, 54, 113
Anna, Claude d', 155, 219
Annabella, 123

Annaud, Jean-Jacques, 16, 117
Anouilh, Jean, 73
Antoine, André-Paul, 58, 114, 192, 212
Appere, Caroline, 208
Aptekman, Igor, 111
Arbillot, Pascale, 103
Arbona, Gilles, 188
Arcand, Diane, 129
Archainbaud, George, 27
Ardant, Fanny, 42, 74, 225
Ardiller, Thierry, 232
Ardisson, Edmond, 40
Arditi, Pierre, 42, 98, 187, 197, 209, 225
Arditi, Rachel, 180
Arena, Samuel, 96
Arestrup, Niels, 88, 119
Argent, Mireille d', 225
Arlaud, Swann, 161
Arletty, 125, 229
Arly, Jacqueline, 73
Armand, Jean-Pierre, 190
Armandy, André, 187
Armanet, François, 125
Armontel, Roland, 62, 192
Arnac, Béatrice, 149
Arnaud, Magali, 43
Arnault, Yves, 134
Arne, Peter, 185
Arnold, Marcelle, 112, 135
Arnoul, Françoise, 91, 168
Arnoux, Alexandre, 51, 220, 221

Arnoux, Robert, 58, 85, 192
Aron, Jean, 222
Arout, Gabriel, 128, 146
Arpé, Jacqueline, 105
Arrabal, Fernando, 133
Artaud, Antonin, 11, 12, 138
Arthuys, Bertrand, 216
Arthuys, Sophie, 216
Asbæk, Plou, 140
Ashworth, Brittany, 125
Aslan, Coco, 98
Aslan, Grégoire, 39, 73
Assal, Anita, 36, 38, 174
Assayas, Olivier, 178, 221
Assche, Laura d', 158
Astier, Alexandre, 136
Astier, Lionnel, 136
Astier, Simon, 228
Astor, Junie, 60, 129
Athanassiadis, Nikos, 47
Atika, Aure, 171
Atkine, Féodor, 101, 150, 152, 219
Atrakchi, David, 125
Attal, Douglas, 80
Attal, Yvan, 68
Atterand, Pierre, 109
Aubert, Leyla, 219
Aublanc, Jean-Jacques, 143
Aubry, Cécile, 58
Auclair, Michel, 59, 216
Auclerc, Florie, 125
Audiard, Jacques, 59, 81
Audiard, Michel, 91, 112
Audiberti, Jacques, 184
Audouard, Yvan, 81
Audran, Stéphane, 64, 70, 137, 138, 146, 147, 161, 165, 173, 184, 198, 209, 217
Audry, Jacqueline, 125
Auer, Misha, 46
Augier, Albert, 120
Aumont, Jean-Pierre, 73, 114, 122, 152
Aumont, Michel, 111
Aumont, Tina, 91
Aurenche, Jean, 202, 211
Auric, Georges, 99
Aurouet, Tristan, 232
Aussey, Germaine, 114, 196
Autant-Lara, Claude, 146, 211
Autant-Lara, Ghislaine, 146
Auteuil, Daniel, 189, 224
Autexier, Hugues, 134
Aveline, Dominique, 115
Avron, Philippe, 108
Aymé, Jean, 191, 223
Aymé, Marcel, 60, 78, 112, 230
Azabal, Lubna, 175
Azaïs, Kévin, 161
Azaïs, Paul, 78
Azéma, Sabine, 42, 197, 225
Azencot, Martine, 181
Aznavour, Charles, 91, 214

Azzopardi, Gilles, 47
Babe, Fabienne, 115, 221
Babilée, Jean, 96
Bach, Simone, 85
Bachelier, Armand, 179
Bachir, Hafida, 191
Back, Yvon, 220
Bacri, Jean-Pierre, 92
Badesco, Sylvia, 119
Badia, Lise, 181
Badin, Jean, 219
Badler, Jane, 227
Bahloul, Abdelkrim, 223
Bahon, Gilbert, 110
Bailargeon, Paule, 172
Baillou, Alfred, 154
Bailly, Raymond, 142
Baines, John, 143
Baiwir, Daphné, 58
Bak, Stéphane, 203
Baker, Kathy, 151
Baker, Lorin, 195
Baker, Scott & Suzy, 139
Balasko, Josiane, 111, 173, 200, 224
Balibar, Jeanne, 79
Ballester, Louis, 96
Balmer, Jean-François, 128
Balpêtré, 69, 105, 143
Balthazar, Jean-Michel, 47
Balutin, Jacques, 82
Balzac, Honoré de, 158, 171
Balzac, Jeanne de, 199
Bandin, Henry, 213
Bang, Nicholas, 209

Bankolé, Isaach de, 36
Banks, Leslie, 221
Banks, Sidney, 138
Baquet, Maurice, 44
Bara, Suzanne, 78
Barançay, Odette, 152
Baratier, Jacques, 184
Barber, Frances, 114
Barbot de Villeneuve, Gabrielle-Suzanne, 59, 60
Barbouth, Joël, 54
Barbulée, Madeleine, 158
Barc, Jean-Christophe, 189
Bardawil, Georges, 39
Bardem, Juan Antonio, 127
Bardine, Patrick de, 68
Bardot, Brigitte, 121
Bardou, Camille, 56, 72, 157
Barge, Paul, 100
Barillet, Pierre, 61, 95
Barjavel, René, 91
Barjol, Jean-Michel, 231
Barjon, Lucien, 149
Barker, Jessica, 148, 206
Barlier, Alexia, 36
Barnett, Florence, 49, 218
Barney, Jean, 102
Baroncelli, Jacques de, 157, 192
Barone, Carina, 155
Baroux, Enya, 228
Baroux, Lucien, 157
Barr, Jean-Marc, 175

Barrault, Jean-Louis, 77, 150, 213
Barrault, Marie-Christine, 177
Barray, Gérard, 199
Barret, André, 215
Barret, Gilles, 87
Barrette, Yvon, 133
Barreyre, Jean, 158
Barsacq, Yves, 149
Barsby, Alice, 47
Barski, Odile, 84
Baruk, Franck, 37
Barzyk, P atricia, 142
Barzyk, Patricia, 141
Basset, Romain, 124
Bataille, Lucien, 56
Bataille, Sylvia, 183
Bates, Alan, 93, 151
Battaglia, Rik, 193
Batut, Stéphane, 226
Bauchau, Patrick, 228
Bauche, Henri, 71
Baudin, Henri, 100
Baudricourt, Michel, 130
Bauer, Belinda, 159
Baur, Harry, 114
Baute, Dominique, 41
Bava, Mario, 85, 205
Baxter, Lindsey, 58, 59
Baye, Nathalie, 69, 141, 148, 161, 228
Baynaud, Erwan, 141
Bazz, Nicolas, 116
Bazz, Yann, 116
Beals, Jennifer, 93

Béalu, Marcel, 47
Béart, Emmanuelle, 88, 227
Beaulieu, Marcel, 86
Beaune, Caroline, 232
Beauvais, Robert, 74
Beccaria, Mario, 64
Becker, Hugo, 89
Becker, Jacques, 40, 49
Becker, Stéphen, 128
Beckers, Betty, 163
Bécue, Nathalie, 180
Bedos, Guy, 39
Bedos, Nicolas, 171
Béhar, Fabien, 224
Beinex, Jean-Jacques, 141
Bejo, Bérénice, 171
Bekhti, Leïla, 80
Belières, Léon, 196
Belin, Bernard, 200
Bélisle, Raymond, 133
Bellanger, Hélène, 95
Belle, David, 57
Bellemare, Pierre, 219
Beller, Georges, 220
Belletto, René, 141
Bellucci, Monica, 80, 172
Belmondo, Jean-Paul, 142, 181
Belmont, Charles, 97
Belmont, Olivier, 216
Belmont, Vera, 69
Belmore, Edwige, 132
Belvaux, Rémy, 32, 68
Bemba, Suzy, 136
Bcmon, Jimmy, 86
Ben Ayed, Aly, 155

Benayoun, Robert, 174
Benedetti, Pierre, 62
Benes, Jean-Patrick, 48
Bénétin, Jacques, 95
Beneyton, Yves, 231
Benga, Feral, 199
Bengell, Norma, 170, 207
Benguigui, Jean, 224
Benhammou, Fouad, 226
Benhamou, Jean-Claude, 77
Benichou, Maurice, 130
Benjamin, André, 118
Benn, Aurore, 181
Bennent, Heinz, 183, 189
Benoît, Jacques, 133
Benoît, Pierre, 50
Benoît, Yves, 214
Bénureau, Didier, 214
Benzina, Gina Lola, 38
Bérangère, Jeanne, 94, 157
Berberian, Alain, 77
Bercot, Emmanuelle, 56
Berg, Marina de, 120
Bergé, Francine, 135, 216
Berger, Deborah, 149
Berger, Helmut, 184
Berger, Pamela, 152
Berger, William, 42, 93
Berhoun, Simane-Baptiste, 228
Berland, Jacques, 168
Berlig, Peter, 190
Berling, Charles, 79
Berlioz, Jacques, 159
Berman, Marc, 216

Bernanos, Georges, 208
Bernard, Armand, 48, 117
Bernard, Jacques, 181
Bernard, Lédon, 140
Bernard, Patrick Mario, 45
Bernard, Paul, 123
Bernard, Raymond, 133, 150
Bernède, Arthur, 14, 61, 134
Bernhardt, Kurt, 220, 221
Bernheim, Emmanuèle, 191
Bernon, Bleuette, 231
Beroard, Jocelyne, 205
Berodot, Philippe, 54
Berreur, François, 74
Berriau, Pierre, 180
Berriau, Simone, 212
Berroyer, Jackie, 83, 96
Berry, Jules, 49, 120, 129, 205, 229
Berry, Mady, 49, 183
Berry, Richard, 224
Bert, Françoise, 105
Bertaux, Louise, 166
Berteau, Marcel, 179
Berthaut, Hanna, 180
Bertheau, Julien, 70, 106, 230
Bertin, Françoise, 45
Bertin, Pierre, 67, 70, 167
Berto, Juliet, 96
Bertrand, Joseph, 179
Bertucelli, Jean-Louis, 15, 128, 209
Berval, Paul, 147

Bervil, André, 212
Beryl, Taïna, 63
Besnard, Éric, 56
Besnard, Jacques, 109
Besnard, Nicole, 59, 153
Besson, Gala, 124
Besson, Luc, 15, 16, 44, 54, 57, 76, 89, 136, 140, 222, 232
Bessy, Maurice, 91, 157
Betbeder, Sébastien, 162
Bettenfeld, Dominique, 224
Betti, Laura, 164
Beucler, André, 126
Beukelaers, François, 207
Beylat, Alice, 122
Bezace, Didier, 210
Bianchetti, Suzanne, 157
Biddle Wood, Clement, 57
Bideau, Jean-Luc, 59, 179
Bidegain, Thomas, 161
Bierce, Ambrose, 52
Bignon, Stéphane, 220
Bijou, Mackenson, 233
Bilal, Enki, 16, 66, 67, 221, 225
Billerey, Raoul, 205
Bills, Teddy, 213
Binet, Alfred, 164
Binet, Catherine, 132
Binoche, Juliette, 118, 132
Biolay, Benjamin, 149
Bioy Casares, Adolfo, 46
Biras, Jeanne, 178, 232
Biraud, Maurice, 101
Birkin, Andrew, 134

Biscary, Thierry, 50
Bisciglia, Paul, 138
Bisset, Jacqueline, 142
Bitsch, Charles, 89
Blackburn, Oliver, 227
Blain, Estella, 86
Blanc, Christina von, 225
Blanc, Éric, 214
Blanc, Erika, 182
Blanc, Michel, 160, 173, 200
Blancan, Bernard, 83
Blanchar, Pierre, 51, 133, 166
Blanchard, Françoise, 42, 155, 160
Blanche, Brigitte, 181
Blanche, Francis, 46, 77, 93, 204
Blanche, Louis, 191
Blanche, Roland, 128
Blasi, Silvana, 142
Bleibtreu, Moritz, 80
Blier, Bernard, 32, 36, 66, 67, 74, 82, 109, 163
Blier, Bertrand, 66, 67, 161, 225
Blin, Roger, 39, 120, 167, 216
Blyth, Jeff, 227
Bocrie, Anne, 65
Boffety, Pierre, 52
Bogarde, Dirk, 185
Bogdan, Adriana, 59, 207
Bogdanoff, Igor & Grichka, 110

Bohringer, Richard, 36, 81, 136, 190, 198, 221
Bohringer, Romane, 96, 180, 206
Boileau, Pierre, 92, 231
Boileau-Narcejac, 91
Boisrond, Michel, 169, 179
Boisseau, Jocelyne, 208
Boisset, Éric, 117
Boisset, Yves, 15, 82, 185
Boisson, Christine, 152, 176
Boivin, Jérôme, 59, 81
Bokanowski, Patrick, 44, 120
Bollo, Joaquin, 81
Bolo, Jean, 130
Bolo, Pierre, 130
Bompard, Barthélémy, 36, 37, 38
Bon, Jean-Marie, 44
Bona, Julie de, 88
Bonello, Bertrand, 233
Bongo, Homère, 181
Bonheur, Gaston, 108
Bonicelli, Vittorio, 57
Bonin, Marie-France, 219
Bonitzer, Pascal, 113, 219
Bonnaire, Sandrine, 208
Bonnard, Damien, 160
Bonnard, Mario, 187
Bonnefous, Jean-Pierre, 188
Bonnet, Manuel, 211
Bonnot, Richard, 69
Bontempelli, Massimo, 79

Bonvoisin, Bérangère, 94
Bonzel, André, 32, 68
Boorman, Charley, 36, 160
Boorman, Katherine, 36, 160
Boorman, Telsche, 160
Bordage, Pierre, 87, 97
Bordas, Arnaud, 123
Borderie, Bernard, 192
Bordier, Philippe, 172
Borel, Raymond, 168
Borges, Suzanna, 148, 221
Borgnine, Ernest, 64
Borlin, Jean, 99, 230
Born, Bernard, 178
Borowczyk, Walerian, 61, 93, 115
Borsche, Dieter, 40
Bory, Jean-Marc, 53, 193
Bosc, Henri, 110
Bosch, Roselyne, 45
Boschero, Dominique, 144
Bossi, Luc, 97
Bost, Jacques-Laurent, 132
Bost, Pierre, 202
Botet, Javier, 125
Botzaris, Roméo, 55
Bouajila, Sami, 45, 80
Bouali, Aïssam, 151
Bouard, Vincent de, 166
Boucaron, Gérard, 95, 120
Bouchitey, Patrick, 174
Boudrioz, Robert, 122
Boughedir, Ferid, 155

Bougosslavsky, Alexander, 98
Bouillaud, Charles, 158
Bouillon, Jean-Claude, 89, 99
Bouise, Jean, 71, 89, 176, 204, 215
Bouix, Évelyne, 229, 230
Boujenah, Laura, 125
Boulanger, Daniel, 121, 128, 168
Boulant-Lemesle, Zélie, 186
Boulay, Muriel, 188
Bouquet, Carole, 66, 160
Bouquet, Jean-Louis, 76, 105
Bouquet, Michel, 110, 145
Bourbeillon, Olivier, 201
Bourdelle, Thomy, 39, 49, 73, 105, 122
Bourdon, Didier, 103, 141, 165
Bourdon, Sylvia, 203
Boureau, Marc, 67
Bourgeois, Gérard, 72
Bourgoin, Louise, 54
Bourseiller, Christophe, 206
Boursinhac, Manuel, 202
Bourvil, 77, 112
Boussac, Marc, 216
Boutefeu, Nathalie, 162
Bouteille, Romain, 43, 139, 214
Bouteron, Pierre, 183
Boutiny, Carlo de, 224
Boutonnat, Laurent, 56, 114
Boutté, Jean-Luc, 201
Bouvette, Alain, 67
Boyer, Benjamin, 116
Boyer, Charles, 126, 138
Boyer, Jean, 112
Boyer, Marie-France, 128
Boyer, Myriam, 227
Bozon, Céline, 96
Bozon, Serge, 141
Bozzuffi, Marcel, 75, 215
Brach, Gérard, 39, 45, 64, 117, 139
Brachlianoff, Nicolas, 103
Bradbury, Ray, 14, 104
Brahim, Suliane, 162
Brainville, Yves, 75
Bral de Boitselieu, Henri, 204
Brana, Frank, 179
Branice, Ligia, 115
Braque, Willy, 138
Brasseur, Claude, 128, 197, 232
Brasseur, Pierre, 48, 58, 109, 115, 126, 177, 183, 192, 207, 232
Bravo, Ermin, 175
Bray, Yvonne de, 99
Brebant, Max, 101
Breillat, Catherine, 58
Breillat, Marie-Hélène, 95, 183
Breitman, Zabou, 197
Brem, Thierry de, 40
Brenner, Muriel, 214

Bréon, 105
Bressol, Pierre, 140
Breton, André, 11
Breton, Guy, 223
Breuil, Dominick, 215
Brialy, Jean-Claude, 50, 69, 88, 91, 106, 116, 128, 173, 209
Briançon, Nicolas, 55
Briand, Annie, 138
Briaux, Hervé, 177
Bride, Djamel, 200
Brill, Corinne, 89
Brindeau, Jeanne, 61
Bringuier, Paul, 164
Brion, Françoise, 207
Brione, Benoist, 74
Brismée, Jean, 182
Brizzi, Paul & Gaëtan, 103
Broca, Philippe de, 142, 149
Brochard, Jean, 92
Brochet, Anne, 81
Brodie, Ryan, 117
Bromberg, Agnès, 166
Bron, Jean-Stéphane, 186
Bronner, Chantal, 79
Bronner, Gérald, 80
Brook, Claudio, 82
Brosset, Colette, 98
Brouer, Jerry, 181
Broustra, Martine, 172
Brouté, Jean- Noël, 197
Brown, Clifford, 183
Brown, Fredric, 126
Brown, John Moulder, 93
Brown, Nathaniel, 207
Brownjohn, John, 160
Bruce, Jean, 167
Bruce, Josette, 168, 170
Brulé, Claude, 57, 99
Brunaux, Olivia, 116
Bruneau, Charlie, 114
Bruneau, Philippe, 98, 200
Brunelle, André, 134
Brunet, Geneviève, 76
Brunet, Paule, 219
Brunet, Philippe, 163
Bruno, 113
Brunot, André, 153
Brunoy, Blanchette, 129
Brynner, Yul, 214
Bujeau, Christian, 228
Bulbul, Zozimo, 207
Buñuel, Juan Luis, 13, 31, 53, 107, 137
Buñuel, Luis, 12, 31, 39, 70, 75, 106, 152, 230
Buron, Annie, 97
Burroughs, William S., 112
Burstyn, Ellen, 185
Busscher, Jean-Marie de, 66
Bussières, Pascale, 150
Bussières, Raymond, 73, 95, 144, 183
Bustillo, Alexandre, 136, 139
Buzek, Agata, 39
Cabel, Stéphane, 80, 172
Cabu, 43
Caccia, Michel, 65

Cadieux, Marc, 177
Caillaud, Laurent, 87
Caillol, Pierrette, 68
Cale, Dominique, 40
Calfan, Nicole, 74
Callas, Jean, 172
Calvé, Jean-François, 146, 217
Calvet, Corinne, 70
Camara, Mohamed, 145
Cambo, Paul, 133
Caméré, Manuel, 73
Cami, 119
Cammage, Maurice, 98
Campan, Bernard, 103
Campillo, Robin, 190
Campos, Christophe, 232
Canale, Gianna-Maria, 39
Candelier, Isabelle, 78
Cantazaro, Veronik, 190
Cantin, Roger, 148, 206
Canto, Marilyn, 98
Canuel, Yvan, 147
Capelier, François, 64
Capellani, Albert, 27, 39, 156
Capone, Alessandro, 200
Cappa, Robert, 211
Caprioli, Vittorio, 142
Cara, Bernard, 222
Carallo, Antonuio, 115
Carax, Leos, 121
Carbonneaux, Norbert, 127
Cardon, Jacques, 103
Carel, Roger, 78, 79

Carette, Julien, 70, 85, 183, 211
Carey, Geoffrey, 106
Carez, Bernard, 206
Carini, Christian, 214
Carl, Renée, 105
Carle, Gilles, 44
Carletti, Louise, 99
Carlevaris, Yves, 48
Carlier, Gérard, 142
Carlisi, Olympia, 100
Carmet, Jean, 40, 66, 83, 152, 173, 208, 230
Carné, Marcel, 135, 149, 183, 229
Caro, Marc, 16, 66, 76, 87, 176
Carol, Martine, 61, 98
Caron, François, 200
Caron, Jean-Luc, 87, 168, 202
Caron, Pierre, 123
Caron, Richard, 168
Caron, Sandrine, 214
Carot, Jacqueline, 78
Carpi, Jezabel, 221
Carr, John Dickson, 69
Carré, Isabelle, 45, 55, 210
Carrel, Dany, 78, 143
Carrier, Roch, 147
Carrier, Suzy, 120, 155
Carrière, Jean-Claude, 31, 41, 67, 70, 86, 106, 107, 110, 128, 137, 152, 221, 230

Carrière, Mathieu, 50, 122, 145, 189
Carruthers, Ben, 128
Carstensen, Margit, 183
Cartier, Caroline, 222
Carton, Pauline, 46, 199
Casanova, Jauris, 116
Casarès, Maria, 74, 123, 167, 202, 214
Cash, Tabatha, 229
Casoar, Phil, 176
Cassel, Jean-Pierre, 50, 70, 145, 151, 210
Cassel, Vincent, 60, 64, 172
Castagnetti, Alexandre, 117
Castaldi, Jean-Pierre, 83, 149
Castanier, Jean, 123
Castel, Marie-Pierre, 225
Castelot, Jacques, 157
Castle, Fred, 184
Cattand, Gabriel, 88, 200
Caty, Micheline, 52
Cauchy, Jean, 166
Caudry, Anne, 65
Caunes, Antoine de, 136
Caussimon, Jean-Roger, 113, 135
Cavanna, 43
Cayatte, André, 84
Cazals, Thierry, 85
Cazenave, Gautier, 125
Ceccaldi, Daniel, 110, 127, 128
Célarié, Clémentine, 38

Celi, Adolfo, 106
Céliat, Madeleine, 191
Céline, Sylvie, 155
Cellier, Caroline, 116
Cenci, Béatrice, 75
Cendrars, Blaise, 129, 130
Cendrier, Luc, 161
Cendrier, Noé, 161
Cerchio, Fernando, 157
Cerf, André, 205
Cerise, 88
Cerrato, Renzo, 170
Ceulemans, Martje, 57
Chabat, Alain, 55, 77, 92, 136, 174
Chabrol, Claude, 13, 32, 40, 64, 84, 93, 122, 137, 138, 147, 161, 165, 166, 179, 209
Chabrol, Thomas, 53
Chaillou, Gérard, 144
Chaîne, Nathalie, 154
Chalonge, Christian de, 41, 94, 144, 216
Chamarat, Georges, 49, 58, 158
Chambon, Jacques, 109, 136
Chamborant, Christian, 196
Champion, Jean, 210
Champreux, Jacques, 127, 135, 164
Champreux, Maurice, 135
Chantal, Marcelle, 105
Chaplin, Charlie, 46
Chaplin, Geraldine, 225

Chaplin, Oona, 187
Chapot, Jean, 75
Chappey, Christine, 234
Chapuis, Eric, 130
Chapuis, Nadia, 216
Chardot, Hubert, 137
Charlier, Jean-Michel, 64
Charlot, Alexandre, 144
Charlots, Les, 69
Charly, Kathryn, 190
Charmetant, Christian, 177
Charpin, Fernand, 108
Charrier, Jacques, 84, 165, 182, 207
Charrière, Christian, 93
Charvey, Marcel, 144
Chase, James Hadley, 63
Chatelain, Hélène, 131
Chaudat, Fabienne, 45
Chauffard, Jacques-René, 100
Chaumette, François, 60, 144, 187
Chaussat, Pierre, 221
Chautard, Émile, 26, 49, 195
Chavance, Louis, 58, 123, 163
Chavane, François, 49, 82
Chavassieux, Gilles, 119
Chazel, Marie-Anne, 228, 229
Chazot, Jacques, 147
Chelton, Tsilla, 41
Chemla, Judith, 226
Chenail, Roland, 147

Chérie, Élodie, 215, 229
Chériguène, Karim, 124
Chérino, Lénie, 228
Cherkis, Ann, 204
Cheryl, Karen, 130
Chesnais, Patrick, 60, 83, 214
Chevalier, Daniel, 103
Chevalier, Pierre, 224
Chevallier, Martine, 56, 96, 98
Chevallier, Philippe, 214
Chevit, Maurice, 144
Chevrette-Landesque, Hugolin, 206
Chevrier, Arnaud, 37
Chevrier, Jean, 68
Cheyney, Peter, 41
Chiba, Omocha, 53
Chiffre, Yvan, 168
Cholewa, David, 87
Cholewa, Laurie, 87
Chomette, Henri, 12
Chomon, Segundo de, 11, 24, 25
Chong, Rae Dawn, 111, 117
Chopel, Farid, 223
Chorfi, Mokhtar, 186
Chrétien de Troyes, 73, 177
Christian-Jaque, 58, 110
Christie, Julie, 61, 104, 154
Christin, Pierre, 66, 67, 222
Christophe, Françoise, 60

Ciampi, Yves, 75
Ciangottini, Valeria, 82
Cisife, Jean-Paul, 188
Civil, François, 52
Clair, Jany, 82, 153
Clair, Laura, 107
Clair, René, 12, 13, 46, 59, 61, 99, 107, 175, 230
Claire, Cyrille, 60
Claisse, Georges, 64, 144
Clariond, Aimé, 58, 105, 106
Clark, Christophe, 229
Clark, Ken, 82
Clary, Gil, 192
Clavier, Christian, 44, 45, 98, 117, 136, 173, 200, 228, 229
Clavier, Stéphane, 200
Clayton, Jane, 198, 217
Clément, Andrée, 78
Clément, Michel, 168
Clémenti, Pierre, 77, 139, 182, 234
Clermont, René, 79
Clermont-Tonnerre, Laure de, 79
Cleven, Harry, 200
Cloche, Maurice, 78, 81, 129, 152, 169, 187
Cloutier, Suzanne, 135
Clouzot, Henri-Georges, 32, 91, 152
Clouzot, Véra, 91, 92

Cocteau, Jean, 12, 13, 58, 59, 99, 167, 199, 213, 214
Coëdel, Lucien, 157
Coeur, Joelle, 88, 181
Coggio, Roger, 59
Cogitore, Clément, 161
Cohen, Catherine, 79
Cohen, Daniel, 90
Cohn, Ethan, 198
Colette, Yann, 145
Colin, Erik, 169, 189
Colin, Grégoire, 96, 210
Collard, René, 207
Collet, Lilou, 153
Collette, Yann, 66
Collin, Maxime, 148
Collin, Mélodie, 216
Colomer, Henry, 119
Colpi, Henri, 127
Coluche, 98, 214
Coluzzi, Francesca, 214
Comar, Esther, 125
Combret, Georges, 144
Compain, Frédéric, 84
Companez, Jacques, 94, 207
Compton, D. G., 16, 154
Comtois, Jean, 44
Condra, Julie, 85
Connery, Jason, 160
Constant, Jacques, 73
Constant, Madeleine, 223
Constantine, Eddie, 41, 67
Constantini, 135
Constantini, Lilian, 100
Continenza, Sandro, 85

Coq, 83
Coquelle, Alexandre, 64
Coqueret, Bernadette, 37
Cordy, Raymond, 46, 157
Cornaly, Anne, 52
Corneau, Alain, 110
Cornelis, Marcel, 179
Cornillac, Clovis, 97, 136, 144
Coronado, José, 90
Corrigan, Shirley, 182
Corthay, Sylvain, 97
Coscia, Marcello, 85
Cosmos, Jean, 214
Côté, Michel, 86
Cottençon, Fanny, 173, 198
Couchard, Jean-Luc, 217
Coudroyer, Philippe, 215
Couilfort, Léo, 176
Coulloud, Chloé, 139
Courant, Gérard, 54
Courcel, Nicole, 100, 207
Courcelles, Pia, 187
Courval, Nathalie, 116
Cousin, Pascal, 120
Cousseau, Thomas, 136
Coutu, Jan, 172
Couture, Martine, 44
Couzinet, Émile, 95
Cowl, Darry, 46, 147, 198
Cowl, George, 195
Cox, Geoff, 118
Cozarinsky, Edgardo, 148
Crauchet, Paul, 122
Creel, Leanna, 232
Cremer, Bruno, 185, 212

Crémer, Bruno, 223
Crémieux, Henri, 177
Cresté, René, 134
Créton, Lola, 58
Creton, Michel, 53
Cristal, Perla, 124
Cristina, Katia, 121
Croheim, Daniel, 209
Cros, Jean-Louis, 64
Cross, Alexandre, 79
Crow, Charlotte, 164
Cuche, Nicolas, 201
Cukier, Serge, 55
Culiersi, Jean-Marc, 90
Cuniot, Alain, 167
Cuny, Alain, 58, 74, 229, 230
Curtelin, Jean, 185, 209
Cusak, Cyril, 104
Cushing, Peter, 116
Cybulski, Zbigniew, 184
Cyprien, Michel, 221
D'Amario, Tony, 57
Dabadie, Jean-Loup, 78
Dac, Pierre, 159, 204
Dacascos, Mark, 85, 172
Dacqmine, Jacques, 81, 82
Daems, Agnès, 98
Dafoe, Willem, 186
Dagan, Robert-Paul, 98
Dahan, Olivier, 180
Dahan, Yannick, 123
Dahlbeck, Éva, 84
Dahlgren, Jeff, 114
Dahm, Yasmine, 53
Daisne, Johan, 207
Daix, Hubert, 179

Daix, Jacqueline, 122, 212
Dalban, Max, 73
Dalban, Robert, 49
Dalbray, Muse, 103
Dali, Salvador, 12, 39
Dalibert, André, 152
Dalio, Marcel, 62, 73, 119
Dalle, Béatrice, 60, 166, 220
Dallesandro, Joe, 62, 186
Dalleu, Gilbert, 72, 157
Dallias, Laurent, 191, 215
Daloz, Thomas, 176
Dalsace, Lucien, 61
Dambrin, Maxime, 125
Damiani, Damiano, 157
Damien, Eva, 120
Damien, Gilbert, 57, 160
Damon, Gabriel, 213
Dang Tran, Quoc, 114
Daniel-Norman, Jacques, 159
Danielsen Lie, Anders, 162, 178
Daninos, Jean-Daniel, 147
Danjou, Henri, 187
Danno, Jacqueline, 100
Danny, Pierre, 52
Dantec, Maurice G., 56
Danton, Sylvie, 208
Daquin, Louis, 197
Darc, Mireille, 167, 231
Dard, Frédéric, 78, 81, 199, 211
Darène, Robert, 67, 73
Darfeuil, Colette, 109, 158
Dargent, Mireille, 194

Dario, Yvonne, 134
Darlan, Eva, 128, 198
Darmon, Gérard, 77, 161, 209
Darmon, Nadine, 74
Darras, Jean-Pierre, 41, 53, 204
Darrieux, Danielle, 91, 137
Darroussin, Jean-Pierre, 68
Darry, France, 46, 147, 198
Dary, René, 115
Dasté, Jean, 42, 69
Daumier, Sophie, 39, 46
Dauphin, Claude, 53, 57, 91, 153
Dauphin, Jean-Claude, 231
Dauvray, Marise, 72, 129
Davert, José, 73
David, Frank, 120
David, Liliane, 212
David, Mario, 113, 142
David, McKell, 41
David, Myriel, 67
Daviot, Tiphaine, 114
Davis, Dolly, 230
Davy, Jean, 144, 203
Day, Josette, 59
De Ro, Jonas, 57
Déa, Marie, 94, 167, 168, 196, 229
Debac, Stéphane, 93
Debary, Jacques, 149
Debbouze, Jamel, 44

Debecque, Serge, 78
Deble, Coline, 121
Debucourt, Jean, 58, 75
Dechamps, Charles, 95
Decoeur, Albert, 192
Decoin, Didier, 149
Decomble, Guy, 120
Degas, Brian, 57
Degen, Michael, 93
Degroot, Serge, 103
Deguy, Madeline-Armelle, 201
DeHaan, Dane, 222
Dehelly, Jean, 195
Dehelly, Suzanne, 85, 196
Deillie, Françoise, 78
Dejean, Max, 135
Dejoux, Christined, 208
Dekeukeleire, Charles, 179
Del Grosso, Remigio, 51
Delachaux, Christophe, 188
Delahaye, Michel, 222
Delaître, Marcel, 130
Delamare, Gil, 82
Delamare, Lise, 59, 78
Delambre, Delphine, 232
Delannoy, Henri, 231
Delannoy, Jean, 99, 132
Delannoy, Philippe, 164
Delanoe, Henri, 14, 159
Delatour, Jean-François, 173
Delay, Florence, 96
Delbo, Jean-Jacques, 85
Delbo, Marion, 135
Delcambre, Marlène, 148
Delcroix, Mireille, 74
Deleau, Colin, 62
Delestrade, Marina, 185
Delevingne, Cara, 222
Delforge, Alain, 103
Dell, Jean, 232
Delmont, Édouard, 40, 108, 135
Delon, Alain, 48, 91, 121, 161, 176, 216, 217
Delon, Nathalie, 142, 152
Delorme, Danièle, 59, 132
Delorme, Guy, 82, 183, 193
Delozier, Mathieu, 86
Delpard, Raphaël, 77, 163
Delpierre, Dominique, 154
Delpierre, Manuel, 231
Delpy, Julie, 150, 221
Delvair, Jeanne, 140
Delvaux, André, 59, 189, 207
Demange, Paul, 152
Demick, Irina, 168
Demongeot, Mylène, 104, 106, 169, 204
Demy, Jacques, 101, 134, 175, 177
Deneuve, Catherine, 80, 84, 96, 101, 107, 113, 128, 177, 180
Deniaud, Yves, 48, 84, 105, 125, 153
Denicourt, Marianne, 201
Denis, Claire, 118, 220
Denis, Jacques, 219

Denner, Charles, 113, 137, 147, 217, 221
Denola, Georges, 191
Deny, Pierre, 151
Depardieu, Gérard, 45, 53, 56, 66, 74, 118, 141, 164, 208, 228
Depardieu, Julie, 181
Depelley, Jean, 96
Deplanche, Philippe, 219
Depp, Johnny, 160
Deprez, Danny, 57
Dequenne, Émilie, 149
Derangère, Gregori, 45
Deréan. Rosine, 49, 166
Derepp, Claude, 219
Dermit, Édouard, 167, 214
Dérou-Bernal, Émilia, 83
Derville, Michel, 190
Desagnat, Jean-Pierre, 69, 170
Desailly, Jean, 211
Desanges, Louis-Paul, 156
Desarthe, Gérard, 110
Descamps, Patrick, 165
Descas, Alex, 220
Deschamps, Hubert, 142, 199
Deschanel, Laure, 220
Deschelles, Paul, 119
Descraques, François, 228
Descraques, Raphaël, 228
Désert, Mariette, 175
Desfossé, Thomas, 108
Desjardins, Maxime, 196
Deslandes, Christophe, 56
Desny, Ivan, 168
Desplechin, Arnaud, 200
Dessailly, Charles, 222
Desvarieux, Jacob, 205
Devaivre, Jean, 39
Deval, Jacques, 51
Devere, Arthur, 135
Deville, Catherine, 227
Deville, Michel, 180
Devilliers, Renée, 130
Devirys, Rachel, 71, 73
Devos, Emmanuelle, 177, 181, 189, 201
Dewaere, Patrick, 173, 214
DeWilder, Audrey, 35
Dharker, Ayesha, 146
Dhem, Bass, 181
Dhéry, Robert, 70, 98, 144
Dhomme, Sylvain, 201
Dhour, Louise, 43, 225
Diafat, Dida, 156
Diamant-Berger, Henri, 49
Diamant-Berger, Jérôme, 221
Dick, Philip K., 81
Didelot, Roger-Francis, 152
Didi, Evelyne, 59
Diefenthal, Frédéric, 61
Diesel, Vin, 56
Dieudonné, Albert, 109
Diffring, Anton, 104
Dillon, Matt, 186
Dimitriadis, Anne, 102
Dix, Richard, 221
Djabri, Aïssa, 205
Doillon, Jacques, 43

Doillon, Lou, 198
Dombasle, Arielle, 40, 178, 219
Donatien, 71, 127
Doniol-Valcroze, Jacques, 122
Donovan, 134
Donovan, Jeffrey, 102
Dopud, Mike, 227
Doret, Thomas, 203
Dorfmann, Jacques, 69
Dória, Diogo, 218
Dorin, Florent, 228
Doris, Pierre, 199
Dorison, Philippe, 37
Dorival, Georges, 191
Dorléac, Françoise, 50
Dory, Christine, 226
Dorziat, Gabrielle, 58, 140
Douglas, Melvyn, 139
Dougnac, Marie-Laure, 87
Douy, Max, 201
Downes, Terry, 169
Dragoumi, Eleni, 47
Drake, Colin, 169
Dréville, Jean, 46, 133
Dréville, Valérie, 201
Dreyfus, Jean-Claude, 76, 87, 178, 223
Dreyfus, Julie, 227
Drouin, Sébastien, 188
Drouot, Jean-Claude, 151
Drouot, Stéphane, 208
Drucker, Léa, 181, 232
Druguet, Valérie, 224
Drye, Jenny, 68
Du Welz, Fabrice, 227

Dubillard, Roland, 60, 65, 72, 110
Dubois, André, 129
Dubois, Bernard, 194
Dubois, Diane, 40
Dubois, Francis, 40
Dubois, Jean-Pol, 220
Dubois, Marie, 116, 204
Dubox, Michel, 144
Dubuquoy, Philip, 54
Duc, Odette, 203
Duchamp, Marcel, 11, 99
Duchaussoy, Michel, 90, 122, 127, 142, 217
Duchesne, Roger, 153
Duchovny, David, 204
Ducos, Jean-Pierre, 69
Ducournau, Julia, 116, 215
Ducret, Arnaud, 228
Ducreux, Louis, 218
Ducrocq, Cécile, 165
Dufilho, Jacques, 49, 77, 128, 184, 230
Duflos, Huguette, 157, 196
Dufourcq, Stéphane, 63
Dugand, Jean-Philippe, 51
Dujardin, Jean, 171
Dulac, Germaine, 12
Dullin, Charles, 123, 132, 133, 150
Dumarçay, Philippe, 67, 97, 164
Dumas, Alexandre, 160
Dumas, François, 79
Dumas, Roger, 49, 66

Dumayet, Pierre, 144
Dumesnil, Jacques, 166
Dumien, Régine, 157
Dumonceau, Jean-Jacques, 232
Dumont, Léa, 105
Dumont, Patrick, 121
Dunoyer, François, 208
DuPac, Jean-Stan, 203
Dupas, Benjamin, 48
Duperey, Anny, 88, 194
Dupeyron, François, 141
Dupieux, Quentin, 198
Dupont, Pierre, 194
Dupontel, Albert, 75
Dupoux, Maryline, 60
Duprez, Gilbert, 37
Dupuis, Jean-Michel, 201
Dupuy-Mazuel, Henry, 133, 150
Duquesne, Edmond, 156
Duran, Michel, 84, 98
Duran, Roxane, 101
Durand, Jean, 11, 27
Duras, Marguerite, 98
Durieux, Jonathan, 200
Durin, Valérie, 74
Duris, Romain, 50, 86, 97, 142, 181
Dussault, Louisette, 129
Dussaux, Laurent, 65, 201
Dussolier, André, 40, 42, 98, 177, 209, 217
Dussollier, André, 60, 225
Dutaillis, Fabien, 138
Duteil, Yves, 104
Dutheil, Marie-Ange, 47
Dutronc, Jacques, 144, 173
Duval, Colette, 67
Duval, Daniel, 57
Duval, Juliette, 232
Duvauchelle, Nicolas, 206, 220
Duverger, Jean-Claude, 205
Duvert, Guy-Roger, 227
Duvic, Patrice, 213
Duvivier, Julien, 13, 69, 70, 91, 114, 146
Dux, Pierre, 142
Earl-Coupey, Ellen, 203
Eastman, George, 170
Ebner, Jacques, 103
Ebouaney, Eriq, 124
Echenoz, Jean, 193
Ede, François, 219
Edison, Thomas, 11
Eggerickx, Marianne, 122
Eidinger, Lars, 178, 186
El Kebir, Abder, 68
Elga, Jean-Pierre, 178
Elloy, Max, 152
Elmaleh, Gad, 97
Eloy, Max, 215
Elvey, Maurice, 221
Elvire, 160, 201
Emilfork, Daniel, 60, 76, 128, 149, 168, 182, 184
Emmanuel, Guy, 161
Enckell, Monique, 204
Engel, Tobias, 134
Engels, Wera, 196
Enrico, Jérôme, 187

Enrico, Robert, 52, 71
Epstein, Jean, 12, 75
Erickson, Christian, 63
Erlanger, Dominique, 203
Escoffier, Paul, 191, 195
Escourrou, Emmanuelle, 55, 137
Escourrou, Pierre, 137
Eskimo, Alexandre, 45
Esmond, Jill, 126
Espiasse, Jean Adrien, 62
Esquenazzi, Jean-Pierre, 160
Etcheverry, Michel, 178, 207
Ettori, Ariakina, 104
Ettori, Magà, 104
Etura, Marta, 90
Evanoff, Lorraine, 165
Evans, Darren, 41
Evans, Madge, 221
Évrard, Claude, 205
Eyquem, Robert, 95
Eyraud, Marc, 47, 177
Fabbri, Diego, 157
Faber, Juliette, 212
Fabian, Françoise, 53, 171
Fabre, Fernand, 132
Fabre, Monique, 103
Fabre, Saturnin, 163, 183, 205
Faburel, Jacques, 68
Fainsilber, Samson, 109
Faithfull, Marianne, 217
Falcon, André, 101
Falconetti, Gérard, 178
Fallet, René, 208

Farahani, Golshifteh, 162
Faraldo, Claude, 130, 214
Fargeau, Jean-Paul, 118
Fargeau, Jean-Pol, 220
Farmer, Mylène, 114
Farnel, Gwenda, 203
Faroux, Bernard, 220
Farrel, Georges, 169
Farro, Dominique, 84
Farrugia, Dominique, 77
Farwagi, André, 212, 214
Fasquelle, Solange, 218
Fau, Michel, 40
Faure, André, 107
Faure, Jacques, 44
Faurez, Jean, 120
Faux, J. A., 163
Fechner, Jean-Guy, 69
Fedor, Tania, 105
Fehrer, Andrei, 185
Féjos, Paul, 105
Fékété, Paul, 110
Féline, Jean, 98
Félix, Zoé, 233
Fellini, Federico, 121
Fennec, Sylvie, 149
Fenriss, 200
Fenton, Leslie, 126
Féraudy, Maurice de, 195
Férié, Bernard, 96, 102
Férié, Mireille, 102
Ferjac, Anouk, 131
Fernandel, 40, 68, 78, 91, 110, 117, 159
Fernandez, Félix, 215
Fernandez, Philippe, 83
Ferone, Pascal, 64

Ferran, Catherine, 59
Ferran, Pascale, 200
Ferrara, Abel, 186
Ferrara, Romano, 153
Ferrara, Stéphane, 218
Ferrari, Pierre, 153
Ferrebeuf, Alexis & Jonathan, 154
Ferréol, Andréa, 111, 185, 209, 218
Ferrer, Mel, 91, 100, 139, 143
Ferrer, Nino, 139
Ferrer, Pascaline, 134
Ferreux, Benoît, 202
Ferro, Salvatore, 176
Ferroukhi, Ismaël, 55
Ferry, Jean, 60, 129, 138, 145, 176
Fersen, Christine, 80, 219
Ferté, René, 135
Fescourt, Henri, 195
Feuillade, Louis, 13, 29, 104, 134, 135, 194, 223
Feuillère, Edwige, 39, 170
Fexis, Dimitri, 100
Fey, Stéphane, 52
Feydeau, Jean-Pierre, 78
Feyder, Jacques, 50
Filippe, Jean-Teddy, 94
Filippelli, Gérard, 69
Fillières, Hélène, 48, 181
Fioravanti, Lucia, 54
Fischer, Madeleine, 85
Fisher, Terrence, 74
Fitoussi, Grégory, 125
Fitz, Peter, 93

Flammarion, Camille, 15, 109
Flaubert, Catherine, 181
Flaubert, Gustave, 198, 199
Flavius, Michel, 163
Flèche, Manuel, 174
Fleischer, Alain, 189, 234
Fleischmann, Peter, 31
Flemyng, Jason, 51
Flepp, Sylvie, 65
Fletcher, Louise, 114, 145
Fleurot, Audrey, 136
Fleury, Louise de, 111
Flint, Olly von, 221
Floche, Sébastien, 66
Floersheim, Patrick, 218
Flon, Suzanne, 60, 230
Flynn, Michael, 179
Flynn, Sean, 169
Folly, Jean-Christophe, 45
Fonda, Jane, 57, 121
Fonda, Peter, 121
Fonjallaz, Soizic, 200
Fontaine, Bruno, 165
Fontaine-Salas, Paul, 165
Fontan, Gabrielle, 135, 143
Fontana, Bepi, 115
Fontana, Patrick, 101, 233
Fontanel, Geneviève, 145
Fontant, Gabrielle, 211
Fonteney, Catherine, 212
Ford, Maria, 159
Ford, Mick, 46
Forde, Jessica, 224

Forest, Jean-Claude, 14, 57
Forestier, Éric, 193
Forestier, Louise, 129, 147
Forlani, Rémo, 215
Fossey, Brigitte, 67, 218, 223
Foster, Robert, 42
Foucaud, Pierre, 106, 157, 168, 169, 170
Fouché, André, 99
Fouchet, Max-Paul, 167
Fougerolles, Hélène de, 156
Foulquier, Jean-Louis, 130
Fox, Matthew, 102
Francem, Rolla, 46
Francen, Victor, 77, 109, 130, 163
Francey, Micheline, 70, 133
Franck, A. M., 35
Franck, Alain, 122
Franck, Dan, 221
Franck, Nino, 129
Franco Manera, Jesus, 183
Franco, Jess, 31, 36, 42, 67, 80, 86, 88, 102, 124, 183, 184, 204, 225, 232
François, Francky, 215
François, Jacques, 74, 113
Franju, Georges, 14, 124, 135, 164, 184, 231
Frank, Catherine, 179
Frankel, Paul, 120
Frankeur, Paul, 70, 106, 179, 230
Frankiel, Éric, 52
Frankiel, François, 52
Franzén, Peter, 148
Frappa, Jean-José, 150
Frappat, Francis, 201
Freda, Ricardo, 82
Freeland, George, 42
Freeman, Morgan, 85, 140
Freiburger, Hervé, 134
Frémont, Kris, 138
Frémont, Thierry, 93, 217
Fresnay, Pierre, 70, 73, 143, 192
Fresson, Bernard, 75, 77, 97, 111, 139, 167, 210
Freund, Karl, 143
Freustié, Jean, 216
Frey, Sami, 96, 151, 221, 222
Fries, Inge, 99
Froissard, Ines, 161
Frot, Catherine, 90, 216
Frot, Dominique, 181
Froug, William, 53
Fruitier, Edgar, 206
Fugain, Marie, 214
Fuller, Samuel, 115
Fulton, Rad, 51
Funès, Louis de, 73, 91, 106, 113, 118, 152, 208
Funès, Olivier de, 118
Furet, Yves, 105, 140
Furey, Lewis, 44
Fusier-Gir, Jeanne, 68, 155
Gabin, Jean, 221
Gaël, Josseline, 143

Gainsbourg, Charlotte, 45, 174
Gainsbourg, Serge, 151
Galabru, Michel, 111, 113, 116, 126, 136, 161, 173, 204
Galán, Mapi, 218
Galiena, Anna, 219
Gallais, Xavier, 53
Galland, Jean, 105
Galli, Ida, 82
Gallienne, Guillaume, 136
Gallo, Vincent, 220
Gallotta, Jean-Claude, 188
Gallotte, Jean-François, 37, 55, 174, 215
Galo, Igor, 77
Gamal, Samia, 40
Gance, Abel, 12, 13, 15, 28, 109, 129, 130
Gance, Marguerite, 75
Gandera, Félix, 157
Gandois, Catherine, 119
Gans, Christophe, 60, 85, 159, 172, 205
Gantillon, Bruno, 154
Garat, Jean, 195
Garcia Lorca, Laura, 186
Garcia, José, 142, 220
Garcia, Nicole, 96
Garcin, Ginette, 161
Gardes, Renée, 189
Gardès, Renée, 158
Gardner, James C., 204
Gardner, Vincent, 164
Garel, Philippe, 139
Garel-Weiss, Marie, 41, 51
Garnier, Christine, 67
Garnier, Dominique, 94
Garnier, Jean-Claude, 204
Garrani, Ivo, 85
Garray, 122
Garrel, Maurice, 144, 207
Garrel, Philippe, 80
Garrigues, Pierre-Alain de, 116
Garrivier, Victor, 190
Gartner, James, 42
Gary, Manuel, 40
Gary, Micheline, 213
Gaspard-Huit, Pierre, 199
Gassener, Alain, 107
Gassman, Vittorio, 149, 225
Gastaldi, Ernesto, 35
Gasté, Philippe, 199, 225
Gastyne, Marc de, 71
Gates, Tudor, 57
Gaubert, Danièle, 174
Gaubert, Ginette, 192
Gautier, Jean-Yves, 219
Gautier, Théophile, 125
Gavin, John, 170
Gaydos, Melanie, 217
Gaylor, Anna, 86
Gazzotti, Bruno, 203
Gébé, 43, 120
Gégauff, Paul, 110, 166, 231
Geisweiller, Gilles, 74
Gélin, Daniel, 83, 98, 151, 212

Gélin, Fiona, 110
Gélin, Manuel, 35, 83
Gélin, Xavier, 83
Gelinas, Isabelle, 92
Gemma, Giulano, 199
Gendron, François-Eric, 218
Gendron, Steve, 148
Genès, Henri, 208
Genevray, Jérôme, 162
Géniat, Marcelle, 155, 157
Genin, René, 135
Gensac, Claude, 118, 208
Georges-Picot, Olga, 114, 131
Gérald, Jim, 122, 192, 230
Gérard, Charles, 60, 217, 229
Gérard, Marc, 122
Gercourt, Albert, 159
Géret, Georges, 208
Gérôme, Raymond, 101, 183
Geromini, Jérôme, 91
Geslot, Roselyn, 55
Ghrenassia, Réphaël, 86
Giavannini, Bettina, 83
Gibrat, Jean-Pierre, 146
Gicca Palli, Fulvio, 192
Giehse, Thérèse, 62
Gielgud, John, 185
Gil, Mateo, 187
Gilbert, Claude, 200
Gilbert, Fernand, 196
Gill, Brian, 117
Giller, Walter, 69
Gilles, Adrien, 87

Gilliam, Terry, 15, 131
Gillot, Alain, 213
Gill-Therrien Charles-André, 206
Gimberg, Louis, 152
Gimpera, Teresa, 179
Ginelly, Leda, 192
Gion, Christian, 130
Giorgetti, Florence, 99
Girard, Rémy, 86
Girardeau, Hippolyte, 81
Girardot, Ana, 165
Giraud, Roland, 98, 151, 206
Giraudeau, Bernard, 216
Girault, Jean, 113, 208
Girod, Francis, 218
Giros, Benoît, 223
Girotti, Massimo, 146
Girouard, Anne, 136
Gitaï, Amos, 115
Glaeser, Henri, 142
Glanz, Richard, 52
Glenn, Julie, 213
Glenn, Pierre-William, 16, 213
Glissant, Djibril, 96
Godard, Jean-Luc, 14, 32, 41, 95, 118, 132, 182, 193, 231
Godbout, Jacques, 129
Godet, Danielle, 73
Godet, Mélisa, 80
Goenaga, Barbara, 226
Goethe, Johann von, 20
Goguey, Isabelle, 163
Goldblum, Jeff, 151

Goldenberg, Luc, 216
Goldstein, Laurent, 68
Gomska, Mascha, 218
Gondry, Michel, 97
Goodis, David, 141
Gora, Claudio, 123, 184
Goretta, Claude, 205
Goscinny, René, 83, 112, 113
Gosselin, Bernard, 147
Gosselin, François, 147
Gosselin, Jean, 186
Gosset, Georges, 105
Goth, Mia, 118
Gouget, Henri, 56
Gouget, Laure, 116
Goujon, Olivier, 111
Goujon, Valérie, 111
Goulet-Robitaille, Anaïs, 206
Goulven, Jérôme, 196
Goupil, Jeanne, 173
Gourmet, Olivier, 197
Goutier, Jean-Michel, 119
Govar, Ivan, 207
Goya, Chantal, 113
Goya, Mona, 110, 123
Goyard, Philippe, 187
Gracq, Julien, 189
Grad, Geneviève, 50, 170
Grall, André, 209
Grandré, Gisèle, 147
Grangé, Jean-Christophe, 80
Grangier, Gilles, 119
Granier, Patrick, 139, 150
Granier-Deferre, Denys, 78
Granier-Deferre, Pierre, 216
Granval, Charles, 163
Gras, Jean, 112
Grasset, Jean-Pierre, 221
Grassian, Dolorès, 111, 210
Gravat, Pascal, 188
Gravina, Carla, 217
Gravone, Gabriel de, 195
Gray, Nadia, 193
Graziano, Laurent, 161
Gréco, Juliette, 167
Grédy, Jean-Pierre, 61, 95
Green, Eugène, 50, 153
Green, Eva, 50, 186
Green, Julien, 85
Green, Marika, 112, 169, 188, 197
Greenhall, Ken, 59
Greenwood, Joan, 112
Greggory, Pascal, 50, 186
Gregorio, Eduardo de, 95, 148, 202
Gregory, Gérard, 185
Greig, David, 227
Grello, Jacques, 46
Grenade, Sylvie, 109
Grendel, Frédéric, 91
Grenier, Serge, 129
Grétillat, Jacques, 133
Gréville, Edmond, 51, 143
Grey, Denise, 46, 78, 84, 198
Gridoux, Lucas, 196

Griffe, Maurice, 40
Griffiths Malin, Emma, 45
Grignard, Olivier, 200
Grimaldi, Caroline, 72
Grimaldi, Eva, 45
Grimblat, Pierre, 93
Grimoin, Michele, 63
Gripari, Pierre, 7
Grobman, Gérard, 65
Groodt, Stéphane de, 62
Grosso, Guy, 113
Ground, Robert, 212
Grousset, Didier, 16, 136
Gruault, Jean, 42, 69, 197, 225
Gründgens, Gustav, 221
Grunstein, Pierre, 116
Gruvman, Henri, 65
Guarino, Giuseppe, 158
Guénin, René, 135
Guerault, William, 64
Guérin, Florence, 87
Guérin, François, 232
Guerlais, Pierre, 85
Guerra, Ruy, 143
Guerra, Tonino, 93
Guers, Paul, 144
Guesmi, Samir, 67
Guez, Jérémie, 162
Guglielmi, Marco, 153
Guignard, Agnès, 233
Guilbeault, Luce, 129
Guillard, Jean-Bernard, 219
Guillard, Marie, 75
Guillot, Gilles, 110
Guilloteau, François, 184
Guimond, Ernest, 147
Guiomar, Julien, 47, 93, 100, 116, 121, 127
Guitty, Madeleine, 140
Gunzbourg, Denis, 121
Gutiérrez, Quim, 90
Guybet, Henri, 43, 127
Guy-Blaché, Alice, 11, 22, 23, 25
Guy-Lou, 179
Guyon, Cécile, 191
Guyot, Albert, 133
Haas, Hugo, 94
Hachard, Cédric, 134
Haddon, Dayle, 208
Hadji-Lazaro, François, 76
Hadzihalilovic, Lucile, 101, 207
Hägele, Jochen, 227
Haggard, H. Rider, 20
Hahn, Jess, 63
Haid, Ijane, 187
Hajdi, Youssef, 226
Halain, Jean, 106, 109, 118, 150, 157, 169, 208
Halat, Héléna, 52
Halberstadt, Michèle, 136
Halbrich, Hugo, 96
Halin, Jean-François, 170, 171
Hall, Deny, 151
Halle, Henri, 173
Haller, Bernard, 204
Hallyday, Johnny, 213
Hamman, Joe, 126, 195
Hampshire, Susan, 145
Hamy, Paul, 89, 160

Hancisse, Thierry, 48
Hancock, Herbie, 222
Hanich, Davos, 131
Hanin, Roger, 142, 147, 150
Hänsel, Marion, 210
Harareet, Haya, 51
Harari, Clément, 128
Hardellet, André, 127
Harduin, Fantine, 86
Hardy, Sophie, 67
Harnois, Béatrice, 203
Harrison, Blaise, 175
Harrison, Cathryn, 62, 134
Harsone, Peter B., 190
Hartl, Karl, 126, 166
Hartman, Paul, 126
Hartnett, Josh, 233
Harwood, Joanne, 159
Hasse, O. E., 49
Haudepin, Sabine, 161
Haudot, Alexia, 130
Hauer, Rutger, 222
Hauller, Véronique, 134
Hauser, Wings, 198
Hautin, Jean-Michel, 111
Haviland, Consuelo de, 81
Hawke, Ethan, 222
Hawks, Howard, 83
Hazanavicius, Michel, 170, 171
Head, Murray, 124
Heck, Dieter Thomas, 185
Heffmann, Gérard, 178
Heinrichsen, Anders, 63
Helm, Brigitte, 51, 166
Helpert, Jean, 125

Helpert, Jonathan, 125
Hembert, Jean-Christophe, 136
Hemmings, David, 57, 138
Hémon, Olivier, 110
Hendricks, Hervé, 115
Henkowa, Nadia, 71
Henrici, Jacques, 173
Henriksen, Lance, 96
Henriques, Elisabeth, 215
Herengt, Catherine, 178
Hergé, 215
Hériat, Philippe, 150
Hérisson, Philippe, 166
Herrand, Marcel, 105, 157, 197, 229
Herré, Henri, 65
Herrera, Jennifer, 45
Herrmann, Fernand, 223
Hersent, Philippe, 192
Hervé, Jean, 191
Herviale, Jeanne, 214
Herzog, Werner, 140
Hessling, Catherine, 181
Heusch, Paolo, 85
Heymann, Claude, 60
Hiegel, Catherine, 145, 224
Higelin, Jacques, 43
Highsmith, Patricia, 84
Hiriart, Lukas, 50
Hiriart, Saia, 50
Hirsch, Robert, 176, 217
Hitchcock, Alfred, 12, 92
Hoffmann, Rémi, 200
Hold, Marianne, 46, 147

Holgado, Ticky, 87, 225
Holm, Ian, 66, 76
Holm, Lali, 107
Holmes, Stéphan, 201
Holt, Jany, 58, 108, 114, 177
Holz, Ortès, 83
Honsou, Djimon, 64
Horackova, Bojena, 109, 194
Hornez, André, 152
Hossein, Robert, 169, 170, 222
Hotz, Nils, 203
Houdin, Robert, 19
Houellebecq, Michel, 184
Houry, Henry, 156
Householder, Jake, 198
Houssin, Jacques, 98
Houssin, Joël, 224, 225
Howard, Arthur, 173
Howard, Trevor, 46
Hubschmid, Paul, 85
Hudson, John, 36, 38, 174
Huerta, Paz de la, 207
Huet, Jacqueline, 123
Huff, Brent, 118
Hughes, Tom, 187
Hugon, Nils, 79, 180
Hulin, Dominique, 130
Hüller, Sandra, 186
Hummel, Lisbeth, 62
Hunebelle, André, 106, 150, 157, 168, 169, 170, 182
Huppert, Isabelle, 43, 79, 142
Huri, Blanche-Neige, 165
Hurt, John, 134, 165
Hussenot, Olivier, 120
Huster, Francis, 166, 175
Hutzler, Paule, 63
Hyams, Leila, 56
Hyndman, James, 150
Icart, Robert, 181
Ickerman, Seth, 63
Ikegami, Ryoichi, 85
Imberdis, Chris, 111
Ionesco, Eugène, 201
Ionesco, Lukas, 131
Iribe, Marie-Louise, 51
Irish, William, 164
Irons, Jeremy, 227
Irving, Washington, 20, 21
Iste, Cyrille, 108
Ito, Keito, 175
Ivanowich, Julien, 63
Ivernel, Daniel, 187
Izzard, Eddie, 64
Jabély, Jean, 62
Jacob, Irène, 200
Jacquemard, Claudine, 200
Jacquemin, Simone, 140
Jacques, Henri, 48
Jacques, Norbert, 93
Jacquet, Roger, 52
Jaeckin, Just, 117
Jakubzcyk, Gilbert K., 178
James, Henry, 69, 106, 217
Janer, Jean-Claude, 189, 210
Janerand, Philippe du, 187

Jannot, Véronique, 216
Janssens, Kevin, 193
Jardel, Pascal J., 36
Jardin, Alexandre, 113
Jardin, Pascal, 82, 216
Jarrett, Catherine, 144, 190
Jasset, Victorin, 11, 25, 26, 27, 33, 56
Jaubert, Pascal, 226
Jaunin, Antoine, 89
Jeanson, Henri, 58, 91
Jeffries, Lang, 82
Jegou, Aurélien, 134
Jehanne, Edith, 133, 195
Jess, Marilyn, 107
Jessua, Alain, 15, 48, 74, 83, 110, 173, 217, 218
Jeunet, Jean-Pierre, 16, 62, 66, 76, 87, 176
Joannon, Léo, 94
Joano, Clotilde, 161
Jobert, Marlène, 128
Joffé, Alex, 159, 176
Joffo, Richard, 163
Johansson, Scarlett, 140
Jolivet, Anne, 151
Jolivet, Pierre, 89, 206
Jonasz, Michel, 55
Joncquet, Gaston, 127
Jonge, Marc de, 200
Joray, Kristine, 211
Jordan, France, 35
Jorre, Colin, 109
José, Édouard, 213
Joseph, Naad, 206
Josserand, Emma, 176
Josso, Fabrice, 186
Jouanne, Patrick, 149
Jouanneau, Jacques, 135
Joubé, Romuald, 129, 150, 195
Jourdan, Catherine, 97, 189, 234
Jourdan, Eric, 85
Journet, Dominique, 164
Jouvet, Louis, 70
Jouy, Samuel, 165
Jovovich, Milla, 76
Joyeux, Odette, 58, 211
Jugnot, Gérard, 69, 95, 149, 173, 200
Julien, André, 187
Julien, Louis, 187
Julien, Pierre, 178
Jullian, Marcel, 179
Jullien, Sandra, 111
Jurgens, Curd, 170
Justice, James Robertson, 121
Justin, John, 123
Juvenet, Pierre, 140
Kaempfert, Waldemar, 42
Kahn, Cédric, 55
Kalfon, Jean-Pierre, 84, 87, 131, 139, 143, 231
Kalfon, Pierre, 169, 170
Kaminka, Didier, 130, 220
Kanakis, Anna, 35, 78
Kane, Carol, 132
Kane, Pascal, 95
Kanen, Robert Mark, 76
Kantof, Albert, 127
Kaplanoglu, Semih, 175

Kapone, Jérémy, 139
Kapoul, Stanley, 42
Karagheuz, Hermine, 96
Karen, Guita, 63
Karina, Anna, 41, 182, 189, 199, 212
Karine, Sabrina B., 90
Karl, Roger, 114
Karlen, John, 138
Karmann, Léo, 90
Karmann, Martin, 90
Karr, Mabel, 86
Karyo, Tchéky, 51, 55, 64, 85, 150, 152, 206, 221
Kassovitz, Mathieu, 56, 68
Kast, Pierre, 15, 42, 143, 207
Kato, Masaya, 85
Kavaïté, Alanté, 101
Kay, Harold, 63
Kay, Suzanne, 129
Kayssler, Friedrich, 166
Kearns, Billy, 212
Kechiche, Abdel, 223
Keen, Jérôme, 177
Keitel, Harvey, 154, 160
Keller, Marthe, 75, 217
Kellermann, Bernhardt, 220
Kelley, Virginia, 152
Kelly, Madeleine, 41
Kelly, Martine, 225
Kempelen, Johann Wolfgang Ritter von, 133
Kemply, Walter, 167
Kenny, Paul, 81

Kensit, Patsy, 217
Keppens, Émile, 72
Ker, Edith, 87
Ker, Nicolas, 40
Keraly, Gildas, 232
Kerbrat, Patrice, 173, 209
Kerchbron, Jean, 197
Keredec, Yann, 48
Kerjean, Germaine, 91, 157
Kermadec, Liliane de, 121
Kerrien, Jean-Pierre, 155
Khunne, David, 204
Kia-Yi, Wang, 68
Kibel, Seth, 160
Kiegel, Léonard, 85
Kier, Udo, 93, 208
Kimura, Keisaku, 53
King, Stephen, 185
Kinnear, Roy, 134
Kinski, Klaus, 82, 234
Kinski, Nastassja, 35, 141
Kirsanov, Dimitri, 12
Kitaen, Tawny, 118
Klapisch, Cédric, 181
Klein, Gérard, 77, 92, 175
Klein, Nita, 94
Klein, William, 151
Klotz, Claude, 65, 95
Knapp, Evalyn, 213
Kohler, Gilles, 149, 211
Koike, Kazuo, 85
Koite, Ramata, 184
Kolldehoff, Reinhard, 112, 170
Kopp, Lionel, 177
Korber, Serge, 72

Korsakova, Tatiana, 232
Koscina, Sylvia, 135
Kosma, Joseph, 183
Kounen, Jan, 64, 224
Kouyaté, Sotiguji, 115
Kramer, Robert, 92
Krauss, Charles, 72
Krawczyk, Gérard, 121, 209
Kriegel, Kathie, 230
Kristel, Sylvia, 40
Kruger, Christiane, 89
Kruger, Diane, 156
Kubler, Ursula, 84
Kuby, Bernard, 87
Kuhne, David, 86, 124
Kumel, Harry, 15, 138, 145
Kurylenko, Olga, 86, 193
Kurys, Diane, 120
Kyrou, Ado, 74, 152
L'Herbier, Marcel, 11, 163, 196
L'Yle, Alain, 167, 229
La Boulaye, Agathe de, 96
La Boulaye, Béatrice de, 134
La Farge, Paul, 63
la Grandière, Georges de, 67
La Haye, David, 86
la Loma, José Antonio de, 82
Laage, Barbara, 81
Laâge, Lou de, 56
Labèque, Louise, 233
Labrèche, Marc, 148

Labro, Maurice, 81, 82, 153
Labry, Michel, 159
Lacambre, Daniel, 200
Lacassin, Francis, 135
Lachapelle, Andrée, 86
Lachens, Catherine, 127, 185, 216, 231
Lachman, Harry, 56
Lacombe, Georges, 177
Lacoste, Philippe, 132
Ladoumègue, Jules, 68
Laferrière, Catherine, 204
Laffon, Yolande, 157
Lafforgue, René-Louis, 77
Lafont, Bernadette, 113, 118, 131, 167, 171, 198, 231
Laforêt, Marie, 147, 179, 221
Lagerlöf, Selma, 70
Lagrange, Louise, 164
Lagrange, Valérie, 193
Lahaie, Brigitte, 91, 107, 108, 164, 184, 187, 209
Lajournade, Jean-Pierre, 134
Laks, Lucile, 93
Lamb, Larry, 221
Lambert, Christophe, 35
Lambert, Henri, 35, 108
Lambert, Vincent, 55
Lambot, Fabrice, 96
Lambrichs, Louise L., 35
Lamorisse, Albert, 108
Lamorté, Morgan, 125

Lamotte, Martin, 83, 98, 173
Lamour, Pénélope, 203
Lamoureux, Robert, 49, 95
Lamy, Alexandra, 191
Lamy, Audrey, 60
Lamy, Charles, 75
Lancelot, Dominique, 190
Lancret, Bernard, 133
Landowski, Stéphane, 206
Landry, Aude, 138
Landry, Gérard, 163
Lane, Sirpa, 62
Lang, Fritz, 82, 93, 138, 139
Langella, Frank, 160
Langlart, Léonie, 63
Langlois, Lise, 138
Lanier, Jean, 84
Lanners, Bouli, 116
Lannes, Georges, 157, 168
Lanniel, Delphine, 125
Lanoux, Victor, 74
Lansac, Frédéric, 107, 203
Lanson, 185
Lanvin, Gérard, 45, 60, 111, 185
Lanvin, Lisette, 196
Lanzi, Paola, 230
Lapière, Denis, 55
Lapiower, Hélène, 106
Lapointe, Isabelle, 206
Lapperousaz, Jérôme, 125
Lara, Joe de, 190
Larivière, Serge, 83
Laroche, Gérald, 144

Laroche, Pierre, 48, 78, 125, 157, 229
Larquey, Pierre, 60, 92, 123, 143, 211, 212
Larriaga, Jean, 194
Larrieu, Arnaud & Jean-Marie, 90
Larsen, Anker, 52
Larson, Georgette, 52
Larue, Claude, 48
Lasowski, Elisa, 63
Laspalès, Régis, 214
Latour, Maria, 109
Latzko, Pierre, 112
Laubier, Jean-Baptiste de, 129
Lauby, Chantal, 77
Laudenbach, Philippe, 144
Laugier, Alexandre, 47
Laugier, Pascal, 198
Launois, Bernard, 126
Laurant, Guillaume, 35, 62
Laure, Carole, 44, 129, 209, 214
Laurendeau, Marc, 129
Laurent, Agnès, 42
Laurent, Gilles, 114
Laurent, Guillaume, 76
Laurent, Mélanie, 56, 172
Lautner, Georges, 127
Lavanant, Dominique, 111, 136, 173
Lavanne, Lisa, 173
Lavant, Denis, 121, 162, 180
Law, John Philip, 57

Lazure, Gabrielle, 60, 185
Le Béal, Robert, 78
Le Bihan, Samuel, 172
Le Bon, Charlotte, 187
Le Chanois, Jean-Paul, 39, 143
Le Coq, Bernard, 214, 216
Le Fanu, Sheridan, 99, 100
Le Gall, André, 105
Le Hénaff, René, 117
Le Marchand, Lucienne, 105, 157
Le Naour, Matthieu, 64
Le Poulain, Jean, 50, 126, 158, 204
Le Vigan, Robert, 123, 159, 221
Le, Paul, 210
Léaud, Jean-Pierre, 66, 80, 171, 182, 214, 231
Léaud, Pierre, 84
Lebas-Joly, Antonin, 83
LeBlanc, Christie, 172
Leblanc, Maurice, 14, 49
Lebon, Yvette, 157
Lebrun, Danièle, 103
Lebrun, Michel, 168
Lecat, Julien, 87
Lechalier, Chantal, 47
Leclerc, Ginette, 115, 208
Leclercq, Julien, 75
Lecocq, Charles, 182
Lederman, Michel, 103
Ledoux, Fernand, 40, 74, 120, 177, 229
Ledoux, Jacques, 131
Ledoux, Mathias, 200
Ledoyen, Virginie, 198
Leduc, Richard, 97, 174
Lee, Christopher, 95, 143
Lee, Margaret, 82, 170
Lee, Patricia, 179
Lee, Robert, 213
Leemans, Ainara, 50
Leep, Michel, 227
Lefaur, André, 58
Lefèbvre, Jean, 109, 127, 128, 135, 142
Lefebvre, Philippe, 171
Lefèvre, René, 63
Leffler, Robert, 187
Léger, Fernand, 11
Legrand, Annie, 214
Legrand, Augustin, 90
Legrand, Gaëlle, 98
Legrand, Lucienne, 71, 127
Legrand, Michel, 167
Legras, Jacques, 118
Lehembre, Philippe, 43
Leigh, Shanyn, 186
Lejeune, Monique, 174
Lellouche, Gilles, 54, 232
Lelouch, Claude, 16, 60, 217, 229
Lemaire, Philippe, 50, 85, 107, 121, 166, 194
Lemaître, Maurice, 222
Lemans, Guillaume, 86, 162
Lemercier, Valérie, 77, 228
Lemieuvre, Richard, 203

Lemoine, Michel, 153, 181, 203
Lemonnier, Meg, 159
Lemorande, Rusty, 217
Lénier, Christiane, 187
Lenoël, Sabine, 148, 163
Lenoir, Alban, 114
Lenoir, Justin, 116
Léon, Jean, 39
Léon, Pierre, 142
Léotard, Philippe, 36, 120, 148, 173, 205
Lepoutre, Raymond, 88
Leprince de Beaumont, Jeanne-Marie, 59, 60
Leprince, Catherine, 60, 93
Leprince-Ringuet, Grégoire, 93
Leroi, Francis, 15, 88, 184
Leroux, André, 170
Leroux, Gaston, 11, 14, 26, 27, 56, 72, 73, 122, 123, 194, 195
Leroux, Maxime, 59, 151
Lesaffre, Roland, 135, 149
Lesaffre, Sofia, 203
Lescot, Micha, 48
Lesoeur, Daniel, 35, 137, 160
Lesret, Catherine, 178
Lestringuez, Pierre, 196
Leto, Jared, 156
Letrong, Ly, 222
Letrou, Bernard, 227
Leubas, Louis, 134, 223
Leurquin, Sabrina, 59

Levallois, Stéphane, 232
Levantal, François, 88
Léveillé-Bernard, Jod, 148
Lévêque, Josianne, 98
Levesque, Marcel, 134, 163, 223
Lévine, Michel, 170
Levinson, Richard, 91
Levitte, Jean, 168
Levy, Bernard, 115
Lewis, Juliette, 64
Lewis, Matthew, 152
Lewish, Sophie, 62
Ley, Sascha, 83
Leysen, Johan, 210, 221
Lhermitte, Thierry, 98, 149, 200
Liberatore, Ugo, 51, 192
Libert, Anne, 48, 88, 225
Libert, Jean, 81
Lichy, Atahualpa, 119
Liebman, Riton, 136
Liebmann, Robert, 138
Ligardes, Patrick, 232
Lilo, 95
Lima, Marilyn, 206
Lime, Jean-Hugues, 214
Lindinger, Natacha, 90, 171
Lindon, Vincent, 55, 60, 215
Lindskog, Camille, 111
Link, William, 91
Linker, Suzanne, 73
Lio, 132
Lionel, Andrée, 157
Liotard, Thérèse, 154

Lippincott, David, 48
Lisi, Virna, 82
Lissou, Fred, 52
Little Brutus, 129
Llopis
   Franck, 111
Llorca, Denis, 73, 74
Llorens, Fabyenne, 233
Lobre, Jane, 69
Lobreau, Pierre, 52
Loca, Jean-Louis, 118
Lockhart, Kim, 203
Lodes, Christine, 185
Loiret, Florence, 220
Lolic, Iliana, 106
Lollobrigida, Gina, 61
Lomay, France, 203
Lombard, Jean-Pierre, 231
Lombard, Robert, 152
Lomeo, Alberto, 176
Lone, Live, 88
Lonsdale, Michael, 106, 114, 118, 128, 132, 171, 193, 197, 224
Lopert, Tania, 72, 185
López, Sergi, 90, 189, 191
Lord, Béatrice, 72, 103
Lord, Jean-Claude, 172
Lorde, André de, 25, 26, 71, 108, 164
Loredana, 192
Loret, Alexis, 153
Loreti, Nicanor, 96
Lorillard, Pauline, 112
Loring, Aude, 170
Loriot, Georges, 215
Lorre, Gaétane, 184

Lorre, Peter, 126, 143
Lorry, Stéphane, 181
Loubet, Michèle, 178
Louimat, Wislanda, 233
Louisa, Marie, 36
Love, John, 115
Lowe, Edmund, 56
Löwensohn, Elina, 39
Loy, Mino, 31
Luc, Jean-Bernard, 118, 159
Lucas, Laurent, 116
Luccioni, Micheline, 72
Luchini, Fabrice, 109, 177
Lucien, Joseph, 76
Lüders, Néa, 176
Lugagne, Françoise, 180
Luguet, André, 123
Luitz-Morat, 76
Lumière, Auguste & Louis, 11, 19, 24
Lumont, Roger, 139
Luna, Paula, 39
Lupo, Alberto, 193
Lupovici, Marcel, 142
Lussac, Robert, 179
Lutz, Alex, 171
Luzi, Maria-Pia, 153
Lvovsky, Noémie, 67, 200
Lynch, Brad, 151
Lynch, Richard, 159
Lyon, Lisa, 219
Lyonne, Natasha, 186
Lys, Lya, 39
M'Dini, Rached, 160
Maatouk, Moïse, 119
Maaz, Érika, 173

Mac Lerie, Allyn Ann, 110
Mac Orlan, Pierre, 146
Macé, Alain, 74
Machard, Alfred, 140
Machiavelli, Nicoletta, 122
Madeddu, Jean-Marie, 37, 38, 174
Madou, Malou, 68
Madsen, Michael, 64
Madys, Marguerite, 158
Maes, Julie, 47
Maffre, Julien, 40
Magdane, Roland, 72
Magee, Patrick, 93
Magier, Fanny, 107, 155
Magimel, Benoît, 184
Magnan, Philippe, 50
Magnet, Cécile, 216
Magnier, Franck, 144
Maguenat, Jeanne, 76
Mahauden, Roland, 103
Mahé, Henri, 63
Maï, Franka, 107
Mai, Natifa, 41
Maicanescu, Simona, 87
Maiden, Rita, 95
Maillan, Jacqueline, 198
Maillet, Dominique, 120, 151
Maillot, Maurice, 196
Maimone, Gérard, 188
Maimone, Jasmine, 87
Maintigneux, Jean, 53
Maintigneux, Pierre, 137
Mairesse, Valérie, 95, 111

Maïs, Suzet, 73, 205
Maistre, François, 70, 169
Malaterre, Bernard, 103
Malatier, Erja, 86
Malaval, Samuel, 65
Malavoy, Christophe, 47, 84
Malet, Laurent, 175, 229
Malet, Léo, 209
Malet, Pierre, 221
Malfille, Pierre, 163
Malherbe, Arnaud, 165
Malidor, Lisette, 234
Malle, Louis, 62, 121
Mallet, Odile, 76
Malone, Roberto, 229
Malzieu, Mathias, 206
Man Ray, 12, 99
Manara, Milo, 87
Manate, Paul, 165
Manchette, Jean-Patrick, 167
Mancini, Maria, 181
Mandico, Bertrand, 38, 112
Manet, Nathalie, 95
Manner, Jeff, 42
Manse, Jean, 78
Manson, Helena, 69, 139, 216
Manuel, Denis, 183
Manuel, Robert, 63, 82, 225
Manzor, René, 16, 42, 176, 209, 218

Marais, Jean, 42, 59, 99, 106, 150, 158, 167, 175, 177, 214
Marboeuf, Jean, 115
Marbot, Philippe, 65
Marcant, Nicolas, 176
Marcas, Dominique, 66
Marceau, Félicien, 62
Marceau, Marcel, 57
Marceau, Sophie, 61
Marcellin, Bernard, 144
Marchal, Arlette, 213
Marchal, Claire, 42
Marchal, Georges, 63, 202, 230
Marchand, Gilles, 55, 96
Marchand, Guy, 116, 209
Marchand, Henri, 46
Marchand, Léopold, 94
Marchat, Jean, 70, 85
Marco, Raoul, 153, 157
Marcoux, Vanni, 150
Marcus, Ed, 209
Marcy, Claude, 211
Maréchal, Marcel, 206
Marengo, Bruno, 79
Maret, Sophie, 178
Mareuil, Philippe, 65
Margot, Stéphane, 180
Marguet, Jean-Marie, 43
Mari, Fiorella, 85
Mariano, Luis, 119
Marias Merli, Alberto, 107
Mariaux, A. L., 42
Marie, André, 215
Marie-Laure, 105
Marie-Laurence, 178
Marielle, Jean-Pierre, 51, 67, 128, 179
Marillier, Garance, 116, 215
Marion, Jean-Marie, 71
Mariotti, Frédéric, 100
Markalé, Jean, 200
Marken, Jane, 48, 153
Marker, Chris, 15, 129, 131
Marks, Lisa, 87
Marlier, Carla, 121
Marlon, Ged, 38
Marmaï, Pio, 80
Marnay, André, 122
Marodon, Pierre, 198
Marquais, Michèle, 130
Marquand, Serge, 100, 187, 231
Marquet, Louise, 164
Marquet, Mary, 149
Marquina, Luis, 169
Marsac, Laure, 223
Marsan, Jean, 82
Marsay, Michel, 140
Marshall, Mike, 155
Marshall, Raymond, 63
Marten, Félix, 187
Martens, G. M., 117
Marthouret, François, 180
Marti Gelabert, Alexandro, 179
Martin, Claude, 99
Martin, Hugues & Sandra, 93
Martin, Jean, 96

Martin, Olivier, 222
Martinelli, Elsa, 100, 170
Martinelli, Jean, 62
Martino, Sergio, 35
Martins, Jean-Pierre, 124
Marx, Gérard, 190
Marzouk, Hachemi, 133
Mas, Victoria, 56
Mascolo, Jean, 98
Masini, Giuseppe, 51
Masini, Julia, 189
Masliah, Laurence, 118
Massard, Laure, 158
Massard, Yves, 123
Massari, Lea, 167
Massimi, Pierre, 127
Massin, Jean, 167
Masson, Han, 133
Masson, René, 91
Masta, Doudou, 124
Mastroianni, Chiara, 219
Mastroianni, Marcello, 101, 219
Mathé, Édouard, 134, 223
Mathé, Gilles, 56, 223
Mathews, Kerwin, 168, 169, 170
Mathot, Léon, 73
Mathot, Olivier, 160
Mattei, Pierre-Olivier, 67
Matthieu, Mireille, 101
Matton, Charles, 208
Mauban, Maria, 113
Maudru, Charles, 192
Mauduit, Allan, 48
Maupassant, Guy de, 74
Maura, Carmen, 210

Maurette, Marc, 40
Maurey, Nicole, 63, 81
Maurin, Mado, 122
Maurois, André, 211
Maury, Julien, 136, 139
Maury, Philippe, 67
Mauvais, Jean, 52
Max, Jean, 130
Maxudian, Max, 192
May, Mathilda, 84, 160
Mayance, Mélusine, 191
Mayans, Anthony, 137
Mayniel, Juliette, 137, 166, 232
Mayo, Alfredo, 67
Mazza, Desdemona, 157
Mazza, Marc, 65
Mazzotti, Pascal, 118
McBain, Ed, 138
McCall, Catriona, 124, 198
McCann, Isabel, 125
McCarthy, Andrew, 93
McCay, Winsor, 160
McColgan, Quinn, 102
McConkey, Sam, 232
McGill, Everett, 117
Meaney, Colm, 64
Medeiros, Maria de, 55, 150
Meersman, Peter, 85
Meersmans, Matthias, 57
Meffre, Armand, 130
Megaton, Olivier, 101
Melchior, Georges, 51, 105, 192

Méliès, Georges, 11, 14, 19, 20, 23, 25, 33, 35, 146, 226, 230, 231
Mélinand, Monique, 113
Melki, Claude, 101
Melki, Gilbert, 44
Mellis, Louis, 64
Mellot, Marthe, 158
Mendaille, Daniel, 76
Mendelssohn, Peter von, 146
Mendes, Eva, 121
Menez, Bernard, 95, 116
Menzer, Ernest, 163
Mercadier, Marthe, 187
Mercer, David, 185
Mercier, Mario, 115, 173
Mercure, Jean, 59
Mercure, Monique, 86
Méré, Charles, 123
Méré, Pierre, 163
Mérelle, Claude, 187, 192
Merenda, Luc, 170
Merenda, Victor, 211
Mergault, Olivier, 69, 141
Mérigny, Marhias, 112
Meriko, Maria, 189
Méril, Macha, 74, 159, 209, 230
Merle, Antoine du, 103
Merle, Robert, 144, 145
Merritt, George, 126
Merry, Arlette, 119
Mesguich, Daniel, 60
Mesnier, Paul, 73
Mesquida, Roxane, 198
Messager, Lucinda, 205
Messica, Vicky, 203
Metzger, Stéphane, 88
Meulemans, Niko, 233
Meurisse, Nina, 180
Meurisse, Paul, 91
Meyer, Hans, 66
Meyrinck, Gustav, 114
Mézières, Jean-Claude, 76, 222
Mézières, Myriam, 219
Mezzogiorno, Vittorio, 115, 141
Michaelis, Dario, 85
Michalik, Alexis, 206
Michaud, Annick, 119
Michaud, Françoise, 54
Michaux, Adrien, 153, 162
Michel, André, 50, 52, 207
Michel, Jean, 105
Michel, Roger, 112
Michel, Vanina, 231
Michelin, Bee, 189
Mieszala, Pascal, 210
Miéville, Anne-Marie, 132
Migenes-Johnson, Julia, 221, 222
Migliar, Adelqui, 158
Mignal, Marie-France, 84
Mihalesco, 135
Mikaël, Ludmila, 83
Milfort, Katiana, 233
Milhou, Sébastien, 134
Milinaire, Catherine, 184
Miller, Lee, 199
Miller, Lion, 65

Milowanoff, Sandra, 107
Minogue, Kylie, 121
Min-sik, Choi, 140
Mionnet, Patricia, 181
Miou-Miou, 116, 214
Mirel, Nicole, 147
Mirmont, Roger, 65
Missolz, Jérôme de, 131
Mitchell, Eddy, 55, 110
Mitchell, Solace, 93
Mitchum, Chris, 184
Mithois, Marcel, 169
Mitterand, Frédéric, 93
Mizrahi, Orit, 56
Moati, Félix, 139
Mocky, Jean-Pierre, 77, 126, 139, 141, 150, 198
Modo, Michel, 113
Modot, Gaston, 39, 59, 71, 91, 105, 133, 150, 157, 213
Moebius, 64, 68, 76
Moerman, Ernst, 105
Moguy, Leonide, 123
Moïssakis, Stéphane, 123
Molinaro, Édouard, 50, 95, 118
Molnar, Ferenc, 138
Mondy, Pierre, 158
Monero, Germaine, 209
Monette, Marie-France, 148
Monnet, Jacques, 98
Monnier, Valentine, 35, 98, 211
Monod, Jacques, 75, 139
Monory, Jacques, 121

Monot, Louise, 171
Monrond, Claude, 103
Monseu, Jacques, 182
Montagne, Jean, 211
Montand, Yves, 146, 151, 183, 207
Monteil, Lynn, 204
Montes, Fernando, 86
Montgomery, Jeff, 35
Monthil, Marcelle, 94
Montoban, Delphine, 148
Montréal, Huguette, 99
Moon, Jean-Yves, 161
Moosmann, Daniel, 212
Morane, Francis, 223
Morat, Michel, 224
Mordellet, Christophe, 151
Morder, Joseph, 54
Moreau, David, 203
Moreau, Jean-Jacques, 230
Moreau, Jean-Luc, 176
Moreau, Jeanne, 42, 125, 150
Moreau, Philippe, 120, 210
Moreau, Roland, 138
Moreau, Yolande, 67, 149
Morel, François, 45, 136
Morel, Pierre, 57, 74
Morelli, Franck, 191
Morello, Anne, 48
Moreno, Dario, 215
Moreno, Marguerite, 132
Morgan, Joanna, 167

Morgan, Michelle, 137, 146
Morgiève, Richard, 92
Morineau, Alain, 212
Morins, Armand, 76
Moriss, Frederik, 223
Morlay, Gaby, 68
Morlet, David, 156
Mosse, Mireille, 76
Mossman, Daniel, 198
Motte, Régine, 154
Mouchet, Catherine, 205
Moukhine, Tatiana, 98
Moulin, Frédéric, 158
Moulin, Guillaume, 203
Moulin, Jean-Pierre, 69
Moullet, Luc, 106
Mouloudji, Marcel, 132
Mousseau, Katerine, 133
Moutier, Norbert, 92, 118
Mouton, Catherine, 181
Moynot, Emmanuel, 83
Muel, Jean-Paul, 136
Muller, Paul, 225
Mulot, Claude, 127, 194, 203
Munchery, Marie-Christine, 37
Munro, Caroline, 184
Murail, Elvire, 201
Murat, Jean, 99
Murst, Jean, 126
Musidora, 134, 223
Mussen, Samuel, 210
Mussine, Marthe, 157
Musson, Bernard, 222
Musy, Alain, 176, 218
Muti, Ornella, 137
Muyl, Philippe, 47
Muyock, Aomi, 131
Myers, Bruce, 162
Mylo, Émile, 191
Myrga, Laurence, 158
Naceri, Bibi, 57
Nadaud, Serge, 46
Nadeau, Claire, 96
Nahon, Philippe, 149, 210
Naish, J. Carrol, 56
Nancel, Nicole, 111
Nanty, Isabelle, 62, 117, 166, 228, 232
Napierkowska, Stacia, 51, 223
Narcejac, Thomas, 92, 231
Nat, Lucien, 192, 197
Nat, Marie-José, 139, 201
Nattier, Nathalie, 70, 183
Naudé, Nicky, 88
Navarre, Louis, 98
Navarre, René, 61, 72, 73, 105, 122, 135
Navo, Manuel, 115
Nazzari, Amadeo, 51
Neal, Raphaël, 220
Nègre, François, 177
Nègre, Mireille, 108
Négret, François, 151
Negroni, Jean, 85, 131
Neill, Sam, 183
Nercessian, Jacky, 54
Nero, Franco, 152, 228
Nerval, Gérard de, 143
Nerval, Nathalie, 46
Nesle, Robert de, 183

Neveux, Georges, 50, 135
Nicati, Adrien, 107
Nichols, Britt, 88, 102, 225
Nicloux, Guillaume, 80
Niddam, Igaal, 219
Niklas, Jan, 93
Niney, Pierre, 171
Nitzer, Alexis, 220
Noblecourt, Noële, 144
Noé, Gaspar, 207
Noé, Yvan, 68, 155, 192
Noël, Magali, 168
Noël-Noël, 46
Noessi, Juliette, 155
Noguez, Dominique, 90
Noiret, Philippe, 78, 113, 151
Nordey, Véronique, 77
Noriega, Eduardo, 60
Norman, Rolla, 157, 192, 199
Norman, Vera, 216
Noro, Line, 108, 130, 166
Nouban, Roxanne, 65
Novak, Ivana, 182
Nuls (Les), 77
Nuridzani, Michel, 137
O'Brady, Frédéric, 112
O'Shea, Milo, 57
Obadia, Thierry, 36
Obey, André, 117
Odier, Daniel, 46
Oger, Frank, 219
Ogier, Bulle, 70, 96, 148, 171, 182, 189, 193, 202
Ogier, Pascale, 182

Ogouz, Philippe, 220
Olbrychski, Daniel, 204
Oldfield, Finnegan, 47
Oldman, Gary, 55, 76
Olenga, Lionel, 226
Olin, Lena, 160
Olive, Philippe, 152
Oliveras, Frank, 82
Olivier, Aude, 184
Olivier, Richard, 103
Ollier, Claude, 96
Ollivier, Paul, 46, 107, 132, 230
Ono, Takahiro, 53
Ophuls, Max, 212
Oppenheim, Antoine, 124
Oppenheimer, Edgar, 194
Orbal, Gaston, 40
Orengo, Antonio, 82
Orléans, Jenny, 215
Orsini, Umberto d', 121
Ortega, Chick, 145, 150
Ortega, Fiametta, 134
Orth, Jacques, 108
Ossang, Frédéric-Jacques, 38, 160, 218
Oufella, Rabah Naït, 116
Ouimet, Danielle, 138
Oumansky, André, 184
Oury, Gérard, 112
Oussadit-Lessert, Lya, 89
Outin, Régis, 119
Ovidie, 163
Owen, Clive, 88, 222
Ozeray, Madeleine, 138, 157
Ozon, François, 191

Pabst, Georg Wilhelm, 51
Pabst, Mickaël, 191
Page, Geneviève, 42
Pageault, Christian, 212
Pagliero, Marcello, 73, 132
Pailhas, Géraldine, 181, 190
Paillardon, Robert, 173
Pain, Didier, 228
Palansky, Marc, 233
Palau, Pierre, 70, 143, 146
Palcy, Euzhan, 205
Pallenberg, Anita, 57
Pallu, Georges, 100
Palma, Rossy de, 206
Palmer, Joe de, 190
Palud, Hervé, 111, 200
Paluzzi, Luciana, 170
Pansard-Besson, Robert, 193
Papagalli, Serge, 136
Pappaert, Hector, 68
Pappaert, Nelly, 68
Paradis, Vanessa, 42, 51
Paraz, Albert, 48
Parédès, Jean, 78, 163
Paredes, Marisa, 219
Parély, Mila, 59, 70
Parent, Jacqueline, 183
Parent, Valérie, 68
Parente, Quélou, 92
Parillaud, Anne, 96
Parisot, Paul, 142
Parker, Sherry, 48
Parking, Gustave, 174
Parlo, Dita, 85
Parmentier, Julie-Marie, 101
Parola, Danièle, 126
Paroldi, Caecilia, 157
Parolini, Marilu, 95
Paroux, Patrick, 87
Parthonnaud, Hugo, 158
Parthonnaud, Olivier, 158
Pascal, Andrée, 122, 191
Pascal, Françoise, 194
Pascal, Jean-Claude, 39, 73
Pascal, Marie-Georges, 187
Pascale, Nadine, 137
Pasco, Isabelle, 83
Pasquale, Frédéric de, 159
Pasquali, Alfred, 204
Pasquier, Arnold, 153
Pasquier, Jean-Pierre, 138
Passalia, Antonio, 64
Passereau, Jean-Luc, 109
Passeur, Steve, 130
Pastor, Alex, 90
Pastor, David, 90
Patisson, Danik, 168
Patorni, Raphael, 157
Patrice, François, 216
Pattinson, Robert, 118
Paturel, Dominique, 82, 201
Paulais, Georges, 61, 164
Paulin, Jean-Paul, 70, 123
Pauly, Rebecca, 84, 209
Pauly, Ursule, 154, 155, 227
Pavan, Marisa, 101

Paviot, Paul, 216
Payet, Alain, 42, 229
Payne, Bruce, 159
Pech, José, 43
Peigné, Daniel, 103
Pelegri, Pierre, 97
Pell, Magali, 185
Pellas, Paul, 210
Pellegrin, Raymond, 158, 169, 193, 229
Penet, Guy, 118
Penot, Jacques, 84
Peploe, Mark, 134
Péra, Janie, 192
Perdriaud, Georges, 138
Perdrière, Hélène, 84, 197
Perello, Michèle, 154, 194
Pérez, Vincent, 204
Pérez-Reverte, Arturo, 160
Périer, François, 167, 211, 212, 214
Perlman, Ron, 76, 117
Pernot, Christian, 214
Perrault, Charles, 20, 58, 177, 179, 180
Perrault, Gilles, 180
Perret, Léonce, 27
Perrey, Mireille, 78
Perrey, Natalie, 138, 163, 178
Perrier, Mireille, 115
Perrin, Jacques, 97, 100, 177
Perron, Claude, 62, 124
Perront, Nadine, 145
Petit, Alain, 119

Petitcuenot, Daniel, 211
Petit-Jacques, Isabelle, 177
Petix, Carmelo, 190
Petrolacci, Jean Pierre, 127
Petterson, Britta, 84
Peufaillit, Nicolas, 114
Peyrelon. Michel, 223, 228
Peyrière, Jean, 192
Pham, Linh-Dam, 156
Pham, Linh-Dan, 87
Phelan, Brian, 146
Philipe, Gérard, 59, 61, 135, 177
Philippe, Jean-Lou, 137
Philippe, Jean-Loup, 138, 163
Philippe, Michele, 63
Philippe, Pierre, 149, 170
Philippenko, Sergei, 158
Philippon, Franck, 35, 75
Philippon, Jean-Louis, 218
Philippot, Just, 162
Pia, Isabelle, 147
Pialat, Maurice, 208
Piat, Jean, 196, 230
Pic, Alexandra, 91
Picabia, Francis, 99
Picasso, Pablo, 214
Picault, Chantal, 47
Piccoli, Michel, 70, 74, 84, 106, 113, 121, 128, 137, 161, 168, 185, 214, 216, 218, 221, 227, 229, 230

Picq, Robert, 153
Piegay, Henri, 75
Pieiller, Jacques, 219
Piéplu, Claude, 70, 78, 97, 106, 118, 128, 139, 161, 167
Piéral, Pierre, 63, 99, 119
Pierangeli, Patrizia, 43
Pierjac, Albert, 151
Pierotti, Piero, 153
Pierre-Dahomey, Nehémy, 233
Pierreux, Jacqueline, 48
Pierro, Marina, 93, 155
Pierrot, 88
Pierrot, Frédéric, 190
Pierry, Marguerite, 95
Pigault, Roger, 68, 129
Pignot, Yves, 124
Piguet, Janine, 104
Pilhes, René-Victor, 128
Pinon, Dominique, 76, 87, 141, 160, 204
Pioutaz, Sylvain, 87
Piquer, Yann, 36, 37, 38, 174
Pirault, Audrey, 228
Pirès, Gérard, 131, 167
Pisani, Anne-Marie, 38, 87
Pisier, Marie-France, 97, 175, 185, 202, 222
Pitiot, Frank, 136
Pitoëff, Sacha, 45, 97, 177, 184
Plate, Roberto, 132

Pleasance, Donald, 134, 138, 151
Pleva, Jörg, 185
Plotnick, Jack, 198
Plume, Christian, 81
Pluot, Fernand, 69
Pluton, Manu, 181
Podalydès, Bruno, 197
Podalydès, Denis, 67, 79, 197
Poe, Edgar Allan, 12, 75, 100, 120, 160
Poelvoorde, Benoît, 32, 51, 68, 80, 90
Poelvoorde, Jacqueline, 68
Poggi, Caroline, 131
Poggi, Daniela, 93
Poggi, Mathieu, 228
Pointeaux, Lilly-Fleur, 124
Poiraud, Didier, 51
Poiraud, Thierry, 41, 51, 114
Poiré, Jean-Marie, 16, 44, 95, 173, 228, 229
Poiret, Jean, 77, 142, 150, 198
Poirier, Léon, 158
Poirier, Mathieu, 223
Poivre, Annette, 84, 144
Poix, Philippe de, 102
Polanski, Roman, 139, 160
Polho, Marquis, 227
Poligny, Serge de, 13, 58, 108, 166
Politoff, Haydée, 159

Pollet, Jean-Daniel, 143
Polley, Sarah, 156
Pollock, Channing, 135, 193
Pons, Vimala, 39, 80, 97, 112, 226
Ponson du Terrail, Pierre-Alexis, 191
Pope, Cassidy, 64
Porcile, François, 102
Portet, Jacques, 149
Portiche, Roland, 110
Portier, Marcel, 126
Potchess, Vernon, 127
Potocki, Jean, 188
Pottier, Richard, 152
Poupaud, Melvil, 79, 113, 219
Pourtalé, Jean, 15, 88
Pozner, Wladimir, 197
Pradal, Bruno, 96
Pradel, Solange, 227
Pradier, Perrette, 169
Préboist, Paul, 60, 74, 118
Preiss, Joanna, 116
Préjean, Albert, 73, 107, 175, 230
Prescott, Julie, 179
Presle, Micheline, 101, 132, 163, 177, 220
Prestia, Jo, 124
Prévert, Jacques, 48, 183, 229
Prévert, Pierre, 39
Prévost, Amélie, 69
Prévost, Daniel, 74, 165
Price, Vincent, 120

Prieur, Jérôme, 182
Prim, Suzy, 49
Prochnow, Jürgen, 213
Proffy, Hugues, 166
Prot, Christelle, 153
Proulx, Marc, 148
Proulx-Cloutier, Émile, 148
Pszoniak, Wojtek, 113
Pucci, Giovanni, 165
Pullicino, Gérard, 55
Pulver, Liselotte, 49
Pushkin, Alexander, 85
Quarxx, 217
Quester, Hugues, 175
Quincey, Thomas de, 120
Quirot, Romain, 89
R., Blaise Michel, 52, 161
Raabi, Manuel, 181
Rabal, Francisco, 147
Rabourdin, Olivier, 103
Radot, Guillaume, 140
Radszun, Alexander, 93
Rafal, Roger, 120
Raffaelli, Cyril, 57
Raguenet, Augustin, 131
Raimondi, Ruggero, 83, 225
Raimu, 117
Rainer, Lorraine, 97
Rambal, Jean-Pierre, 113
Rambaux, Sylviane, 98
Ramm, Haley, 198
Rampling, Charlotte, 56, 229
Ramuz, Charles-Ferdinand, 205

Randone, Salvo, 121
Rapace, Ola, 48
Rappeneau, Jean-Paul, 49
Rasmussen, Rie, 44
Rataud, Dimitri, 144
Rau, Andréa, 138
Ray, Jean, 15, 77, 145
Rayfiel, David, 154
Reading, Béatrice, 141
Réal, Denise, 99
Rebe, Martial, 135
Recoing, Aurélien, 124
Redgrave, Colin, 202
Redon, Jean, 81, 231, 232
Reeves, Sandra, 179
Régent, Benoît, 93
Reggiani, Serge, 78, 147, 183, 197
Règne, Marie-Hélène, 181
Rego, Luis, 69, 224
Reisch, Walter, 126
Rémy, Constant, 157
Renant, Simone, 212
Renard, Maurice, 143
Renaud, 98
Renaud, Francis, 156
Renaud, Madeleine, 221
Renaud, Véronique, 126
Renault, Brune, 56, 119
Rendina, Massimo, 153
René, Fernand, 135
Renier, Jérémie, 161, 172
Rénier, Yves, 45
Reno, Jean, 42, 89, 228, 229
Renoir, Jean, 12, 180, 213
Renoir, Pierre, 78, 140

Renot, Delphine, 191
Renucci, Robin, 50
Resnais, Alain, 14, 42, 43, 45, 131, 185, 225
Revelin, Pierre, 86
Rexlane, Marcelle, 143
Rey, Fernando, 67, 70, 93, 107, 170, 199
Reyer, Walter, 165
Rhomm, Patrice, 182
Riaboukine, Serge, 137
Rialet, Daniel, 59
Ribaut, Simone, 157
Riberolles, Jacques, 169
Rich, Catherine, 203, 212
Rich, Claude, 131, 197
Richard, Bruno, 66
Richard, Claude Marcel, 82
Richard, Émilien, 192
Richard, Franck, 149
Richard, Jacques, 194
Richard, Jean, 73, 142
Richard, Jean-Louis, 87, 104, 201
Richard-Willm, Pierre, 108
Riche, Daniel, 225
Richez, Serge, 55
Rico, John, 88
Ridoret, Marianne, 179
Riel, Van, 187
Rigal, Françoise, 223
Rigaud, Georges, 105, 179
Rignault, Alexandre, 105, 138, 157, 232
Rihanna, 222

Rinaldi, Gérard, 69
Riordan, Fergus, 41
Ripert, Colette, 99, 132
Risch, Maurice, 113
Rispal, Jacques, 48
Riva, Emmanuelle, 133, 155, 167
Riva, Marie, 79
Rival, Catherine, 178
Rivault, Pascale, 62
Rivero, Enrique, 199
Rivette, Jacques, 95, 171, 182
Rivière, Caroline, 204
Roanne, André, 187
Robak, Alain, 37, 55, 174
Robart Thimotée, 226
Robbe-Grillet, Alain, 13, 45, 46, 60, 97, 114
Robert, Jacques, 62
Robert, Yves, 49, 78, 128, 135
Robert-Dumas, Charles, 152
Roberts, Lynne, 56
Robin, Anastasia, 50, 98, 190
Robin, Dany, 158, 183
Robin, Michel, 86, 179
Robin, Muriel, 229
Robin, Olivia, 194
Robiolles, Jacques, 109, 194
Roby, Daniel, 86
Rocalve, Marie-Thérèse, 43
Rocca, Robert, 46

Rochant, Eric, 45
Rochard, Julien, 111
Roche, France, 42
Rochefort, Jean, 67, 110, 159, 212, 228
Rocher, Benjamin, 114, 123
Rocher, Dominique, 162
Rocher, Karole, 142
Rode, Thierry, 132, 221
Rodon, François, 157
Rodrigue, Madeleine, 107, 175
Rohmer, Éric, 177
Roland, Bernard, 84
Roland, Noëlle, 192
Rollan, Henri, 157, 175
Rollin, Georges, 48, 163
Rollin, Jean, 14, 88, 91, 92, 107, 108, 111, 137, 148, 155, 163, 164, 178, 187, 194, 222, 225, 227
Rollin, Marie-Simone, 148
Romain, Nicole, 227
Roman, Jacqueline, 119
Romand, Béatrice, 214
Romans, Pierre, 94
Romay, Lina, 80, 183, 204
Romer, Jean-Claude, 55, 139, 150
Romo, Marcello, 207
Roncoroni, Jean-Louis, 82
Rondard, Patrice, 168
Ronet, Maurice, 207
Ropert, Axelle, 141
Roquevert, Noël, 46, 92, 119, 143, 158

Rosay, Françoise, 133
Rosca, Gabriel, 192
Rosé, Jean-Christophe, 109
Rosny Aîné, J.-H., 16, 117
Rossini, Gabriel, 35
Rossi-Stuart, Giacomo, 85
Rosson, Richard, 56
Roth, Léon, 192
Rothpan, Mitchell David, 55
Rouan, Brigitte, 88
Roubaix, Pierre de, 52
Roubakha, Rémy, 200
Roudier, Brigitte, 211
Rouffio, Jacques, 218
Rougerie, Jean, 118
Rougerie, Sylvain, 189
Rouleau, Raymond, 77, 84, 94
Roullet, Jacques, 140
Roussel, Henry, 108
Roussel, Myriem, 132
Roussel, Nathalie, 206
Rousselle, Agathe, 215
Roussillon, Jean-Paul, 59, 200
Rouve, Jean-Paul, 54
Rouvel, Catherine, 137, 197
Roux, Jean-Michel, 150
Roux, Michel, 153
Roux, Stéphane, 134
Rouxel, Diane, 112
Rovère, Liliane, 181
Roy, Ginette, 157
Roy, Jean-Louis, 128

Royer, Guy, 130
Rozenberg, Sylviane, 68
Rozmann, Owen T., 88
Ruchaud, Frédérique, 52
Rudel, Roger, 64
Ruder, Ken, 179
Ruellan, André, 74, 125, 126, 173, 203
Rufus, 41, 139, 145, 151, 221, 234
Ruiz, Raoul, 79, 95, 113, 165, 188, 219
Rumeau, Jean-Pierre, 205
Rumilly, France, 113
Rumpf, Ella, 116
Sabatier, Pierre, 207
Sabel, Virgilio, 85
Sacha, Jean, 105, 168
Sacy, Agnès de, 189, 210
Sadoyan, Isabelle, 41
Sagan, Françoise, 137
Saidi, Karim, 151
Saint-Arnaud, Huguette, 123
Saint-Clair, Marie-Ange, 115
Saint-Cyr, Renée, 73, 127
Saint-Germain, Macel, 129
Saint-Simon, Lucile, 143
Sainval, Claude, 58
Saitô, Hiroshi, 205
Sala, Henri, 48
Salacrou, Armand, 59
Salem, Lionel, 39
Salfati, Pierre-Henri, 65
Salik, Rachel, 65

Salinger, Emmanuel, 200, 201
Salmirs, Deborah, 188
Salomé, Jean-Paul, 50, 61
Salou, Louis, 140, 211
Salvador, Thomas, 39, 226
Salvatori, Renato, 48
Salvy, Jean, 172
Samie, Catherine, 113, 190, 224
Samuel, Susan, 105
San Martin, Conrado, 124
San Martin, Mariola, 54
Sands, Julian, 146, 217
Sanson, Charlotte, 80
Santiago, Hugo, 96
Santini, Bertrand, 180
Santini, Pierre, 88
Santoni, Joël, 128
Sanz, Gabrielle, 180
Sanz, Jean-François, 131
Sanz, Joséphine, 180
Sapin, Louis, 216
Sapriel, Ariane, 227
Sapritch, Alice, 101
Sarapo, Théo, 135
Sarcey, Martine, 122
Sarno, Joseph, 71
Sarolie, Mériem, 136
Sarrus, Jean, 69
Sartène, Raymonde, 98
Sartre, Jean-Paul, 125, 132
Satie, Erik, 99
Satou, Alain, 75
Saugeon, Nathalie, 54
Saulnier, Jean-Pierre, 133
Saunin, Mireille, 154

Saurel, Pierre, 129
Sauter, Claude, 231
Sauvajon, Marc-Gilbert, 199, 205
Savalas, Telly, 184
Savin, ëric, 151
Sax, Guillaume de, 143
Sazie, Léon, 26
Sbille, Jean-Louis, 116
Scarfoglio, Paul, 203
Scarpelli, Umberto, 168
Scheroff, Misha, 176
Schiaffino, Rosanna, 150, 168
Schiavelli, Vincent, 151
Schiffman, Suzane, 152
Schmid, Philippe, 212
Schmitz, Sybille, 126
Schneider, Maria, 66, 145, 218
Schneider, Romy, 154
Schüler, Stefanie, 83
Schulmann, Patrick, 189
Schulmann, Tristan, 114
Schwartz, Gary, 117
Schwarzenegger, Arnold, 101
Schygulla, Hanna, 115
Sciamma, Céline, 180
Scob, Edith, 121, 135, 230, 232
Scott, Alan, 170
Ségur, Rolande, 147
Seigner, Emmanuelle, 160
Seignolle, Claude, 107, 119, 120, 151
Selhami, Talal, 151

Sélignac, Arnaud, 15, 113, 160
Semas, Jacques, 58
Semler, Peter, 141
Semonin, Laurence, 214
Sentier, Jean-Pierre, 130
Sepulveda, Sebastian, 165
Sergyl, Yvonne, 150, 157
Seria, Joël, 199
Serling, Rod, 53
Sermonne, Bruno, 162
Serrault, Michel, 61, 66, 74, 92, 94, 109, 113, 126, 142, 144, 150
Serre, Henri, 112, 142, 169
Serres, Charles, 43
Serres, Francis, 43
Serry, Viviane, 188
Servais, Jean, 67, 82, 83, 182, 202, 203, 207
Serval, Claude, 166
Setbon, Philippe, 83, 151
Séty, Gérard, 39, 74, 228
Seuzaret, Hélène, 116
Séverin-Mars, 129
Sevilla, Joëlle, 136
Sewell, Rufus, 227
Seweryn, Andrzej, 113
Seydoux, Léa, 60
Seyfferlitz, Gustav von, 56
Seyfried, Robert, 188
Seyrig, Delphine, 45, 70, 93, 138, 151, 177, 230
Seyvos, Florence, 67
Sfez, Philippe, 38

Shandor, Stéphane, 116
Shannon, George, 133
Sheckley, Robert, 15, 185
Shemesh, Ophrah, 115
Sherley, Pierre, 138
Shidor, Dieter, 213
Shirley, Helen, 107, 130
Sibirskaïa, Nadia, 157
Sibony, Clément, 210
Sieger, Jacqueline, 227
Signe, Jean, 223
Signoret, Simone, 84, 91, 92, 105, 229
Signoter, Gabriel, 49
Sigurðsson, Pétur, 125
Sijie, Dai, 145
Silva, Maria, 124
Silvestre, Gaston, 191
Simas, Joseph, 56
Simenon, Marc, 204
Simon, Christian, 183
Simon, Jean-Daniel, 127
Simon, Malka, 115
Simon, Marcel, 195
Simon, Michel, 59, 126
Simon, Pascal, 126
Simoneau, Yves, 86
Simonet, Eve, 100
Simonet, Julien, 117
Simonin, Albert, 49
Simonnet, Hélène, 200
Simono, Albert, 198
Sinclair, Eva, 118
Singer, Anne, 55
Siniac, Pierre, 121
Sinniger, Christian, 55
Siodmak, Curt, 126

Sire, Gérard, 74
Siry, Jean-Étienne, 99
Sisbane, Philippe, 79
Smagghe, André, 75
Smaïn, 174
Smith, Thomas, 108
Snoek, Anaël, 112
Solaar, MC, 154
Solar, Emilio de, 219
Solar, Silvia, 82
Solo, Bruno, 232
Sologne, Madeleine, 85, 99, 140, 153
Sopkiw, Michael, 35
Soral, Agnès, 92
Sorano, Daniel, 39
Sorrente, Sylvia, 170
Soualem, Zinedine, 232
Soubise, Gérard, 192
Souchon, Janine, 216
Souplex, Raymond, 112, 144
Southern, Terry, 57
Souvestre, Pierre, 14, 104
Souza, Roger, 68
Spaak, Charles, 69
Spiesser, Jacques, 59, 166
Spinella, Stephen, 198
Stafford, Frederick, 169
Stamp, Terence, 121, 125
Stanczak, Wadeck, 83
Stanford, Pamela, 183
Stanton, Harry Dean, 154
Starenios, Dimitrios, 215
Steeman, Stanislas-André, 98
Steffen, Valérie, 71

Stegers, Bernice, 46
Steinbicker, Reinhart, 220
Steiner, Kurt, 74, 203
Stelli, Jean, 212
Stephens, Robert, 36, 164
Sterckx, Pierre, 145
Sternberg, Jacques, 7, 131
Stévenin, Jean-François, 96, 161, 182
Stevenson, Robert-Louis, 141, 213
Stewart, Alexandra, 62, 97, 127, 193, 207
Stewart, Cathy, 115, 130
Stewart, Kristen, 178
Sting, 136
Stoker, Bram, 132
Stone, Sharon, 92
Stoppa, Paolo, 59
Storm, Jean, 181
Stritch, Elaine, 185
Stroyberg, Anita, 207
Stubbs, Neil, 216
Subor, Michel, 85
Sue, Eugène, 156
Sun, Sabine, 82
Surgère, Hélène, 100, 223
Sussfeld, Jean-Claude, 98
Swaim, Bob, 51
Swift, Jonathan, 20
Swinn, Monica, 204
Sy, Omar, 97
Sydow, Max von, 154, 220
Sylva, Lolita de, 63
Sylvia, Gaby, 125
Sylvie, Louise, 78

Syring, Anke, 71
Szabo, Laszlo, 41
Szajner, Bernard, 48
Szekely, Étienne, 196
Szulzinger. Boris, 145
Tabet, André, 51
Tadic, Radovan, 66
Taghmaoui, Saïd, 93
Takita, Yojiro, 205
Talansier, Jean, 138
Talba, Suzanne, 195
Talbot, Jean-Pierre, 215
Tallet, Gérard, 54
Tamiroff, Akim, 41, 147
Tanner, Alain, 46
Tanzler, Franz, 152
Tara, Isabelle, 190
Tarbès, Monique, 142
Tardi, Jacques, 54, 55
Tati, Jacques, 211
Taurand, Gilles, 84
Tautou, Audrey, 97
Tauveron, Guillaume, 53
Tavernier, Bertrand, 16, 154
Tavezzano, Frankie, 38
Tavier, Vincent, 51, 68
Taylor, Jack, 80
Taylor, Lili, 204
Tcherina, Ludmilla, 163
Tchernia, François, 53
Tchernia, Pierre, 112
Teal, Sonne, 184
Teboul, Isabelle, 91
Teillot, Carla, 37
Temerson, Jean, 78
Teodori, Muriel, 216

Térac, Solange, 105, 153
Terrier, Vincent, 63
Terry, Ethel Grey, 195
Terzieff, Laurent, 230
Tessier, Elisabeth, 194
Tessier, Valentine, 70
Testa, Karina, 53
Teynac, Maurice, 105
Théophane, Stanley, 52
Théophile, Robert, 119
Theret, Christa, 226
Thierry, Mélanie, 54, 56, 75
Thierry, Rose, 220
Thirlby, Olivia, 204
Thomas, Arlette, 206
Thomas, Dominique, 58
Thomas, Kristin Scott, 50
Thompson, Christopher, 51
Thompson, Danièle, 61
Thomson, Richard J., 52, 161, 191, 215
Thoquet, Sandrine, 108
Thorel, Renée, 123
Thorèze, Maurice, 192
Thouin, Lise, 172
Thouvenin, Cyrille, 226
Tieck, Ludwig, 137
Tifo, Marie, 86
Tijou, Brigitte, 190
Tiller, Nadja, 69, 152
Tison, Pascale, 210
Tissier, Jean, 99, 129, 155, 205
Tissot, Alice, 110, 122
Titoyo, 179

Todeschini, Bruno, 201
Toelle, Tom, 185
Tognazzi, Ugo, 57
Tolo, Marilu, 182, 199, 214
Tolzac, Jean, 160
Tomneer, Chris, 47
Tonnerre, Jérôme, 61, 149
Toomey, Patrick, 50
Topart, Jean, 82, 213
Topor, Roland, 139, 140, 219
Torkelli, Sophia, 89
Torok, Jean-Paul, 119
Torres, César, 115
Torres, Henri, 123
Torreton, Philippe, 57
Toublanc-Michel, Bernard, 169
Toumarkine, François, 68
Tourneur, Maurice, 13, 26, 27, 108, 143, 164, 195
Toussaint, Jean-Marc, 37
Toutain, Roland, 138, 196
Tozzi, Fausto, 199
Trabaud, Pierre, 179
Tramel, 68
Tramont, Émile, 108
Treil, Laurence, 230
Tréjean, Guy, 62, 75
Tremain, Rose, 191
Tremblay, Hugues, 133
Trembleau, Romain, 80
Trench, Charlotte, 155
Trenet, Charles, 68
Trévières, Martin, 179
Tréville, Georges, 49
Trimble, Laurence, 189
Trintignant, Jean-Louis, 51, 66, 114, 144, 167, 221, 229
Trissou, Dominique, 130
Tristan, Pierre, 67
Trividic, Pierre, 45
Troyat, Henri, 70
Truffaut, François, 14, 69, 104
Tsirbas, Aristomenis, 233
Tua, Lionel, 38
Tucker, Chris, 76
Tudal, Antoine, 68
Tulard, Jean, 32
Turckheim, Charlotte de, 163
Turi, Mathieu, 124, 148
Turine, Jean-Marc, 98
Turlure, Marcelle, 208
Turner, Dick, 158
Turner, Laurent, 89
Ulliel, Gaspard, 160
Ullman, Liv, 137
Ulmer, Edgar G., 51
Urbizu, Enrique, 160
Urzendowsky, Sebastian, 131, 165
Uytterhoeven, Pierre, 217
Vacarisas, François, 53
Vachaud, Laurent, 50
Vadim, Annette, 100
Vadim, Christian, 79
Vadim, Roger, 14, 57, 99, 120
Vailland, Roger, 99

Vaillant, Sophie, 155
Vajda, Ladislao, 51
Val, Germán, 96
Valbel, Marc, 212
Valbrune, Raphaëlle, 55
Valcke, Serge-Henri, 210
Valera, Dominique, 213
Valère, Simone, 59, 108
Valette, Éric, 144
Vallardy, André, 159
Vallée, Marcel, 84, 95, 135, 175
Valli, Alida, 49, 116, 166, 232, 234
Vallier, Maurice, 178
Van Belle, Jean-Louis, 198
Van Daële, Edmond, 158, 196, 221
Van den Hoof, Adriaan, 233
Van Doren, Fernande, 195
Van Dormael, Jaco, 156, 210
Van Eyck, Peter, 39
Van Khache, Matthias, 137
Van Rijckeghem, Jean-Claude, 57
Van Severen, Gunther, 62
Van, Adrien de, 180
Van, Marina de, 180
Vanberg, Roland, 103
Vandel, Jean Gaston, 81
Vandenpanhuyse, Gaston, 81
Vaneck, Pierre, 147, 203

Vanel, Charles, 40, 91, 92, 127, 164, 198, 205, 215
Vankeerberghen, Laurette, 210
Vanloo, Rolf E., 166
Vannier, Agathe, 194
Varda, Agnes, 84
Varennes, Jacques, 159, 167
Varèse, Anne, 115
Vargas, Daniele, 121
Varini, Célian, 216
Varupenne, Stéphane, 180
Vassiliu, Pierre, 231
Vauclin, Jean-Marie, 118
Vaudry, Simone, 157
Vaughan, Peter, 134
Vaultier, Georges, 107
Vautier, Elmire, 61
Vayssié, César, 233
Vayssière, Marie, 65
Veber, Francis, 142
Veber, Pierre, 123, 196
Vecchiali, Paul, 32, 100, 188
Vehlmann, Fabien, 203
Veidt, Conrad, 126, 133, 143
Veillot, Claude, 82
Velle, Gaston, 11, 24, 25
Velle, Joseph, 24
Venantini, Venantino, 51
Ventonderen, Trudi, 105
Ventura, Lino, 81, 91, 211
Verdier, Guillaume, 142
Verez, Michèle, 147
Vergez, Laurent, 149

Verhaeghe, Jean-Daniel, 47
Verissimo, Dany, 57
Verley, Bernard, 118, 230
Verley, Renaud, 99
Vernay, Robert, 105
Verne, Jules, 11, 20, 21, 22, 25, 127, 226, 227, 231
Vernier, Pierre, 74
Vernon, Howard, 41, 93, 102, 124, 128, 137, 160, 181, 184, 194, 224, 225
Vernoux, Marion, 116
Véron, Alain, 107
Véry, Pierre, 177
Vessel, Edy, 193
Vessey, Tricia, 220
Vestiel, Franck, 97
Vial, Alice, 134
Vialèles, Philippe, 73
Vialle, Franck, 88
Vialle, Max, 48, 225
Vian, Boris, 97
Viard, Karin, 87
Vicas, Victor, 122
Victor, Franck, 162
Vidal, Gil, 147
Vidal, Henri, 81, 211
Vidalie, Albert, 216
Videau, Frédéric, 226
Vierne, Jean-Jacques, 215
Viguier, 71
Vila, Monique, 48
Vilar, Antonio, 199
Vilar, Jean, 183
Vilbert, Henri, 40, 147
Vilbert, Marcel, 196
Vilers, Vania, 170
Vilfrid, Jacques, 113, 118, 147
Villalonga, José-Luis de, 220
Villalonga, Marthe, 72
Villard, Franck, 60, 99, 125, 157
Villard, Jean, 152
Villeret, Jacques, 111, 144, 173, 200, 208
Villiers de L'Isle-Adam, Auguste, 223
Villiers, Aruna, 35
Villiers, François, 146
Villiot, Bernard, 65
Vina, Victor, 199
Vincent, Jean-Marc, 137
Vincent, Louise, 151
Vincent, Maria, 231
Vincent-Bréchignac, Francis, 140
Vinci, Raymond, 78
Vinel, Jonathan, 131
Vinour, Pierre, 210
Vinter, Georges, 39
Violet, Edouard E., 73
Viot, Jacques, 135
Virlojeux, Henri, 50, 72, 169
Virly, Joan, 42, 160
Vissieres, Charles, 68
Vital, Jean-Jacques, 46
Vitez, Antoine, 69
Vitold, Michel, 50, 74, 110, 135, 196, 213

Vitray, Georges, 157, 212
Vittet, Judith, 76
Vitti, Monica, 106
Vivas, Miguel Angel, 102
Vlady, Marina, 67, 132, 169, 207
Vo, Patrick, 60
Vo-Anh, Sandra, 60
Vogler, Rüdiger, 171
Voisin, Benjamin, 56, 90
Volckman, Christian, 193
Voltaire, 167
Volter, Philippe, 206
Von Sternberg, Josef, 27
Von Stroheim, Erich, 39, 153
Von Trier, Lars, 31
Voutsinas, Andréas, 69, 121
Vuillermoz, Michel, 67, 224
Vyridar, Axel, 52
Wajnberg, Alexandre, 145
Wajnberg, Marc-Henry, 145
Waked, Amr, 140
Walker, Jennie-Anne, 112, 176
Warner, David, 165, 185
Warnier, Mathilde, 112
Watschenko, Katia, 132
Watson Barr, Bob, 212
Watson, James Sibley, 75
Webber. Melville, 75
Weber, André, 82, 142
Weber, Jacques, 107

Weingarten, Isabelle, 66, 224
Weiss, Gaia, 148
Welles, Orson, 145
Wells, Claudia, 220
Wells, H. G., 126, 149, 228
Wendling, Isabelle, 205
Wenger, Alan, 209
Wepper, Fritz, 89
Werber, Bernard, 188, 189
Werner, Oskar, 104
Werner-Kahle, Hugo, 187
Wheeler, René, 98, 119
White, André, 185
White, Pearl, 213
White, Stanley, 107
White, Ulrika, 65
Wiazemsky, Anne, 224
Wiene, Robert, 143
Wiener, Elisabeth, 47
Wiik, Aurélien, 93
Wild, Jack, 134
Wilde, Oscar, 183
Wilkening, Catherine, 64, 210
Williamson, Nicol, 152
Willie, John, 117
Willis, Bruce, 76
Wilms, Dominique, 169
Wilson, Andreas, 45
Wilson, Georges, 74, 91, 215, 230
Wilson, Lambert, 56, 79, 87, 154, 230
Winberg, Rachel, 42
Winfield, Peter, 201

Wing, Anna, 185
Winocour, Alice, 186
Winters, Shelley, 139
Woerner, Natalia, 141
Wolfrom, Fabian, 87
Wu, Kris, 222
Wyler, Richard, 82
Yaccelini, Alberto, 178
Yanne, Jean, 48, 64, 74, 128, 170, 231
Yaru, Marina, 121
Yd, Jean d', 99, 109
Yeoh, Michelle, 56
Yonnel, Jean, 147, 164
Yoshida, Mari, 53
Yoshimura, Tetsuko, 169
Young, Terence, 169
Yung, Élodie, 57
Yve, Christian, 147
Zabou, 98, 118, 200, 209
Zaccaï, Jonathan, 190
Zacharias, Ann, 110
Zapponi, Bernardino, 121
Zavatta, Achille, 144
Zavattini, Cesare, 40
Zazie, 48
Zazou, 139
Zecca, Ferdinand, 11, 23, 24
Zeff, Alexandre, 79
Zeiger, Nathalie, 181
Zeitlin, Laurence, 173
Zeller, Jean-François, 52
Zerah, Laurent, 65
Zéro, Karl, 220
Zeta-Jones, Catherine, 149
Zidi, Hélène, 130
Zidi, Malik, 172
Ziental, Isabelle, 158
Zimmer, Bernard, 138
Zimmer, Pierre, 97
Zingg, Gérard, 36, 164
Zischler, Hanns, 93
Zorin, 176
Zouzou, 45, 80
Zucco, George, 56
Zulawski, Andrezej, 183
Zürn, Unica, 132
Zwobada, André, 14, 85, 202
Zylberstein, Elsa, 62, 79, 80

www.ingramcontent.com/pod-product-compliance
Lightning Source LLC
Chambersburg PA
CBHW030135170426
43199CB00008B/70